Escape Stories

Escape Stories

Sundial

This edition first published in
Great Britain in 1980 by

Sundial Publications Limited
59 Grosvenor Street
London W1

The arrangement of this collection is
© 1980 Hennerwood Publications Limited
© 1980 illustrations Hennerwood Publications Limited
Illustrated by Tony Masero

ISBN 0 906320 49 6

Second Impression 1981

Printed in the United States of America by
R. R. Donnelley and Sons Company

Contents

Contents

They have their exits

AIREY NEAVE

Imprisoned in the legendary Colditz Castle during the Second World War, Airey Neave recounts the way in which he and a fellow prisoner escaped.

We waited till the door was locked behind us and we could no longer hear his muffled steps. Then we crept carefully to the top of stone spiral stairs at an open door on the other side of the attic. A wireless in the guard-room on the ground floor was playing organ music. It was the moment to go down, for the music was loud. We walked quickly down the first flight of stairs, past the door of the officers' mess on the first floor where a light showed beneath. We waited, then stepped confidently down through darkness, into the passage beside the guard-room. The guard-room door was half-open, and I caught a glimpse of German uniforms inside, as we marched smartly into the blinding whiteness of the snow under the arc lights.

The testing time had come. I strode through the snow trying to look like a Prussian. There stood the sentry, the fallen snow covering his cap and shoulders, stamping his feet, just as I had pictured him. He saluted promptly, but he stared at us, and as our backs were turned I felt him watching. We walked on beneath the first archway and passed the second sentry without incident. Then, between the first and second archways, two under-officers talking loudly came from the Kommandantur. They began to march behind us. I felt Luteyn grow tense beside me. I clasped my hands behind my back with an air of unconcern. I might have been casually pacing an English parade ground. In a moment of excitement I had forgotten my part. 'March with your hands at your sides, you bloody fool,' came a fierce sharp whisper from my companion.

Again I saw the bicycles near the clock tower. Could they be ridden fast in this thick snow? We passed beneath the tower, saluted by the sentry, and came to the fateful wicketgate. As Luteyn opened it I watched the under-officers, their heads bowed to the driving snow, march on across the moat bridge. Down we went into the moat, stumbling and slipping, until we reached its bed. A soldier came towards us from the married quarters. He reached us, stopped and stared deliberately. I hesitated for a moment ready to run, but Luteyn turned on him quickly and in faultless German said crossly, 'Why do you not salute?'

The soldier gaped. He saluted still looking doubtful and began to walk up the side of the moat towards the wicket-gate. We did not look back but hastened up to the path on the far side, and, passing the married quarters, came to the high oak paling which bordered the pathway above the park. We were still within the faint glare of searchlights. Every moment that we stayed on the pathway was dangerous. Lifting ourselves quickly over the paling, we landed in thick snow among the tangle of trees. My cardboard belt was torn and broken and with it into the darkness vanished the holster.

Groping among the trees we struggled through frozen leaves down the steep bank and made for the outer stone wall. It was five minutes before we were at the bottom of the slope. Helped by Luteyn, I found a foothold in the stones of the wall and sat astride the coping. The wall, descending steeply with the tree-covered slope, was shrouded in snow and ice. Each time that I tried to pull Luteyn on top, I lost my foothold and slid backwards through the steep angle of the wall. Then with numbed hands, I caught him beneath the armpits and, after great efforts, hoisted him up beside me. For a minute we sat breathless in the cold air clinging to the coping, and then jumped a distance of twelve feet. We fell heavily on the hard ground in the woods outside the castle grounds. I was bruised and shaken and frightened. I stood leaning against a tree looking at Luteyn. Another minute passed in the falling snow.

'Let's go,' I said, and we began to climb towards the east seeking the direction of Leisnig, a small town six miles away.

At ten o'clock the snow was falling less thickly and the moon showed us a way through the trees as we continued to climb towards the road to Leisnig. Beyond the trees we stumbled over frozen fields with hearts uplifted. The headlights of a car, yellow in the bright moonlight, turned in our direction. We lay flat in the snowdrifts till the lights swung towards the east. As we felt the hard surface of the road, I turned up the collar of my dark blue jacket against the cold. I had left the warm green overcoat behind me buried with the rest of the uniform beneath a pile of leaves and snow. The blue jacket was made from an officer's uniform of the Chasseurs Alpins. Shorn of silver galons and badges it became a rough workman's coat of serviceable cloth. I was given it by a Jewish officer, Capitaine Boris, who sacrificed his smart uniform for my escape. Boris was an elderly business man, a reserve officer in the Chasseurs Alpins and a great patriot. Such was the splendid comradeship of Colditz and one of the results of my interference in the Jewish Row.

On my head I wore a ski cap made of blanket and my Royal Air Force trousers were now turned down over my Army boots. From this moment Luteyn and I were Dutch electrical workers with papers permitting us to change our place of occupation from Leipzig to Ulm in South-Western Germany. Leipzig was twenty-two miles from the castle. We planned to reach it by walking the six miles to Leisnig, and there to take an early workman's train. Foreign workers, it was said, were numerous in Leipzig and some were to be transferred to the south.

We had no papers for the journey to Leipzig. Success depended on our safe arrival at the main station for the south. Pausing a while beside the road, we recovered money, maps and papers from the containers concealed in our bodies and then trudged smartly along the road. After two hours we passed a row of cottages close to Leisnig and came to what appeared to be a barracks. A faint light shone from the entrance gate and in the moonlight we saw a sentry. We stopped, turned from the road, and floundered through deep snow towards a belt of trees on higher ground. We stood there, sheltering among the trees against the sharp winds of the night. The ingenious Dutch officers in Colditz had acquired by bribery a timetable of the trains from Leisnig to Leipzig. We therefore knew that the first workmen's train was due to start at five o'clock. Three hours passed. It was too cold to talk. We waited silently for the train, looking towards the town and listening to the sound of shunting on the railway.

There was not a stir in all that crystal stillness as we climbed down the slope, broke through a hedge, and came back to the road. The road descended into a valley and walking boldly down the main street to the station we passed an early morning traveller and exchanged greetings. There was peace in the little town with its spires and snow-covered roof-tops. I thought of an illustration to the children's tale, *The Tailor of Gloucester* where a lone figure waure walks through the sleeping city. We had half an hour to wait. There was no one at the station so we walked away to the outskirts of the town unnoticed.

When the train was due we came slowly back to the entrance of the station where a small group of German working people had collected at the gate. As is the custom, the travellers were not allowed on the platform until the train was due to start. We stood silently aside from the others sheltering from the cold beside a wooden hut. When it was nearly five o'clock the doors opened, and the crowd surged forward to the ticket office. We followed in their wake and Luteyn, who spoke the best German, stopped at the *guichet* and bought two workmen's tickets to Leipzig. I followed him on to the platform where we stood apart from the others, men and women carrying small baskets or bags of tools.

The orange front light of an engine appeared. It was a scene of true romance. Here were we, escaped enemy prisoners of war, standing on the platform of the little station, mingling with ordinary people travelling to their daily work. The train, puffing with determination through the snow, halted and we climbed into a wooden carriage.

We were herded together in the semi-darkness of air-raid precautions. The warmth inside the carriage covered the windows with moisture so that I could hardly see the dawn. I bowed my head and dozed beside an old, and evil-smelling market-woman. Suddenly I was awakened by a sharp kick on my shins and looked up in fear. I met the half-smiling eyes of Luteyn. He sat hunched in a short tight overcoat, his ski cap on one side. Then I realised that I must have been talking English in my sleep. No one had noticed or even listened to my murmurs. I watched the thin, strained faces of the working-men as they dozed shoulder to shoulder, and saw the dawn slowly appear through the sweaty windows.

I felt ashamed that Luteyn was more alert and awake. He was strongly-built with humorous grey eyes and long dark hair. He was a strong and buoyant character whose life was spent in laughter and good fellowship. Yet he had a Dutch quality of thoroughness which made him a great escaper. He had staying power and resourcefulness and his great advantage lay in his superior knowledge of Germany and its language, so that he could take each fence with boldness and aplomb. He had a gay, attractive manner of speaking which disarmed the enemy and saved us both in the many dangerous situations which were to follow. For my part, rebellious by temperament though I was, I found him easy to work with and we seldom argued with each other.

Escape Stories

At six o'clock we drew in to the great station of Leipzig. The travellers, woken by shrill whistles, began to yawn and swear in low exhausted voices. We looked around us and followed the crowd towards a barrier where we gave up our tickets. There came upon me a sense of alarm and bewilderment. It was twenty months since I had seen the outside world, except for my adventures in the wild desolate country of Poland. Here, among the silent crowds of people moving in the dim light of the station, I was aghast at my helplessness. I felt like a peasant come for the first time to a city, unable to comprehend the paraphernalia of civilisation.

We wandered timidly round the station watching the indicators for a train to Ulm and found that no train left until 10.30 in the evening. It slowly dawned on us that we must stay in Leipzig with nowhere to shelter or sleep for many hours. We tried to find refreshment. Entering a tea-room we ordered coffee, supplied with a small envelope of saccharine. This was all we could obtain, for every other article of food required coupons. The coffee warmed us as we looked shyly at each other, smiling a little, and not daring to speak in any language. After paying for our coffee we wandered to a waiting-room crowded with travellers, mostly poor, who sat among their luggage and children, silent and obedient. I looked at these victims of Hitler's war and felt a great pity. The hopelessness in their faces brought a stark realisation of suffering. We had heard rumours of their plight in the camp, they were now confirmed beyond our belief. Musing I took from my pocket a huge bar of Red Cross chocolate and began to eat.

A young woman with fierce hysterical eyes, gazed at the chocolate as if she had seen a ghost. I stared back at her uncomprehending. She spoke to an old woman beside her and they looked at me in anger. Immediately the crowd near us began to talk in threatening whispers. I heard the word *tchokalade* many times. Luteyn turned to me and frowned angrily. Slowly realising the danger of my position, I put the chocolate back in my pocket. I had committed a terrible

Immediately the crowd near us began to talk in threatening whispers

blunder. Chocolate had been unknown to working Germans for many months. Goering himself may well have tasted little. We British prisoners were well supplied. To sit eating this forbidden delicacy in the waiting-room of a great station made one not only an object of envy but of deep suspicion. We rose awkwardly and walked out of the waiting-room into the town.

Leipzig at nine in the morning on January the 6th, 1942. The snow was cleared from the streets and there was a distant hum of traffic in the sunshine. Military vehicles sped by us filled with hard-looking men in steel helmets who ignored the civilians. The sidewalks were a mass of field grey and the mauve-blue of the Luftwaffe. We stared into the shop windows, gazing like children at expensive dresses and furs. Around us stiff, bourgeois, young men in uniform tapped their smart black boots on the pavement, as they stood before the shops. Blonde girls, in short skirts, looked up at the soldiers with fiercely possessive blue eyes and clutched them tightly.

We entered a big emporium and moved among bright lights and dance music and tinsel finery. We watched the people strolling by the counters. The Germans were young, confident and hopeful and we, mere beggars with a few bars of precious chocolate, had only our own high courage between us and the enemy on every side. Only a few sad civilians of an older generation, shabby and worn, crept among the counters like wraiths. The Nazi Revolution of Destruction was at hand.

We were bitterly disappointed to see no sign of bombing, yet the civilians looked hungry and unhappy. We threaded our way through the crowd and came to a square of gardens where a few old men and women walked in the sunshine with their dachshunds. I could read memories in their worn faces and their hatred of Hitler's New Order. I sat beside Luteyn on a seat watching their slow, hopeless perambulation among the snow-bound flower beds and shrubs. For me the months of imprisonment were gone and past. I was a detached spectator watching Life go by. New sights and sounds, fresh and clear, came to me after the darkness of prison. Elderly business men and lawyers with briefcases under their arms marched past muttering sombrely to each other. A girl left the procession of Life and sat beside me.

She was young and blonde and plainly of the working class. She looked at me sharply as she sat on the wooden seat. She wore a torn old overcoat and her short tight skirt was above her bare knees. She looked down at her shoes with *ersatz* wooden heels and kicked at a heap of snow. Her mouth was set in a hard determined line. I struggled to look at her calmly but with an inwardly beating heart. Her prominent blue eyes had ruthlessness.

'Good morning,' she said.

I dared not answer or risk conversation. She pouted.

'You are unsociable, my friend.'

I turned to see Luteyn had already risen from the seat and was walking slowly away. I followed him in dismay and embarrassment and, for a moment, turned towards the girl. She was looking hard at us. I felt her blue eyes watching, deep with suspicion and annoyance. We hurried away and wandered among the side streets of Leipzig till it was noon.

A cinema in enemy territory is a fine hiding place for the fugitive. After a lunch of *ersatz* coffee we came to a cheap stuffy cinema at the bottom of an arcade. Luteyn bought the tickets. Our small stock of German marks was enough for only the cheapest seats. We stood, obediently waiting for the performance, regimented by a commissionaire. In a few minutes, we took our seat among German soldiers and sailors and their girls and waited for the curtain, and, as the lights went out, a tall young German officer came in alone and sat next to me.

We saw first on the programme a news-film of events in Libya. Rommel, standing beside a staff car in the desert, talking decisively; then excellent shots of panzers in action and a British plane being shot down. Close ups followed of a British pilot taken prisoner by the Germans and waving encouragement to his friends still fighting in the air. In my excitement I clutched the seat in front of me and was rewarded by the occupant turning round with a harsh whisper of protest.

The feelings of a prisoner who for many months has been shut out from the war and accustomed only to the crudest enemy propaganda, are hard to describe. I could have wept from joy. At least the war was not yet lost. In the next part of the news-film there came a most shattering revelation. The scene was set in a Russian winter. Up a long snowbound hill German soldiers struggled against the blizzard, dragging guns and vehicles. There were photographs of frozen bodies and men's limbs swollen to unrecognisable size with frost-bite. If Goebbels wanted to impress the Germans with the sufferings of their troops to inspire them to greater sacrifices at home, he hid no detail of their hardships.

There was a shocked silence when the news-film came to an end. The lights went up in the shabby hall while martial music played from a cracked loudspeaker. Young men and girls chanted Nazi songs and around us their clear voices sounded in perfect harmony. Only the old people were glum and quiet. The music changed to

'We are marching against England!'

For a moment I caught my companion's eye and, with a faint grin on our faces, Luteyn and I sang loudly with the rest.

The remainder of the programme was a film set in early nineteenth-century Germany. The heroine, a hard-faced simpering creature, was surrounded by heavy Prussian admirers. The scene which won the most applause was that in which the witty girl took refuge in an earth closet at the bottom of the garden to repel their advances. It was a hut with two heart-shaped holes cut in the door to which she pointed knowingly as she entered. The Germans roared without restraint and we, unimpressed by their lavatory humour, were constrained to do the same for fear of detection.

In the early afternoon the snow began to fall again and the streets of Leipzig seemed full of foreboding for us. A policeman watched us, and followed stealthily until we evaded him among dark alleyways. Working our way back towards the big shops and the crowds, we came to another cinema where there was an atmosphere of plush warmth, antiseptic and wurlitzer music. We saw the same news-film again as we sat high in the gallery among more German troops on leave. Then came a royal fanfare of trumpets and Hermann Goering appeared on the screen appealing for higher output for the war. He wore the grey uniform in which I was later to see him in his cell at Nuremberg, but with a lavish display of decorations. His throaty voice rasped out propaganda to an audience which remained quiet if respectful. When his vulgar performance had lasted ten minutes there came shots of goose-stepping battalions of Nazis and someone struck up the *Horst Wessel Lied*. But the singing was cheerless and half-hearted.

From the cinema we walked again into the blackout of the city. The moon had not yet risen and only the soft whiteness of the snow guided us through public gardens to the main station. Often at corners of the streets we caught the faint reflection of a policeman's polished helmet and edged away among the crowds or dodged the trams to cross the street.

We came again to the station waiting-room and sat there tired and cold and anxious. The numerous passengers in the waiting-room, many poor and infirm, assembled for the night trains. Then came the men in uniform, elbowing all the civilians aside. I watched them closely. The bullying S.S. men, the clod-like infantrymen, and the pale, and spectacled administrative clerks. All in uniform, they tramped over the gloomy station like locusts, demanding refreshment or newspapers or anything they wanted. Such is total war.

Luteyn bought the tickets to Ulm. We had decided to change there and, if all went well, to take tickets to the Swiss frontier. At the barrier of the platform for the train to the south, military police stood to check the soldiers but there seemed no control of civilians. We waited beside the train before it started, preferring to find standing room than risk conversation in a compartment. As it began to move we climbed the steps of a carriage and stood in the corridor.

The compartment opposite was occupied by a single figure in the uniform of the S.S. I could see the man as we stood outside, a great ape-like person with a heavy jaw. His uniform was new and spotless and he crossed his legs which were in fine black boots as he read a newspaper with screaming red and black headlines. I caught only the word 'Rommel.' So that he should not watch us, we moved into the shadow at the end of the corridor and looked into the darkness where only a few pin-points of light showed the effective blackout of the city. The train jolted over the points and gathered speed with piercing whistles. Above its rattle I heard the door of the compartment open, and turning my head saw the big S.S. man standing in the doorway. His hands were on each side of the entrance door and he spoke to us in a soft voice.

'Are you Jews?'

'Certainly not. We are Dutch,' replied Luteyn.

'Good. Come in and sit here. This compartment was reserved, but my friends are not coming.'

We took our seats beside the big man who spoke very slowly to us, using simple phrases. His friendliness alarmed me.

'Where are you travelling?'

'To Ulm.'

'Why?'

'We are Dutch electrical workers transferred there from Leipzig.'

Luteyn was doing the talking. He had his genuine Dutch passport ready to produce in an emergency. Then the man turned to me and his stupid eyes examined my face, searching for something he did not understand.

'You are Dutch, too?'

'Yes.'

'How are things in Holland?'

'We have not been there for some months. We have been in Leipzig since the summer.'

They have their exits

It was Luteyn who spoke. The S.S. man turned to me. 'I am going to Munich,' he said unexpectedly. 'Then I go to Vienna for a conference.'

We nodded politely and the conversation stopped. Men and women passengers were walking up and down the corridor and were soon invited into the reserved compartment. They bowed respectfully to the high S.S. officer, took their seats and gave our shabby clothes a scornful stare.

There was no further conversation about Holland. I was glad of this. My sole visit to that country had been the journey in the barge up the River Waal to Germany as a prisoner in 1940. As soon as the passengers began to snore, Luteyn stayed awake according to our arrangement and I slept for a few hours until his turn came to sleep. I was awakened by a loud tapping on the glass of the door and two military policemen looked in. They checked the passes of the soldiers and even scrutinised the documents of the S.S. officer. They stopped for a moment to stare at our queerly tailored clothes. I wondered for a moment whether they would recognise the colour of R.A.F. trousers, but the S.S. officer intervened importantly.

'These are foreign workers (*fremdarbeiter*). Dutch,' he said with conviction.

The military police hesitated, then turned away as if suspicious civilians were nothing to do with their department. Now it was Luteyn's turn to sleep and I listened to the endless rattle of the express as we passed through Plauen and Hof and sped southwards into Bavaria. Lifting the blind, I glimpsed the snow outside or studied the sleeping faces in the dim light of the compartment. Towards four in the morning the train began to slow and came to a halt amid the sounds of a large station. I woke Luteyn, rose and stretched my limbs, and walked over to the doorway. In the gloom there was shouting and the bustle of passengers. I leant out of the window and saw on a sign before me the word 'Regensburg.'

It was here that we were due to change for the train to Ulm and we stepped on to the platform in the sharp cold.

'Good-bye, Dutchmen,' said the S.S. man pompously from inside the compartment.

We went into a waiting-room and sat down at a table. Passengers with their luggage came with us, and promptly fell asleep with their heads resting on the tables. Opposite, a man in railway police uniform stared at us in unfriendly fashion. We did not wait for him to speak but walked out again on to the platform and entered the booking-hall. We sat on the floor with other travellers leaning against a wooden partition. A man and a girl smelling of spiced sausages and garlic lay near us in a close embrace.

When the train to Ulm had filled with passengers it left the station in a cloud of steam and we found seats in a compartment, again taking turns to keep awake. When dawn came I saw that we were travelling through the wintry countryside of Bavaria. The snow, collecting along the edges of the windows, framed a picture of white roofs and towers set in the hollows of the hills. Sometimes beside the track an *autobahn* stretched like a tape threading through the forest and long convoys of military vehicles moved into the mist.

At nine on the second morning of the escape the train drew into Ulm and we left it, making our way towards the booking office. Luteyn calmly asked the girl for two tickets to Singen on the Swiss frontier. She frowned and my heart began to sink. She asked for papers and we showed our papers to her.

'I must fetch the railway police. Stay here.'

We did not wish to run away, hoping that our papers would satisfy them. A fat, red-faced railway policeman in his dark blue uniform asked us why we wished to go to the frontier zone. Luteyn explained that we were due to begin work in Ulm on the morrow and wished to spend a short vacation. The policeman, looking baffled, released us and we started to leave the station, walking across the big square in front. There was a shout behind us.

'Come back, gentlemen! I want to speak to you again.'

The policeman took us to an office in the goods-yard where a thin, tight-lipped German railway police lieutenant sat at a desk.

They have their exits

He examined our false papers with bewilderment. It appeared to me that the writing on them did not make sense to him. I could hardly stop myself from laughing as he lifted them to the light, looking, no doubt, for water marks. He was, however, impressed by Luteyn's Dutch passport and there seemed no inkling in his mind that we were escaped prisoners of war.

'I don't understand these men at all,' he said helplessly. 'Take them to the Labour Office. I wish someone would control these foreign workers more efficiently.'

We walked across the square outside the station escorted by another policeman with a revolver. We chatted gaily in German, complimenting the man on the beauties of the town of Ulm. He was flattered and asked us about our own country of Holland. So much did we win his confidence that when we reached the State Labour Office, where men in brown uniforms with spades stood guard at the entrance, he bade us walk up the steps on our own, saying he would wait for us. His parting words were:

'You speak good German. Go and report to the office on the first floor and I shall wait for you here.'

Smiling to ourselves and hardly able to believe our good fortune, we climbed to the top floor of the building and it was not long before we discovered some stairs on the far side from the entrance. Hurrying down them we left by another door. Avoiding the policeman and the guards with spades, we made for the back streets of Ulm, and Luteyn bought a map of the surrounding country in a small shop.

The cold had now become intense and, walking beyond the suburbs of Ulm, we left the snow-capped roofs of the university town behind us and hurried towards the town of Laupheim. It was nearly dusk when we reached the market square and, asking the way to the station, we took tickets to Stockach, a village as near to the Swiss frontier as we dared to go. The country folk on the platform watched us in silence as we sat upon the bench sleepily waiting for the train. When it arrived we entered a wooden compartment too tired to be able to take turns to stay awake. The train jolted on into the night. We wakened only at the sound of a halt, and after passing the village of Pfullendorf we reached Stockach about nine in the evening.

Of Stockach I only remember white cottages in the moonlight and a doubtful station master watching us as we walked into the hills hoping to reach the frontier town of Singen when the moon went down and the frontier was in darkness. The road began to rise steeply through the forests and great banks of snow were on either side of us. Even by two o'clock in the morning we still had many miles to go, struggling along the icy road as the moon began to wane. The road slowly descended towards Singen.

It seemed hopeless to try to cross the frontier that night and we determined to look for somewhere to hide until the following evening. At five o'clock on the morning of January 8th, we were still moving towards Singen. Lights showed ahead of us in the roadway and to our tired eyes they seemed welcoming and kind. Then the figures of four men appeared. They were woodcutters walking to work from Singen. They hailed us and we wished them good morning. Something about us surprised them.

'Are you Poles?' said one of them.

'Yes,' replied Luteyn.

'I don't believe it,' said another. 'Poles are not allowed out of their camp at five in the morning.'

Evidently there was a Polish labour camp in the neighbourhood. The four woodcutters looked startled and undecided. As for me, I was near to surrender. My feet seemed to be frozen in my boots as if in blocks of ice. I hardly cared that we had come so far only to be recaptured. I could only think of warm fires and beds.

'Go, Hans, fetch the police,' said the oldest woodcutter. The man called Hans who wheeled a bicycle, mounted it and rode off towards Singen. The remainder confronted us uncertainly. They did not try to detain us but stood irresolute and dumb. We suddenly realised that they were frightened of us. Without a word we dashed to the side of the road and into the forest, running in the snow until we sank exhausted. My breath came painfully and my head began to swim. I could not look at the whiteness around me without pain. We rose to our feet after a

minute and began to move across a clearing. There was no sign
of the woodcutters. As I walked there came over me a kind of
delirium between sleep and waking. I thought that I was on
some parade ground in England. I felt a figure beside me and
turned to see my old Colonel marching in the snow in his
uniform and field boots. I spoke to him and addressed him
respectfully.

'What the hell?' said Luteyn.

'It's all right,' I said ashamed.

Luteyn grunted impatiently, and a few paces across the
clearing we came to a large wooden hut surrounded by a fence.
There was the outline of a pathway, shrubs and flower beds in
the snow, and beside the hut were beehives. We walked up to the
hut and tried the doors which were all locked, but a small
window in the wall was open. We lifted ourselves in and
staggered crazily around the hut in the faint light of dawn.
There was no sound of life. We found a kitchen and two rooms
in one of which there was a bed. Tired and faint, we lay together
on the bed in the intense cold and with an old blanket over us fell
into a deep sleep, not waking until the afternoon.

When we awoke there had been another heavy fall of snow
which luckily concealed our footsteps leading to the hut. From
outside it seemed that we could hear the far-off sound of dogs
and we got ready to escape into the woods. But as the hours
passed no one came in sight and the sound of barking grew faint.
Searching the hut, we found in one corner of the kitchen, spades
and shovels, and hanging behind the door, two long white coats
evidently used by the bee-keeper.

According to our map, we were in the middle of a forest, two or
three miles from Singen. We planned, therefore, to leave the hut
at dusk and walk along the road to the town. West of the town
and to the south lay woods through which ran the road and
railway line to Schaffhausen in Switzerland. At some points the
road formed the frontier between Switzerland and Germany.

Shortly before five o'clock on this afternoon of the eighth of
January, we shouldered spades, and carrying the two white

coats under our arms we cut through the forest to the road to Singen. For more than a mile we saw no one on the road, then the lights of bicycles came towards us and a voice called 'Halt.' In the glow of the bicycle lamps I could see two boys in the uniform of the Hitler Youth, each armed with truncheons. I felt no fear of them. Refreshed by sleep, I was determined they should not stop us. The boys spoke in a hectoring fashion.

'What are your names and where are you going?'

'We are Westphalians working in the neighbourhood and we are going back to our lodgings in Singen,' said the resourceful Luteyn. This was a good choice of disguise for the Dutch accent resembles that of the Westphalians. The boys seemed doubtful.

'What is wrong?' I said, trying to imitate Luteyn's accent.

'We have been told to look for two British prisoners who have escaped and are thought to be trying to cross the frontier tonight.'

We both laughed.

'They won't get far,' said Luteyn, 'it is much too cold for prisoners of war!'

The boys laughed uncertainly and rode off towards Singen and as we reached the town they turned again and came towards us. One said to the other:

'There are the Westphalians.'

As this conversation was taking place in the road I reflected that these boys alone stood between us and freedom. Afterwards I asked Luteyn what was in his mind.

'For me to kill one with my spade and you the other,' he said, 'what did you intend to do?'

'Exactly the same.'

We passed through Singen in the black-out, without incident, and skirting a great dark mound which seemed to be a slag heap we set off southwards through the wood, marching upon a compass bearing to the frontier. At two o'clock in the morning on the ninth of January we crossed the railway to Schaffhausen about two miles north of a point where the road forms the frontier. It was a fine, cold night and the moon was full.

They have their exits

Wrapping ourselves in the white bee-keeper's coats for camouflage, we slowly advanced until we could see a gap in the trees and lights of cars passing along the road ahead. Not far to the east were voices and lanterns and what appeared to be a frontier post.

For an hour we crouched in a ditch beside the road and watched a sentry pacing up and down only forty yards away. Here we ate the remainder of our chocolate and swallowed a few mouthfuls of snow. Black clouds began to hide the moon and the cold increased with a rising wind. I watched the German buttoning the collar of his overcoat and saw him move towards the sentry-box beside the frontier barrier.

Before us across the roadway was a smooth plain of snow surrounded by distant trees. Beyond this few hundred yards of open No Man's Land was freedom. At half-past four in the morning the sentry turned away from us. I could no longer hear his footsteps against the wind.

'Do you agree to cross now?' said Luteyn.

'This is the moment,' I whispered.

We crawled from the ditch and across the road still dressed in our white coats. We continued crawling across the field in front of us, ploughing on hands and knees through the deep snow. After what seemed an eternity we rose to our feet, and surged forward into Switzerland.

The Scarlet Pimpernel

BARONESS ORCZY

PARIS:
SEPTEMBER, 1792

A surging, seething, murmuring crowd, of beings that are human only in name, for to the eye and ear they seem naught but savage creatures, animated by vile passions and by the lust of vengeance and of hate. The hour, some little time before sunset, and the place, the West Barricade, at the very spot where, a decade later, a proud tyrant raised an undying monument to the nation's glory and his own vanity.

During the greater part of the day the guillotine had been kept busy at its ghastly work: all that France had boasted of in the past centuries, of ancient names, and blue blood, had paid toll to her desire for liberty and for fraternity. The carnage had only ceased at this late hour of the day because there were other more interesting sights for the people to witness, a little while before the final closing of the barricades for the night.

And so the crowd rushed away from the Place de la Grève and made for the various barricades in order to watch this interesting and amusing sight.

It was to be seen every day, for those aristos were such fools! They were traitors to the people, of course, all of them, men, women, and children who happened to be descendants of the great men who since the Crusades had made the glory of France:

28

her old *noblesse*. Their ancestors had oppressed the people, had crushed them under the scarlet heels of their dainty buckled shoes, and now the people had become the rulers of France and crushed their former masters – not beneath their heel, for they went shoeless mostly in these days – but beneath a more effectual weight, the knife of the guillotine.

And daily, hourly, the hideous instrument of torture claimed its many victims – old men, young women, tiny children, even until the day when it would finally demand the head of a King and of a beautiful young Queen.

But this was as it should be: were not the people now the rulers of France? Every aristocrat was a traitor, as his ancestors had been before him: for two hundred years now the people had sweated, and toiled and starved, to keep a lustful court in lavish extravagance; now the descendants of those who had helped to make those courts brilliant had to hide for their lives – to fly, if they wished to avoid the tardy vengeance of the people.

And they did try to hide, and tried to fly: that was just the fun of the whole thing. Every afternoon before the gates closed and the market carts went out in procession by the various barricades, some fool of an aristo endeavoured to evade the clutches of the Committee of Public Safety. In various disguises, under various pretexts, they tried to slip through the barriers which were so well guarded by citizen soldiers of the Republic. Men in women's clothes, women in male attire, children disguised in beggar's rags: there were some of all sorts: *ci-devant* counts, marquises, even dukes, who wanted to fly from France, reach England, or some other equally accursed country, and there try to rouse foreign feeling against the glorious Revolution, or to raise an army in order to liberate the wretched prisoners in the Temple, who had once called themselves sovereigns of France.

But they were nearly always caught at the barricades. Sergeant Bibot especially at the West Gate had a wonderful nose for scenting an aristo in the most perfect disguise. Then, of course, the fun began. Bibot would look at his prey as a cat looks upon the mouse, play with him, sometimes for quite a quarter of an hour, pretend to be hoodwinked by the disguise, by the wigs and other bits of theatrical make-up which hid the identity of a *ci-devant* noble marquise or count.

Oh! Bibot had a keen sense of humour, and it was well worth hanging round that West Barricade, in order to see him catch an aristo in the very act of trying to flee from the vengeance of the people.

Sometimes Bibot would let his prey actually out by the gates, allowing him to think for the space of two minutes at least that he really had escaped out of Paris, and might even manage to reach the coast of England in safety: but Bibot would let the unfortunate wretch walk about ten metres towards the open country, then he would send two men after him and bring him back stripped of his disguise.

Oh! that was extremely funny, for as often as not the fugitive would prove to be a woman, some proud marchioness, who looked terribly comical when she found herself in Bibot's clutches after all, and knew that a summary trial would await her the next day, and after that the fond embrace of Madame la Guillotine.

No wonder that on this fine afternoon in September the crowd round Bibot's gate was eager and excited. The lust of blood grows with its satisfaction, there is no satiety: the crowd had seen a hundred noble heads fall beneath the guillotine to-day, it wanted to make sure that it would see another hundred fall on the morrow.

Bibot was sitting on an overturned and empty cask close by the gate of the barricade: a small detachment of citoyen soldiers were under his command. The work had been very hot lately. Those cursed aristos were becoming terrified and tried their hardest to slip out of Paris: men, women and children, whose ancestors, even in remote ages, had served those traitorous Bourbons, were all traitors themselves and right food for the guillotine. Every day Bibot had had the satisfaction of unmasking some fugitive royalists and sending them back to be tried by the Committee of Public Safety, presided over by that good patriot, Citoyen Foucquier Tinville.

Robespierre and Danton both had commended Bibot for his zeal, and Bibot was proud of the fact that he on his own initiative had sent at least fifty aristos to the guillotine.

But to-day all the sergeants in command at the various barricades had had special orders. Recently a very great number of aristos had succeeded in escaping out of France and in reaching England safely. There were curious rumours about these escapes; they had become very frequent and singularly daring; the people's minds were becoming strangely excited about it all. Sergeant Grospierre had been sent to the guillotine for allowing a whole family of aristos to slip out of the North Gate under his very nose.

It was asserted that these escapes were organized by a band of Englishmen, whose daring seemed to be unparalleled and who, from sheer desire to meddle in what did not concern them, spent their spare time in snatching away lawful victims destined for Madame la Guillotine. These rumours soon grew in extravagance; there was no doubt that this band of meddlesome Englishmen did exist; moreover, they seemed to be under the leadership of a man whose pluck and audacity were almost fabulous. Strange stories were afloat of how he and those aristos whom he rescued became suddenly invisible as they reached the barricades, and escaped out of the gates by sheer supernatural agency.

No one had seen these mysterious Englishmen; as for their leader, he was never spoken of, save with a superstitious shudder. Citoyen Foucquier Tinville would in the course of the day receive a scrap of paper from some mysterious source; sometimes he would find it in the pocket of his coat, at others it would be handed to him by some one in the crowd, whilst he was on his way to the sitting of the Committee of Public Safety. The paper always contained a brief notice that the band of meddlesome Englishmen were at work, and it was always signed with a device drawn in red – a little star-shaped flower, which we in England call the Scarlet Pimpernel. Within a few hours of the receipt of this impudent notice, the citoyens of the Committee of Public Safety would hear that so many royalists and aristocrats had succeeded in reaching the coast, and were on their way to England and safety.

The guards at the gates had been doubled, the sergeants in command had been threatened with death, whilst liberal rewards were offered for the capture of these daring and impudent Englishmen. There was a sum of five thousand francs promised to the man who laid hands on the mysterious and elusive Scarlet Pimpernel.

Every one felt that Bibot would be that man, and Bibot allowed that belief to take firm root in everybody's mind; and so, day after day, people came to watch him at the West Gate, so as to be present when he laid hands on any fugitive aristo who perhaps might be accompanied by that mysterious Englishman.

'Bah!' he said to his trusted corporal, 'Citoyen Grospierre was a fool! Had it been me now, at that North Gate last week...'

Citoyen Bibot spat on the ground to express his contempt for his comrade's stupidity.

'How did it happen, citoyen?' asked the corporal.

'Grospierre was at the gate, keeping good watch,' began Bibot, pompously, as the crowd closed in round him, listening eagerly to his narrative. 'We've all heard of this meddlesome Englishman, this accursed Scarlet Pimpernel. He won't get through *my gate*, morbleu! unless he be the devil himself. But Grospierre was a fool. The market carts were going through the gates; there was one laden with casks, and driven by an old man, with a boy beside him. Grospierre was a bit drunk, but he thought himself very clever; he looked into the casks – most of them, at least – and saw they were empty, and let the cart go through.'

A murmur of wrath and contempt went round the group of ill-clad wretches who crowded round Citoyen Bibot.

'Half an hour later,' continued the sergeant, 'up comes a captain of the guard with a squad of some dozen soldiers with him. "Has a cart gone through?" he asks of Grospierre, breathlessly. "Yes," says Grospierre, "not half an hour ago." "And you have let them escape," shouts the captain furiously. "You'll go to the guillotine for this, citoyen sergeant! that cart held concealed the *ci-devant* Duc de Chalis and all his family!" "What!" thunders Grospierre, aghast. "Aye! and the driver was none other than that cursed Englishman, the Scarlet Pimpernel." '

A howl of execration greeted this tale. Citoyen Grospierre had paid for his blunder on the guillotine, but what a fool! oh! what a fool!

Bibot was laughing so much at his own tale that it was some time before he could continue.

'"After them, my men," shouts the captain,' he said, after a while, '"remember the reward; after them, they cannot have gone far!" And with that he rushes through the gate, followed by his dozen soldiers.'

'But it was too late!' shouted the crowd, excitedly.

'They never got them!'

'Curse that Grospierre for his folly.'

'He deserved his fate!'

'Fancy not examining those casks properly!'

But these sallies seemed to amuse Citoyen Bibot exceedingly; he laughed until his sides ached, and the tears streamed down his cheeks.

'Nay, nay!' he said at last, 'those aristos weren't in the cart; the driver was not the Scarlet Pimpernel!'

'What?'

'No! The captain of the guard was that damned Englishman in disguise, and every one of his soldiers aristos!'

The crowd this time said nothing: the story certainly savoured of the supernatural, and though the Republic had abolished God, it had not quite succeeded in killing the fear of the supernatural in the hearts of the people. Truly that Englishman must be the devil himself.

The sun was sinking low down in the west. Bibot prepared himself to close the gates.

'En avant the carts,' he said.

Some dozen covered carts were drawn up in a row, ready to leave town, in order to fetch the produce from the country close by, for market the next morning. They were mostly well known to Bibot, as they went through his gate twice every day on their way to and from the town. He spoke to one or two of their drivers – mostly women – and was at great pains to examine the inside of the carts.

'You never know,' he would say, 'and I'm not going to be caught like that fool Grospierre.'

The women who drove the carts usually spent their day on the Place de la Grève, beneath the platform of the guillotine, knitting and gossiping, whilst they watched the rows of tumbrils arriving with the victims the Reign of Terror claimed every day. It was great fun to see the aristos arriving for the reception of Madame la Guillotine, and the places close by the platform were very much sought after. Bibot, during the day, had been on duty on the Place. He recognized most of the old hags, 'tricotteuses,' as they were called, who sat there and knitted whilst head after head fell beneath the knife, and they themselves got quite bespattered with the blood of those cursed aristos.

'Hé; la mère!' said Bibot to one of these horrible hags; 'what have you got there?'

He had seen her earlier in the day, with her knitting and the whip of her cart close beside her. Now she had fastened a row of curly locks to the whip handle, all colours, from gold to silver, fair to dark, and she stroked them with her huge, bony fingers as she laughed at Bibot.

'I made friends with Madame Guillotine's lover,' she said with a course laugh, 'he cut these off for me from the heads as they rolled down. He has promised me some more to-morrow, but I don't know if I shall be at my usual place.'

'Ah! how is that, la mère?' asked Bibot, who, hardened soldier though he was, could not help shuddering at the awful loathsomeness of this semblance of a woman, with her ghastly trophy on the handle of her whip.

'My grandson has got the small-pox,' she said with a jerk of her thumb towards the inside of her cart, 'some say it's the plague! If it is, I shan't be allowed to come into Paris to-morrow.'

At the first mention of the word small-pox, Bibot had stepped hastily backwards, and when the old hag spoke of the plague, he retreated from her as fast as he could.

'Curse you!' he muttered, whilst the whole crowd hastily avoided the cart, leaving it standing all alone in the midst of the place.

The old hag laughed.

'Curse you, citoyen, for being a coward,' she said. 'Bah! what a man to be afraid of sickness.'

'Morbleu! the plague!'

Every one was awe-struck and silent, filled with horror for the loathsome malady, the one thing which still had the power to arouse terror and disgust in these savage, brutalized creatures.

'Get out with you and with your plague-stricken brood!' shouted Bibot, hoarsely.

And with another rough laugh and coarse jest the old hag whipped up her lean nag and drove her cart out of the gate.

This incident had spoilt the afternoon. The people were terrified of these two horrible curses, the two maladies which nothing could cure, and which were the precursors of an awful and lonely death. They hung about the barricades, silent and sullen for a while, eyeing one another suspiciously, avoiding each other as if by instinct, lest the plague lurked already in their midst. Presently, as in the case of Grospierre, a captain of the guard appeared suddenly. But he was known to Bibot, and there was no fear of his turning out to be a sly Englishman in disguise.

'A cart...' he shouted breathlessly, even before he had reached the gates.

'What cart?' asked Bibot, roughly.

'Driven by an old hag... A covered cart...'

'There were a dozen...'

'An old hag who said her son had the plague?'

'Yes...'

'You have not let them go?'

'Morbleu!' said Bibot, whose purple cheeks had suddenly become white with fear.

'The cart contained the *ci-devant* Comtesse de Tournay and her two children, all of them traitors and condemned to death.'

'And their driver?' muttered Bibot, as a superstitious shudder ran down his spine.

'Sacré tonnerre,' said the captain, 'but it is feared that it was that accursed Englishman himself—the Scarlet Pimpernel.'

The Bald Archaeologist

JOHN BUCHAN

On his return to England in 1912, Richard Hannay has become embroiled with sinister foreign agents and plots he only half understands. Scudder has been killed by these agents and Richard Hannay is on the run in the Highlands: both from the police who believe he has committed the murder and from Scudder's enemies. Looking for refuge, he has had the bad luck to walk into his enemies' headquarters and has been imprisoned despite his disguise. Now he must escape before they identify him.

'I do not propose to let you go. If you are what you say you are, you will soon have a chance of clearing yourself. If you are what I believe you are, I do not think you will see the light much longer.'

He rang a bell, and a third servant appeared from the veranda.

'I want the Lanchester in five minutes,' he said. 'There will be three to luncheon.'

Then he looked steadily at me, and that was the hardest ordeal of all.

There was something weird and devilish in those eyes, cold,

malignant, unearthly, and most hellishly clever. They fascinated me like the bright eyes of a snake. I had a strong impulse to throw myself on his mercy and offer to join his side, and if you consider the way I felt about the whole thing you will see that that impulse must have been purely physical, the weakness of a brain mesmerized and mastered by a stronger spirit. But I managed to stick it out and even to grin.

'You'll know me next time, guv'nor,' I said.

'Karl,' he spoke in German to one of the men in the doorway, 'you will put this fellow in the storeroom till I return, and you will be answerable to me for his keeping.'

I was marched out of the room with a pistol at each ear.

The storeroom was a damp chamber in what had been the old farmhouse. There was no carpet on the uneven floor, and nothing to sit down on but a school form. It was black as pitch, for the windows were heavily shuttered. I made out by groping that the walls were lined with boxes and barrels and sacks of some heavy stuff. The whole place smelt of mould and disuse. My gaolers turned the key in the door, and I could hear them shifting their feet as they stood on guard outside.

I sat down in that chilly darkness in a very miserable frame of mind. The old boy had gone off in a motor to collect the two ruffians who had interviewed me yesterday. Now, they had seen me as the roadman, and they would remember me; for I was in the same rig. What was a roadman doing twenty miles from his beat, pursued by the police? A question or two would put them on the track. Probably they had seen Mr. Turnbull, probably Marmie too; most likely they could link me up with Sir Harry, and then the whole thing would be crystal clear. What chance had I in this moorland house with three desperadoes and their armed servants?

I began to think wistfully of the police, now plodding over the hills after my wraith. They at any rate were fellow-countrymen and honest men, and their tender mercies would be kinder than these ghoulish aliens. But they wouldn't have listened to me.

The Bald Archaeologist

That old devil with the eyelids had not taken long to get rid of them. I thought he probably had some kind of graft with the constabulary. Most likely he had letters from Cabinet Ministers saying he was to be given every facility for plotting against Britain. That's the sort of owlish way we run our politics in this jolly old country.

The three would be back for lunch, so I hadn't more than a couple of hours to wait. It was simply waiting on destruction, for I could see no way out of this mess. I wished that I had Scudder's courage, for I am free to confess I didn't feel any great fortitude. The only thing that kept me going was that I was pretty furious. It made me boil with rage to think of those three spies getting the pull on me like this. I hoped that at any rate I might be able to twist one of their necks before they downed me.

The more I thought of it the angrier I grew, and I had to get up and move about the room. I tried the shutters, but they were the kind that lock with a key, and I couldn't move them. From the outside came the faint clucking of hens in the warm sun. Then I groped among the sacks and boxes. I couldn't open the latter, and the sacks seemed to be full of things like dog-biscuits that smelt of cinnamon. But, as I circumnavigated the room, I found a handle in the wall which seemed worth investigating.

It was the door of a wall cupboard – what they call a 'press' in Scotland, – and it was locked. I shook it, and it seemed rather flimsy. For want of something better to do I put out my strength on that door, getting some purchase on the handle by looping my braces round it. Presently the thing gave with a crash which I thought would bring in my warders to inquire. I waited for a bit, and then started to explore the cupboard shelves.

There was a multitude of queer things there. I found an odd vesta or two in my trouser pockets and struck a light. It went out in a second, but showed me one thing. There was a little stock of electric torches on one shelf. I picked up one, and found it was in working order.

With the torch to help me I investigated further. There were bottles and cases of queer-smelling stuffs, chemicals no doubt for experiments, and there were coils of fine copper wire and yanks and yanks of a thin oiled silk. There was a box of detonators, and a lot of cord for fuses. Then away at the back of a shelf I found a stout brown cardboard box, and inside it a wooden case. I managed to wrench it open, and within lay half a dozen little grey bricks, each a couple of inches square.

I took up one, and found that it crumbled easily in my hand. Then I smelt it and put my tongue to it. After that I sat down to think. I hadn't been a mining engineer for nothing, and I knew lentonite when I saw it.

With one of these bricks I could blow the house to smithereens. I had used the stuff in Rhodesia and knew its power. But the trouble was that my knowledge wasn't exact. I had forgotten the proper charge and the right way of preparing it, and I wasn't sure about the timing. I had only a vague notion, too, as to its power, for though I had used it I had not handled it with my own fingers.

But it was a chance, the only possible chance. It was a mighty risk, but against it was an absolute black certainty. If I used it the odds were, as I reckoned, about five to one in favour of my blowing myself into the tree-tops; but if I didn't I should certainly be occupying a six-foot hole in the garden by the evening. That was the way I had to look at it. The prospect was pretty dark either way, but anyhow there was a chance, both for myself and for my country.

The remembrance of little Scudder decided me. It was about the beastliest moment of my life, for I'm no good at these cold-blooded resolutions. Still I managed to rake up the pluck to set my teeth and choke back the horrid doubts that flooded in on me. I simply shut off my mind and pretended I was doing an experiment as simple as Guy Fawkes fireworks.

I got a detonator, and fixed it to a couple of inches of fuse. Then I took a quarter of a lentonite brick, and buried it near the door below one of the sacks in a crack of the floor, fixing the detonator in it. For all I knew half of those boxes might be dynamite. If the cupboard held such deadly explosives, why not the boxes? In that case there would be a glorious skyward journey for me and the German servants and about an acre of the surrounding country. There was also the risk that the detonation might set off the other bricks in the cupboard, for I had forgotten most that I knew about lentonite. But it didn't do to begin thinking about the possibilities. The odds were horrible, but I had to take them.

I ensconced myself just below the sill of the window, and lit the fuse. Then I waited for a moment or two. There was dead silence – only a shuffle of heavy boots in the passage, and the peaceful cluck of hens from the warm out-of-doors. I commended my soul to my Maker, and wondered where I would be in five seconds. . .

A great wave of heat seemed to surge upwards from the floor, and hang for a blistering instant in the air. Then the wall opposite me flashed into a golden yellow and dissolved with a rending thunder that hammered my brain into a pulp. Something dropped on me, catching the point of my left shoulder.

And then I think I became unconscious.

My stupor can scarcely have lasted beyond a few seconds. I felt myself being choked by thick yellow fumes, and struggled out of the debris to my feet. Somewhere behind me I felt fresh air. The jambs of the window had fallen, and through the ragged rent the smoke was pouring out to the summer noon. I stepped over the broken lintel, and found myself standing in a yard in a dense and acrid fog. I felt very sick and ill, but I could move my limbs, and I staggered blindly forward away from the house.

A small mill lade ran in a wooden aqueduct at the other side of the yard, and into this I fell. The cool water revived me, and I had just enough wits left to think of escape. I squirmed up the lade among the slippery green slime till I reached the mill wheel. Then I wriggled through the axle hole into the old mill and tumbled on to a bed of chaff. A nail caught the seat of my trousers, and I left a wisp of heather mixture behind me.

The mill had been long out of use. The ladders were rotten with age, and in the loft the rats had gnawed great holes in the floor. Nausea shook me, and a wheel in my head kept turning, while my left shoulder and arm seemed to be stricken with the palsy. I looked out of the window and saw a fog still hanging over the house and smoke escaping from an upper window. Please God I had set the place on fire, for I could hear confused cries coming from the other side.

But I had no time to linger, since this mill was obviously a bad hiding-place. Any one looking for me would naturally follow the lade, and I made certain the search would begin as soon as they found that my body was not in the storeroom. From another window I saw that on the far side of the mill stood an old stone dovecot. If I could get there without leaving tracks I might find a hiding-place, for I argued that my enemies, if they thought I could move, would conclude I had made for open country, and would go seeking me on the moor.

I crawled down the broken ladder, scattering chaff behind me to cover my footsteps. I did the same on the mill floor, and on the threshold where the door hung on broken hinges. Peeping out, I saw that between me and the dovecot was a piece of bare cobbled ground, where no footmarks would show. Also it was mercifully hid by the mill buildings from any view from the house. I slipped across the space, got to the back of the dovecot and prospected a way of ascent.

That was one of the hardest jobs I ever took on. My shoulder and arm ached like hell, and I was so sick and giddy that I was always on the verge of falling. But I managed it somehow. By the use of out-jutting stones and gaps in the masonry and a tough ivy root I got to the top in the end. There was a little parapet behind which I found space to lie down. Then I proceeded to go off into an old-fashioned swoon.

I woke with a burning head and the sun glaring in my face. For a long time I lay motionless, for those horrible fumes seemed to have loosened my joints and dulled my brain. Sounds came to me from the house – men speaking throatily and the throbbing of a stationary car. There was a little gap in the parapet to which I wriggled, and from which I had some sort of

I felt myself being choked by yellow fumes and struggled out of the debris to my feet

prospect of the yard. I saw figures come out – a servant with his head bound up, and then a younger man in knicker-bockers. They were looking for something, and moved towards the mill. Then one of them caught sight of the wisp of cloth on the nail, and cried out to the other. They both went back to the house, and brought two more to look at it. I saw the rotund figure of my late captor, and I thought I made out the man with the lisp. I noticed that all had pistols.

For half an hour they ransacked the mill. I could hear them kicking over the barrels and pulling up the rotten planking. Then they came outside, and stood just below the dovecot, arguing fiercely. The servant with the bandage was being soundly rated. I heard them fiddling with the door of the dovecot, and for one horrid moment I fancied they were coming up. Then they thought better of it, and went back to the house.

All that long blistering afternoon I lay baking on the roof-top. Thirst was my chief torment. My tongue was like a stick, and to make it worse I could hear the cool drip of water from the mill lade. I watched the course of the little stream as it came in from the moor, and my fancy followed it to the top of the glen, where it must issue from an icy fountain fringed with ferns and mosses. I would have given a thousand pounds to plunge my face into that.

I had a fine prospect of the whole ring of moorland. I saw the car speed away with two occupants, and a man on a hill pony riding east. I judged they were looking for me, and I wished them joy of their quest.

But I saw something else more interesting. The house stood almost on the summit of a swell of moorland which crowned a sort of plateau, and there was no higher point nearer than the big hills six miles off. The actual summit, as I have mentioned, was a biggish clump of trees – firs mostly, with a few ashes and beeches. On the dovecot I was almost on a level with the tree-tops, and could see what lay beyond. The wood was not solid, but only a ring, and inside was an oval of green turf, for all the world like a big cricket field.

The Bald Archaeologist

I didn't take long to guess what it was. It was an aerodrome, and a secret one. The place had been most cunningly chosen. For suppose any one were watching an aeroplane descending here, he would think it had gone over the hill beyond the trees. As the place was on the top of a rise in the midst of a big amphitheatre, any observer from any direction would conclude it had passed out of view behind the hill. Only a man very close at hand would realize that the aeroplane had not gone over but had descended in the midst of the wood. An observer with a telescope on one of the higher hills might have discovered the truth, but only herds went there, and herds do not carry spy-glasses. When I looked from the dovecot I could see far away a blue line which I knew was the sea, and I grew furious to think that our enemies had this secret conning-tower to rake our waterways.

Then I reflected that if the aeroplane came back the chances were ten to one that I would be discovered. So through the afternoon I lay and prayed for the coming of darkness, and glad I was when the sun went down over the big western hills and the twilight haze crept over the moor. The aeroplane was late. The gloaming was far advanced when I heard the beat of wings and saw it volplaning downward to its home in the wood. Lights twinkled for a bit and there was much coming and going from the house. Then the dark fell, and silence.

Thank God it was a black night. The moon was well on its last quarter and would not rise till late. My thirst was too great to allow me to tarry, so about nine o'clock, so far as I could judge, I started to descend. It wasn't easy, and half-way down I heard the back door of the house open, and saw the gleam of a lantern against the mill wall. For some agonizing minutes I hung by the ivy and prayed that whoever it was he would not come round by the dovecot. Then the light disappeared, and I dropped as softly as I could on to the hard soil of the yard.

I crawled on my belly in the lee of a stone dyke till I reached the fringe of trees which surrounded the house. If I had known how to do it I would have tried to put that aeroplane out of action, but I realized that any attempt would probably be futile. I was pretty certain that there would be some kind of defence round the house, so I went through the wood on hands and knees, feeling carefully every inch before me. It was as well, for presently I came on a wire about two feet from the ground. If I had tripped over that, it would doubtless have rung some bell in the house and I would have been captured.

A hundred yards farther on I found another wire cunningly placed on the edge of a small stream. Beyond that lay the moor, and in five minutes I was deep in bracken and heather. Soon I was round the shoulder of the rise, in the little glen from which the mill lade flowed. Ten minutes later my face was in the spring, and I was soaking down pints of the blessed water.

But I did not stop till I had put half a dozen miles between me and that accursed dwelling.

Flight to Freedom

MICHAEL DONNET

Two young Belgian fliers grounded after the Germans' occupation of their country in the Second World War discover an aeroplane hidden in the grounds of a chateau. Unobserved by the Germans who have requisitioned the chateau, the boys set to work to restore the plane and fly it to England.

Two nights later we were back again. This time Miche Jansen had got something else for us, or rather someone else. Pierre Nottet was an aircraft engineer as well as an air force pilot and he had volunteered to try and find out why the Stampe engine would not start.

Divoy, Nottet and Miche worked in the hangar whilst I kept watch outside. So accustomed had we become to carrying on our clandestine activities that at first I couldn't believe it when I detected footsteps in the distance coming from the Chateau. I hissed a hurried warning to the others and they slipped out. I just had time to close the doors before joining them in a thick patch of bushes nearby. The unknown walker came nearer. He was whistling softly to himself. I remember it was the 'Radetzky March' and he was a bit out of key. As he came nearer I tightened my hand round the butt of my revolver and beside me

Divoy had a spanner ready. The man, whoever he was, walked steadily on and we heard his footsteps pass into the forest and his whistle float away into the darkness. He never knew how near death he was at that moment.

Half-an-hour later the mystery of the engine was solved. The Stampe had been fitted with special throttles for inverted flying and we had inadvertently connected up the linkage the wrong way so that when we thought the throttle was open it was in fact shut!

It was again too late to do anything that night. We tidied up and covered our traces and melted back into the forest and headed home. This time we set a date and it was to be the following Friday, the 4th July. Someone reminded me it was American Independence Day and I thought it was as good a date as any.

Jansen persuaded us to change our usual routine. We should have done it long ago, but hadn't thought about it in our eagerness to get things ready.

Divoy and I were to meet up and go together to Jansen's house. He would then drive us out in his car and leave it in the garden of a friend's house for his return journey.

Once again we counted the hours and felt the tension build up and our stomachs get tighter. So often had we made the trip out to Terbloc and so often had our hopes been dashed at the last minute. Just what could go wrong next? We couldn't think of anything but no doubt Lady Luck would still have a nasty one up her sleeve!

There were only two people on the rear platform of the tram out to Miche's home. Myself and a German S.S. officer. All the way, he never took his eyes off me and carefully inspected every inch, taking in my raincoat, my red scarf and my boots. I had hoped his eyes were not too penetrating for in my grip were the revolvers and under the raincoat I was in uniform.

I decided to take the initiative and smiled at him. Unexpectedly under his peaked cap his face broke into an answering tight-lipped smile and he moved off inside the tram and sat down. I got off at the next stop just to get out of the way of those eyes.

It was a lovely evening with the sort of sunset which promises a fine night and a day to follow. As planned Divoy, Miche and I got out to Groenendael in Jansen's car. To wait for darkness we sat on the terrace of the village café and drank a beer or two, chatting with forced nonchalance about anything we could think of to take our minds off what might lie ahead.

Following our usual route down the lane and through the trees we quickly opened the shed after fixing the instruments. Jansen and Divoy embarked on the last check of the aircraft and then we sat and waited until the exact time we had planned came round. That was the worst. The waiting, with the meadow in bright moonlight and the lights from the Chateau. The windows were obviously open and we could hear voices louder than usual.

Two a.m. We got to our feet and, pushing and grunting, got the Stampe moving across the grass. We could still see the wheel marks left when we had pushed her out last. Why in God's name had no one else noticed them?

We got her down to the end of the field. Then it was handshakes again and Divoy and I climbed up to the cockpit.

Jansen handed up to us the papers we had to take to London and I stowed them away securely. We had wrapped them in a petrol-soaked rug so we could destroy them easily if necessary.

The hands of Divoy's beloved alarm clock on the instrument panel ticked off the last few minutes to 2.45 a.m. This was it!

'Ready?'

'All set.'

'Switches off.'

'Switches off. Suck-in.'

A couple of turns of the propeller.

'Contact?'

'Contact.'

Jansen took a firm grip on the propeller blade, heaved it over compression, then skipped quickly back.

The motor coughed, spluttered, fired and then Divoy had it

caught on the throttle and it broke into an ear-splitting roar! The night's silence was shattered. Jansen ran round to the side of the cockpit and punched each of our arms in turn.

'Bon voyage!' he yelled above the engine. No need to whisper now. We knew that if the Germans came running it would take them five minutes to reach us but the engine had to warm up. I saw Jansen by now running away into the shadows and I was half out of my seat with impatience for Divoy to get that throttle open. We held it for two minutes, then the fuselage vibrated as the throttle went wide and the engine took on a louder roar. Slowly we began to trundle forward over the grass, then faster and faster. The Stampe bounced along and I felt the tail lift. Bounce, thud, bounce, another thud. The black shadowy trees were beginning to blur past now and I thought I could hear shouting. I had my revolver cocked and ready over the side. Nothing, no one was going to stop us now! I felt the control column ease back. She rose, sank again then came up and suddenly the jolting had ceased and we were airborne!

Then the stick jolted forward and we pitched down into a dive heading straight for the trees. We both had our hands on the control column. I was in front and Divoy with the dual control was in the rear cockpit. We pulled hard and she came up, wheels and wings brushing the leaves. Then we were up and over the trees. I saw the ground drop away and the forest and Terbloc and the shed and the field fall into the dark behind. Up, up through the night sky we climbed, the little engine roaring away as if it, too, was joyous at being in the air again. At 10,000 feet Divoy levelled off. I don't know what he felt like but my mind was a whirl of excitement, relief, and sheer unmitigated surprise that we seemed to have done it. I twisted round and I could see his face split in a triumphant grin. He reached one arm forward over the cowling between the two cockpits. I reached mine back and we grasped hands. I leaned my head back, looked up at the stars and laughed outright.

I checked our course as best I could. About sixty degrees left of the Pole Star would give us a true course of about three-zero-

zero degrees and this would bring us to England. The little engine sang sweetly. Now it was everything to us. All our hopes and our future, in this world or the next, hung on that engine.

We could make out Ghent and the Scheldt estuary. This meant we had drifted too far north and had to correct. Divoy banked to port until we thought it was about right, then levelled off again. Suddenly we both shot bolt upright as the aircraft, us and the sky were bathed in a sudden white glare. Then we realised it was a searchlight groping for us across the sky. It missed us and the beam swept on leaving us in the dark as we crossed the coast and saw the dull, silver glimmer of the sea.

Then the motor died away! All at once silence, emptiness and despair. We madly jerked throttles, switched on and off, turned fuel-cocks every way. Nothing happened. We continued gliding silently through the night: the sea which now looked cold and hostile, waiting for us below. Suddenly I remembered we had forgotten to bring the two old car inner tubes which were to be our survival gear. 'I can't swim,' came Divoy's voice over the headphones. He sounded gloomy. I didn't know if he were joking or not. By now it was too late to consider a forced landing inland or on a beach. We were down to a thousand feet and bracing ourselves for a wet, crash landing.

Then, as suddenly as it had stopped, the engine picked up! The unbelievable had happened. Why or how we never knew but there were all the pistons pumping up and down again like mad and all the valves popping open and shut and that blessed roar of power once again.

Slowly we regained altitude and with every revolution of the propeller our escape grew more certain. Even if that engine did it again on us surely we could now glide down to somewhere where a British ship or aircraft would see us.

As we cruised along under the stars I wondered about that engine. What had caused it to stop at that crucial moment and why was it running rough now and cutting intermittently? Luck had been on our side, as when the engine cut first the sudden silence must have put off the anti-aircraft sound detectors which were used by the Germans to bring the guns to bear and start shooting. Then when it picked up low this might have been a trick of Lady Luck. If at all she would keep her keen 'supervision' of our flight a little longer. This was my prayer.

Divoy had a splendid sense of occasion and it did not fail him on this one. He groped around in his cockpit and reached his arm forward to me again. This time, it was a bottle of brandy and together under the stars, at several thousand feet and half-way to England, we drank our toast to freedom!

Nevertheless we were not out of trouble even yet. Every time we reached 3,000 feet the motor started to cough and splutter. It began to feel very cold. Just before sunrise I took over the controls and behind me the blackness of the sky began to pale as a hint of the coming dawn. Ahead and above the stars continued to glitter. It seemed as if a million eyes were watching us with amused interest; just to see if we would make it, or plunge into the grey sea stretching from horizon to horizon.

I realised all at once that the horizon ahead was broken slightly here and there from its level line. It must be the English coast. Nearer and nearer came the faint line where sky and sea joined and then suddenly it was a line no longer but the loom of a flat, muddy coast pierced with watery inlets. I pored over the map but could find nothing resembling what I saw below. I could now make out sandbanks and mud flats with flocks of gulls roosting at the end of their night's sleep. At this moment the rim of the sun slid above the horizon behind us and all at once it was green fields below. I made out a road and a farmhouse or two. If only the coast defences let us alone, we had it made! Come to think of it, where were those defences? We had thought to find the English coast bristling and alert and that we would certainly be intercepted by fighters. It seemed almost an insult to have come in an hour or two from enemy-occupied Europe and to be greeted with such sleepy, morning indifference.

This quiet had me worried. Had something gone wrong with our navigation? Had we unknowingly in the dark gone round in a circle. Was the land below not a welcoming England but a very inhospitable Holland or France?

The engine began spluttering again and we realised that we would have to make a landing somewhere; preferably in a spot of our own choosing while we still had some power. In any event we had only about fifteen minutes' fuel left so the matter was really beyond any decision we might make.

We peered over the side, Divoy to port and I to starboard. Then I called Divoy to my side and he saw exactly what we had been looking for. A nice, level-looking field between a road and a railway line. We flew round it in approved, initial flying school manner, inspecting the surface. It looked O.K. Divoy continued round across the downwind end of the field, flew back up then turned in, sideslipping to lose height. He straightened out, cut the motor, and eased the stick back. There was a gentle shiver, a bump, then another bump and we were down. We rolled jerkily a few yards then slowed to a stop. The engine cut and we sat there in silence. Somewhere a bird commenced his morning song and a little wind rippled the grass of the field.

'Good man,' I said to Divoy. 'Another landing like that and you'll be fit for solo.'

We still were not sure if we had made it. It might not be England.

We scrambled stiffly from the machine. Over to one side there was a small wood, ideally placed to hide fugitive aviators not sure which country they are in. We made a bee-line for it and hid our belongings. Then we took a careful look around.

At one end of the field we saw something we had not noticed before. It was a farm-house with a red tiled roof. Obviously that should be our first port of call. Stepping cautiously across the grass we could see a farm cart standing in the yard. It had something on the side. 'Smith Brothers & Sons.' Divoy read it slowly. 'Sounds English enough,' he said. I nodded. We pushed open the gate. Then I nudged Divoy. 'This is England all right.'

'How can you tell?'

I chuckled.

'Look at those bedroom windows. Open. Only the English

sleep with their windows open all night!'

As for the English people, their first representative came round the corner at that moment. He was an oldish man with a white moustache. I summoned up my best English. 'Good morning. Please, where is this place?'

He looked startled and replied automatically, never taking his eyes off us.

'Thorpe-le-Soken.'

'Is that in England?'

He seemed astonished at such a question.

''Course it is. In Essex.'

An Act of God

GEOFFREY KILNER

For Joe Burkinshaw in 1930 there was no choice; at the age of seven he had to join his brother, Jud, working in the coal mine with little hope of escaping from the darkness, the toil and the danger.

On that day in July when it had happened there had been nothing in the half-light before dawn to suggest that this day was different from any other. They were in a spell of hot weather, but that made little difference underground, too deep for the hottest sun to reach. Joe and Jud had gone down in the cage as usual.

The winding engine jetted steam and the sheer drop of the cage past the shaft-works sent them plunging into darkness. Joe and Jud worked together. Jud could protect him a bit with his good humour, even though he was nothing special as a fighter.

Joe didn't remember anything about that day; it had been like any other. But then in the afternoon there came a shout down the shaft: 'Bring everybody out!' it said to the pit-bottom man. The word passed, travelling on the blown air, and everywhere work stopped. The candles were put out. What could it be but gas?

Stumbling, elbowing in darkness, all going too fast, they clogged and crushed their way to the pit-bottom. There, they

55

gathered, waited, knowing nothing. Fear and anger mounted until the place was a din that baffled any effort to understand.

William Lamb shouted, roared out over the confusion, and beat down the noise and fear. 'Don't press!' he told them when he had quiet. 'Move out a bit, there are kiddies being crushed. Listen! Listen for their shout!' He called up the shaft to the top, and everybody listened. But the shaft gave no answer.

''t engine's stopped! How can they get us up?' A voice broke the silence. They pressed together. Joe found himself lifted off his feet, squeezed, his ribs pressed in fit to crack. The voices rose now in panic. ''t Fountain Shaft!' It was a quarter of a mile away. There, they would be taken up. The press moved, carrying Joe away from the wide space where everyone had gathered.

He let himself be bundled along until he could duck out of the crowd into the shelter of a niche between two props. Here, he waited until all had gone by, and then he followed on behind. Other children had sought safety this way, but he could not find Jud. William Lamb came along after them. He had taken a lamp from the pit-bottom, and he walked with a group of stragglers towards the Fountain Shaft.

Again, when they arrived, William Lamb bore down on the shouting and compelled a silence. But to his call up the shaft there was no answer. There was no sound from the top, either of engine or of men.

The children had gathered together, and, keeping close, quiet, they decided what they must do. 'Ask William Lamb, ask 'im if we can go.' At first William Lamb wouldn't hear of it. 'We don't know what t'trouble is. It might be gas, but we don't know where. Stop here a bit.'

But they went in ones and twos and pestered him: 'Why not? We'll come back if there's owt wrong.' And, at last, he agreed.

Over half a mile away there was a walk-in entrance to the pit. There was a road that followed the stratum of the coal seam and rose gradually to this entrance. The children had been given permission to follow it and walk out into daylight on the hillside at the place called Haigh Moor Dayhole.

Free from the restraint of waiting about they went quickly. Joe found Jud, and the brothers went together. There was barely any talk, just a common will to travel the distance and get out of the darkness after so much fear and uncertainty.

It was the way the ponies went to the surface; it was wide enough, and the roof was high. The children kept close, but there seemed to be no danger. At each air-door they feared what they might meet; but everything was as usual. When they came to the last door it seemed that whatever danger there had been was left behind them; they had shut doors on it. Soon they would see the light of day.

Someone held open the last door until everyone was through, and they began to climb the last of the slope in a ragged line. There were forty of them.

Joe heard it, and that was strange, because he was not one of the leaders of the line; he and Jud walked about the middle. It was the sound of water, racing, hissing, a first wave thrust on by the thick force of a torrent behind.

There was a side-slit a little raised from the level of the road. Props stood in open space there, for it was an old working. It took Joe a little time to think, and then he grabbed Jud's arm and dragged him towards the space at the side. Jud resisted a fraction too long; falling bodies and the force of the water had struck him before he realised his danger. He snatched at Joe who had one arm safely hooked around a prop.

The water nearly dragged Joe free; it pushed his legs and unbalanced him, swirling round his knees. But he clung to his prop and had the advantage of Jud in being a foot higher. Jud was torn from his hold and swept with all those who had failed to anchor themselves. The torrent crashed by where Joe had fastened himself; it burst over the others and beat them back against the air-door which they had just closed behind them. There, it builded over them to the roof, sealed them off, and deepened back until its flow was cut. Then it began to leak away slowly under the door into the pit.

Suddenly, where Joe clung, mindless of everything but the

need to resist the pull of the water, the force diminished until there was no torrent, nothing but water pooled deep about his legs. Gingerly, he took a step into the road and upwards towards the way out. There were others moving cautiously, the same, bewildered by what had happened to them. Nobody dared to think of what had happened to the rest in the blackness behind.

When their first steps were permitted – no force of water pressing them down, no second wave threatening from above – they all began to thrust and splash their way upward until they were clear, running now over a wet but firm floor. And they all went frantically upwards, towards the light, pushing and stumbling as the light of day appeared and invited them ahead.

Joe flung his arms wide as he burst out into day, and then he fell down onto the sodden ground, lying in mud, and panting to recover breath. But he was exultant to have escaped, safe; until his breath came back he had no thought but joy.

When he stood and looked about him, he thought of finding people, men, to whom he could give the responsibility for Jud and the others back there, beyond that entrance which he dare not even turn to see. But the world that Joe saw before him in the hot glare of light was a world that seemed empty of people, and terribly, crazily changed.

In the distance the hills were white with snow. Snow on a hot July day! Nearer at hand, the land was flooded in its hollows, water swirled, trees were down, some floating in new-made lakes, others, whole rows of them, lay and leaned in crazed collapse. Dry-stone walls were tumbled, their heaviest stones swept by torrents out into the road. It was all too much to understand, all crazy, too mad to be believed.

Joe stood with the rest of the survivors. They spoke together in cowed voices, lest the mad force that had caused all this to happen should decide to start again. They wanted to show themselves content with the present state of glowering calm. But they were uneasy here, near to the scene of the disaster, and away from people. All of them wanted to find protection and

The water nearly dragged Joe free

comfort. Cautiously, they moved away, going with stealthy haste towards houses.

They met a man trying to steer water out of his garden; he dug a channel through the gap where his wall had been. The door of the house was open on a flood, and several window-panes were broken, downstairs and up.

'Where've you come from?' he asked wearily. One of the big lads told him, and described how the water had met them coming out, how a lot of the young 'uns were still in there 'drownded'.

The man stopped digging. 'Go an' tell iverybody you can see,' he said. 'Send 'em up to t'day hole. I'll go an' have a look.'

They went into the village telling everybody. Soon there were men on their way to the scene. It was too late to save anyone. Joe knew that Jud was dead. He got away on his own, and set off home. He daren't go back to the pit; he dreaded having to say it at home: 'Our Jud's got drownded.'

His mam raised herself from where she leaned over the table. Joe saw her hand pressed into her back as she made the effort to straighten herself. 'Have they sent you out?' she asked, and showed alarm, noticing the expression on his face.

He said it: 'Some young'uns have got drownded. Our Jud—'

'Where is he?' Her voice went high with dread.

'He's there'

'Where is he?'

'In Haigh Moor Dayhole. I couldn't hold him. T'water came in—' He tried to tell it, but she wasn't listening, she was shouting out her grief and painfully moving about getting herself ready to go. Suddenly she noticed him standing miserable and wet, wretched, with a black hand on the table. 'Tha're niver goin' back down that pit. Niver as long as I live. Niver, niver!' And she held out her arms to him, and Joe rushed forward to her, and buried his face in her body and wept.

All confusion for long afterwards. The hailstones, as big as walnuts, lay unmelted on the hills for days. They had broken windows, and people couldn't stop recounting the marvels that had been seen in this sudden, freak storm, whose brief fury had devastated a whole sweep of country along a path no more than a few hundred yards broad.

The day had dawned without the sun showing. Yet heat had inflamed a heavy air that was too thick to flow. It was a sour, glaring light that had hung over South Yorkshire all morning, and the sky made flashings and crackling. It leaned ominously over the land.

In the afternoon the clouds split and instant rain crashed down. Great stones of hail came too and flattened the ripening wheat in the fields. Windows, sky-lights, were burst in, and the hot-house glass at Wentworth Hall nearby was smashed as with hammers. But it was the rain that people talked of longest. It carried away the very earth, baring tree roots and toppling the growth into a sweeping flood. A line of poplars, thirty years old, was so felled. At Wentworth Hall again, the rain dropped through shattered rooflights and cascaded down the great staircase. At Wharncliffe Pit the rising water filled the sump that took the winding engine's waste. The level rose and so swamped the fire. This was the warning that went down the shaft when the engine stopped. The same thing happened at the Fountain Shaft.

The storm lasted two hours. Damage was beyond calculation; but when the carts rolled down the streets bringing the dead children women tore their hair. Jud, his face wiped clean, his body clothed, was one of the twenty brought into Silkworth.

Where Eagles Dare
ALISTAIR MACLEAN

Major Smith, his girl-friend Mary Ellison and an American lieutenant called Schaffer have been sent with three British agents, Carraciola, Thomas and Christiansen to invade an 'impenetrable' gestapo commando post. The mission is to discover which of the three British agents is working for the Nazis and to rescue Corporal Carnaby-Jones who is being held prisoner. The only way to leave the Schloss Adler is by cable car and when they discover that all the agents are Nazis, they try to escape with their three prisoners. But as they climb down the cable-car header station, Schaffer is overpowered and the agents take the cable-car. The only way to stop them is for Smith to jump onto the roof of the car as it moves off on its journey down the mountain.

'No!' For perhaps two dazed, incredulous seconds that were the longest seconds she had ever known, Mary had quite failed to gather Smith's intention: when shocked understanding did come, her voice rose to a scream. 'No! No! For God's sake, no!'

Smith ignored the heart-broken voice, the desperate clutching hand and walked to the end of the flat section of the roof. At the lower edge of the steeply sloping roof section the leading edge of the cable-car had just come into view: a cable-car with, inside it, three men who were exchanging delighted grins and thumping one another joyously on the back.

Smith ran down the ice-coated pitch of the roof, reached the edge and jumped. The cable-car was already seven or eight feet beyond him and almost as far below. Had the cable-car not been going away from him he must surely have broken both legs. As it was, he landed with a jarring teeth-rattling crash, a crash that caused the cable-car to shudder and sway and his legs to buckle and slide from beneath him on the ice-coated roof. His injured right hand failed to find a purchase on the suspension bracket and in his blindly despairing grab with his left hand he was forced to drop his Luger. It slid to the edge of the roof and fell away into the darkness of the valley below. Smith wrapped both arms round the suspension bracket and fought to draw some whooping gasps of air into his starving lungs: he had been completely winded by the fall.

In their own way, the three men inside the cable-car were as nearly stunned as Smith himself. The smiles had frozen on their faces and Christiansen's arm was still poised in mid-air where it had been arrested by the sound and the shock of Smith's landing on the cable-car roof. Carraciola, predictably was the first to recover and react. He snatched the Schmeisser from Christiansen and pointed it upwards.

The cable-car was now forty to fifty feet clear of the castle and the high wind was beginning to swing it, pendulum-like, across the sky. Smith, weakened by the impact of the fall, the pain in his hand and the loss of blood, hung on grimly and dizzily to the suspension bracket, his body athwart the roof of the car. He felt sick and exhausted and there seemed to be a mist in front of his eyes.

From shoulder to knee and only inches from his body a venomous burst of machine-pistol fire stitched a pattern of holes in the cable-car roof: the mists cleared away from Smith's eyes more quickly than he would have believed possible. A Schmeisser magazine held far more shells than that. They would wait a second or two to see if a falling body passed any of the side windows – with that violently swinging transverse movement it was virtually impossible for anyone to fall off over the leading or trailing ends of the car – and if none came, then they would fire again. But where? What would be the next area of roof chosen for treatment? Would the gunman fire at random or to a systematic pattern? It was impossible to guess. Perhaps at that very moment the muzzle of the Schmeisser was only two inches from the middle of his spine. The very thought was enough to galvanise Smith into a quick roll that stretched him out over the line of holes that had just been made. It was unlikely that the gunman would fire in exactly the same place again, but even that was a gamble, the gunman might figure just as Smith was doing and traverse the same area again. But he wasn't figuring the same as Smith, the next burst was three feet away towards the trailing end of the car.

Using the suspension bracket as support, Smith pulled himself to his feet until he was quite vertical, hanging on to the cable itself. This way, the possible target area was lessened by eighty per cent. Quickly, soundlessly, sliding his hands along the cable, he moved forward until he was standing at the very front of the car.

The cable-car's angle of arc through the sky was increasing with every swing of the pendulum. The purchase for his feet was minimal, all the strain came on his arms, and by far the greater part of that on his sound left arm. There was nothing smoothly progressive about the cable-car's sideways motion through the sky, it jumped and jerked and jarred and jolted like a Dervish dancer in the last seconds before total collapse. The strain on the left arm was intolerable, it felt as if the shoulder sinews were being torn apart: but shoulder sinews are reparable whereas the effects of a Schmeisser blast at point blank range were not. And it seemed, to Smith, highly unlikely that anybody would waste a burst on the particular spot where he was standing, the obvious position for any roof passenger who didn't want to be shaken off into the valley below was flat out on the roof with his arms wrapped for dear life round one of the suspension arm's support brackets.

His reasoning was correct. There were three more bursts, none of which came within feet of him, and then no more. Smith knew that he would have to return to the comparative security of the suspension arm and return there soon. He was nearly gone. The grip of his left hand on the cable was weakening, this forced him to strengthen the grip of his right hand and the resulting agony that travelled like an electric shock from his hand up his arm clear to the right hand side of his head served only to compound the weakness. He would have to get back, and he would have to get back now. He prayed that the Schmeisser's magazine was empty.

And then, and for another reason, he knew that he had no option but to go now: and he knew his prayer hadn't been answered. The leading door of the cable-car opened and a head and a hand appeared. The head was Carraciola's: the hand held the Schmeisser. Carraciola was looking upwards even as he leaned out and he saw Smith immediately: he leaned farther out still, swung the Schmeisser one-handedly until the stock rested on his shoulder and squeezed the trigger.

Under the circumstance accurate aiming was impossible but at a distance of four feet accurate aiming was the last thing that mattered. Smith had already let go of the cable and was flinging himself convulsively backward when the first of the bullets ripped off his left hand epaulette. The second grazed his left shoulder, a brief burning sensation, but the rest of the burst passed harmlessly over his head. He landed heavily, stretched out blindly, located and grasped one of the suspension arms and scuttled crab-like round the base of the suspension arm until he had it and what little pathetic cover it offered between him and Carraciola.

For Carraciola was coming after him and Carraciola was coming to mak' siccar. He had the gun still in his hand and that gun could have very few shells indeed left in the magazine: it would be no part of Carraciola's plan to waste any of those shells. Even as Smith watched, Carraciola seemed to rise effortlessly three feet into the air – a feat of levitation directly attributable to the powerful boost given to him by Thomas and Christiansen – jack-knifed forward at hip level and flattened his body on top of the cable-car roof: his legs still dangled over the leading edge. A suicidal move, Smith thought in brief elation, Carraciola had made a fatal mistake: with neither hand hold nor purchase on that ice-coated roof, he must slide helplessly over the edge at the first jerk or jolt of the cable-car. But the elation was brief indeed for Carraciola had made no mistake. He had known what Smith hadn't: where to find a secure lodgement for his hand on the smooth expanse of that roof. Within seconds his scrabbling fingers had found safety – a gash in the cable-car roof that had been torn open by one of the bursts from the Schmeisser. Carraciola's fingers hooked securely and he pulled himself forward until he was in a kneeling position, his toes hooked over the leading edge.

Smith reached up with his wounded hand and clawed desperately for a grenade in the canvas bag slung over his left shoulder, at the same time pushing himself as far back as his anchoring left hand, clutched round a suspension bracket, would permit: at that range a grenade could do almost as much damage to himself as to Carraciola. His legs slid back until his feet projected over the trailing edge and he cried out in pain as a tremendous pressure, a bone-breaking, skin tearing pressure, was applied to his shins, half-way between knees and feet: someone had him by the ankles and that someone seemed determined to separate his feet from the rest of his body. Smith twisted his head round but all he could see was a pair of hands

66

round his ankles, knuckles bone-white in the faint wash of moonlight. And no one man's weight, Smith realised, could have caused that agonising pain in his shins. His companion must have had him by the waist, whether to increase the pressure or to ensure his safety if Smith did slide over the end. The reasons were immaterial: the effect was the same. He tried to draw up his legs but with a pinning weight of well over 200 lbs., any movement was quite impossible.

Smith risked a quick glance forward, but Carraciola hadn't moved, the cable-car was now half-way between the header station and the top pylon, the pendulum swing was at its maximum and Carraciola, still in his kneeling position, was hanging on for his life. Smith abandoned his attempt to reach for a grenade which could now serve no purpose whatsoever, unsheathed his knife, clasped the haft in the three good fingers of his right hand, twisted round and tried to strike at those hands that were causing him such excruciating agony. He couldn't get within fifteen inches of them.

His legs were breaking: his left arm was breaking: and his clenched grip on the support was slowly beginning to open. He had only seconds to go, Smith knew, and so he had nothing in the world to lose. He changed his grip on his knife, caught the tip of the blade between his broken thumb and the rest of his fingers, turned and threw the knife as powerfully and as accurately as his smashed hand and pain-dimmed eyes would permit. The stinging pain in his left ankle and the scream of pain from the trailing door were simultaneous: immediately, all the pressure on his ankles vanished: a second later, Christiansen, whom Thomas had managed to drag back inside the cable-car, was staring stupidly at the knife that transfixed his right wrist.

In that one instant Smith had won and he had lost. Or so it most surely seemed, for he was defenceless now: Carraciola had bided his time, calculated his chances and flung himself forward until he had reached the safety of the suspension bracket. Now he pulled himself slowly to his feet, his left arm round the suspension arm itself, his left leg twined securely round one of the brackets. The Schmeisser pointed into Smith's face.

'Only one bullet left.' Carraciola's smile was almost pleasant. 'I had to make sure, you see.'

Perhaps he hadn't lost, Smith thought, perhaps he hadn't lost after all. Because of the pinioning effect of Christiansen's hands on his ankles he'd been unaware, until now, how much less difficult it had become to maintain position on that ice-sheathed roof, unaware how much the pendulum swaying of the cable-car had been reduced. And it seemed that, even now, Carraciola was still unaware of it, or, if the change of motion had registered with him, the reason for it had not. With a conscious effort of will Smith shifted his by now half-hypnotised gaze from the staring muzzle of the Schmeisser to a point just over Carraciola's shoulder. The suspension arm of the first pylon was less than twenty feet away.

'Too bad, Smith.' Carraciola steadied the barrel of his machine pistol. 'Comes to us all. Be seeing you.'

'Look behind you,' Smith said.

Carraciola half-smiled in weary disbelief that anyone should try that ancient one on him. Smith glanced briefly, a second time, over Carraciola's shoulder, winced and looked away. The disbelief vanished from Carraciola's face as if a light had been switched off. Some sixth sense or instantaneous flash of comprehension or just some sudden certainty of knowledge made him twist round and glance over his shoulder. He cried out in terror, the last sound he ever made. The steel suspension arm of the pylon smashed into his back. Both his back and inter-twined leg broke with a simultaneous crack that could have been heard a hundred yards away. One second later he was swept from the roof of the cable-car but by that time Carraciola was already dead. From the open rearward door of the car, Thomas and Christiansen, their shocked faces mirroring their stunned disbelief, watched the broken body tumbling down into the darkness of the valley below.

Shaking like a man with the ague and moving like an old man in a dream, Smith slowly and painfully hauled himself forward until he was in a sitting position with an arm and leg wound round one of the after arms of the supporting bracket. Still in the same dream-like slow motion he lifted his head and gazed down the valley. The other cable-car, moving up-valley on its reciprocal course, had just passed the lowermost of the three pylons. With luck, his own cable-car might be the first to arrive at the central pylon. With luck. Not, of course, that the question of luck entered into it any more: he had no options or alternatives left, he had to do what he had to do and luck was the last factor to be taken into consideration.

From his kit-bag Smith extracted two packets of plastic explosives and wedged them firmly between the roof of the car and the two after arms of the suspension bracket, making sure that the tear strip igniters were exposed and ready to hand. Then he braced himself, sitting upright, against the suspension bracket, using both arms and legs to anchor himself and prepared to sit it out once more as the cable-car, approaching midsection of its second lap between the first and central pylons, steadily increased its swaying angle of arc across the night sky.

It was foolish of him, he knew, to sit like that. The snow had momentarily stopped, and the full moon, riding palely in an empty sky, was flooding the valley with a wash of ghostly light. Sitting as he was he must, he realised, be clearly visible from either the castle or the lower station: but apart from the fact that he doubted whether concealment mattered any longer he knew there was nothing he could do about it, there wasn't the strength left in his one good arm to allow him to assume the prone spread-eagled position that he and Schaffer had used on the way up.

He wondered about Schaffer, wondered about him in a vaguely woolly detached way for which exhaustion, loss of blood and the bitter cold were almost equally responsible. He wondered about the others, too, about the elderly man and the girl perched on top of the header station roof, about the two men inside the cable-car: but Mary and Carnaby-Jones were helpless to do anything to help and the chances of the unarmed Thomas and Christiansen carrying out another roof-top sortie were remote indeed: Carraciola had carried a Schmeisser, and they had seen what had happened to Carraciola. Schaffer, it was Schaffer who mattered.

Schaffer was feeling even more vague and woolly than Smith, for different reasons. He was waking, slowly and painfully, from a very bad dream and in this dream he could taste salt in his mouth and hear a soft urgent feminine voice calling his name, calling it over and over again. In normal times Schaffer would have been all for soft feminine voices, urgent or not, but he wished that this one would stop for it was all part of the bad dream and in this bad dream someone had split his head in half and he knew the pain wouldn't go until he woke up. He moaned, put the palms of his hands on the floor and tried to prop himself up. It took a long time, it took an eternity, for someone had laid one of the girders from the Forth bridge across his back, but at last he managed to straighten both his arms, his head hanging down between them. His head didn't feel right, it didn't even feel like his head, for, apart from the fact that there seemed to be a butcher's cleaver stuck in it, it seemed to be stuffed with cotton wool, grey and fuzzy round the edges. He shook his head to clear it and this was a mistake for the top of his head fell off. Or so it felt to Schaffer as the blinding coruscation of multi-coloured lights before his eyes arranged themselves into oddly kaleidoscopic patterns. He opened his eyes and the patterns dimmed and the lights began to fade: gradually, beneath his eyes the pattern of floorboards began to resolve themselves, and, on the board, the outlines of hands. His own hands.

He was awake, but this was one of those bad dreams which stayed with you even when you were awake. He could still taste salt – the salt of blood – his head still felt as if one incautious shake would have it rolling across the floor and that soft and urgent voice was still calling.

'Lieutenant Schaffer! Lieutenant Schaffer! Wake up, Lieutenant, wake up! Can you hear me?'

He'd heard that voice before, Schaffer decided, but he couldn't place it. It must have been a long time ago. He twisted his head to locate the source of the voice – it seemed to come from above – and the kaleidoscopic whirligig of colours were back in position again, revolving more quickly than ever. Head-shaking and head-twisting, Schaffer decided, were contra-indicated. He returned his head slowly to its original position, managed to get his knees under him, crawled forward in the direction of some dimly-seen piece of machinery and hauled himself shakily to his feet.

'Lieutenant! Lieutenant Schaffer! I'm up here.'

Schaffer turned and lifted his head in an almost grotesque slow motion and this time the whole universe of brightly dancing stars was reduced to the odd constellation or two. He recognised the voice from the distant past now, it was that of Mary Ellison, he even thought he recognised the pale strained face looking down from above, but he couldn't be sure, his eyes weren't focusing as they should. He wondered dizzily what the hell she was doing up there staring down at him through what appeared to be the bars of a shattered sky-light: his mind, he dimly realised, was operating with all the speed and subtle fluency of a man swimming against a river of black molasses.

'Are you—are you all right?' Mary asked.

Schaffer considered this ridiculous question carefully. 'I expect I shall be,' he said with great restraint. 'What happened?'

'They hit you with your own gun.'

'That's right.' Schaffer nodded and immediately wished he hadn't. He gingerly fingered a bruise on the back of his head. 'In the face. I must have struck my head as—' He broke off and turned slowly to face the door. 'What was that?'

'A dog. It sounded like a dog barking.'

'That's what I thought.' His voice slurred and indistinct, he staggered drunkenly across to the lower iron door and put his ear to it. 'Dogs,' he said. 'Lots of dogs. And lots and lots of hammering. Sledge-hammers, like enough.' He left the door and walked back to the centre of the floor, still staggering slightly. 'They're on to us and they're coming for us. Where's the Major?'

'He went after them.' The voice was empty of all feeling. 'He jumped on to the top of the cable-car.'

'He did, eh?' Schaffer received the news as if Smith's action had been the most natural and inevitable thing in the world. 'How did he make out?'

'How did he make—' There was life back in her voice now, a shocked anger at Schaffer's apparent callousness. She checked herself and said: 'There was a fight and I think someone fell off the roof. I don't know who it was.'

'It was one of them,' Schaffer said positively.

'One of—how can you say that?'

'The Major Smiths of this world don't drive over the edge of a cliff. Quotation from the future Mrs Schaffer. The Major Smiths of this world don't fall off the roofs of cable-cars. Quotation from the future Mrs. Schaffer's future husband.'

'You're recovering,' Mary said coldly. 'But I think you're right. There's still someone sitting on top of the cable-car and it wouldn't be one of them, would it?'

'How do you know there's someone sitting—'

'Because I can see him,' she said impatiently. 'It's bright moonlight. Look for yourself.'

Schaffer looked for himself, then rubbed a weary forearm across aching eyes. 'I have news for you, love,' he said. 'I can't even see the damn' cable-car.'

The cable-car was ten yards away from the central pylon. Smith, upright now, stooped, tore off the two friction fuses, straightened and, holding the cable in his left hand, took up position just on the inner side of the car roof. At the last moment he released his grip on the cable and stretched both arms out before him to break the impact of his body against the suspension arm. The ascending car on the other cable was now almost as close to the central pylon as his own. It didn't seem possible that he could make it in time.

The impact of the horizontal suspension arm drove the thought from his mind and all the breath from his body; had it

72

not been for the buffering effect of his outstretched arms, Smith was sure, some of his ribs must have gone. As it was, he was almost completely winded but he forced himself to ignore the pain and his heaving lungs' demand for oxygen, swung his feet up till they rested on the lower cross-girder, hooked his hands round the upper girder and made his way quickly across to the other side. At least, his hands and his feet moved quickly, but the steel was so thickly coated in clear smooth ice that his scrabbling feet could find almost no purchase whatsoever on the lower girder. He had reached no farther than the middle when the ascending car began to pass under its suspension arm. For the first time that night Smith blessed the brightness of the moon. He took two more slipping, sliding steps and launched himself towards the ice-coated cable that glittered so brightly in the pale moonlight.

His left hand caught the cable, his right arm hooked over it and the cable itself caught him high up on the chest. He had made no mistake about the location of his hand and arm, but his sliding take-off had caused his body to fall short and the cable slid up under his chin with a jerk that threatened to decapitate him. His legs swung out far beneath him, swung back and touched the roof as he lowered himself to the full extent of his left arm. He released his grip on the cable, dropped on all fours and reached out blindly but successfully for one of the arms of the suspension bracket. For long seconds he knelt there, retching uncontrollably as he was flooded by the nausea and pain from his throat and still winded lungs: then, by and by, the worst of it passed and he lay face down on the floor as the cable-car began to increase its pendulum swing with the increasing distance from the central pylon. He would not have believed that a man could be so totally exhausted and yet still have sufficient residual strength and sufficient self-preservation in-stinct to hang on to that treacherous and precarious hand-hold on that ice-coated roof.

Long seconds passed and some little measure of strength began to return to his limbs and body. Wearily, he hauled himself up into a sitting position, twisted round and gazed back down the valley.

The cable-car he had so recently abandoned was now hardly more than fifty yards from the lowermost pylon. Thomas and Christiansen sat huddled in the middle, the latter wrapping a makeshift bandage round his injured hand. Both fore and aft doors were still open as they were when the abortive attack on Smith had been made. That neither of the two men had ventured near the extremities of the car to try to close either of the doors was proof enough of the respect, if not fear, in which Smith was now held.

From the roof of the cable-car came a brilliant flash of light, magnesium-blinding in its white intensity: simultaneously there came the sound of two sharp explosions, so close together as to be indistinguishable in time. The two rear supports of the suspension bracket broke and the car, suspended now by only the two front supports, tilted violently, the front going up, the rear down.

Inside the angle of the floor of the car changed in an instant from the horizontal to at least thirty degrees. Christiansen was flung back towards the still open rear door. He grabbed despairingly at the side – but he grabbed with his wounded hand. Soundlessly, he vanished through the open doorway and as soundlessly fell to the depths of the valley below.

Thomas, with two sound hands and faster reactions, had succeeded in saving himself – for the moment. He glanced up and saw where the roof was beginning to buckle and break as the forward two suspension arm support brackets, now subjected to a wrenching lateral pressure they had never been designed to withstand, began to tear their retaining bolts free. Thomas struggled up the steeply inclined floor till he stood in the front doorway: because of the tilt of the car, now almost 45° as the front supports worked loose, the leading edge of the roof was almost touching the car. Thomas reached up, grabbed the cable with both hands, and had just cleared his legs from the doorway when the two front supports tore free from the roof in a rending screech of metal. The cable-car fell away, slowly turning end over end.

Despite the cable's violent buffeting caused by the sudden release of the weight of the car, Thomas had managed to hang on. He twisted round and saw the suspension arm of the lowest pylon only feet away. The sudden numbing of all physical and mental faculties was accurately and shockingly reflected in the frozen fear of his face, the lips drawn back in a snarling rictus of terror. The knuckles of the hands gleamed like burnished ivory. And then, suddenly, there were no hands there, just the suspension arm and the empty wire and a long fading scream in the night.

As his cable-car approached the header station, Smith edged well forward to clear the lip of the roof. From where he crouched it was impossible to see the east wing of the Schloss Adler but if the columns of dense smoke now drifting across the valley were anything to go by, the fire seemed to have an unshakable hold. Clouds were again moving across the moon and this could be both a good thing and a bad thing: a good thing in that it would afford them cover and help obscure those dense clouds of smoke, a bad thing in that it was bound to high-light the flames from the burning castle. It could only be a matter of time, Smith reflected, before the attention of someone in the village or the barracks beyond was caught by the fire or the smoke. Or, he thought grimly, by the increasing number of muffled explosions coming from the castle itself. He wondered what might be the cause of them: Schaffer hadn't had the time to lay all those distractions.

The roof of the cable-car cleared the level of the floor of the header station and Smith sagged in relief as he saw the figure standing by the controls of the winch. Schaffer. A rather battered and bent Schaffer, it was true, an unsteady Schaffer, a Schaffer with one side of his face masked in blood, a Schaffer who from his peering and screwed-up expression had obviously some difficulty in focusing his gaze. But undoubtedly Schaffer and as nearly a going concern as made no odds. Smith felt energy flow back into him, he hadn't realised just how heavily he had come to depend on the American: with Schaffer by his side it was going to take a great deal to stop them now.

Smith glanced up as the roof of the header station came into view. Mary and Carnaby-Jones were still there, pressed back against the castle wall. He lifted a hand in greeting, but they gave no sign in return. Ghosts returning from the dead, Smith thought wryly, weren't usually greeted by a wave of the hand.

Schaffer, for all the trouble he was having with his eyes and his still obviously dazed condition, seemed to handle the winch controls immaculately. It may have been – and probably was – the veriest fluke, but he put the gear lever in neutral and applied the brake to bring the cable-car to rest exactly halfway in under the lip of the roof. First Mary and then Jones came sliding down the nylon rope on to the roof of the car, Jones with his eyes screwed tightly shut. Neither of them spoke a word, not even when Schaffer had brought them up inside and they had slid down on to the floor of the station.

'Hurry! Hurry!' Smith flung open the rear door of the cable-car. 'Inside, all of you!' He retrieved Schaffer's Luger from the floor, then whirled round as he heard the furious barking of dogs followed by the sound of heavy sledges battering against the iron door leading from the station. The first of the two defences must have been carried away: now the second was under siege.

Mary and a stumbling Schaffer were already inside the cable-car. Jones, however, had made no move to go. He stood there, Smith's Schmeisser in his hand, listening to the furious hammering on the door. His face seemed unconcerned. He said, apologetically: 'I'm not very good at heights, I'm afraid. But this is different.'

'Get inside!' Smith almost hissed the words.

'No.' Jones shook his head. 'You hear. They'll be through any minute. I'll stay.'

'For God's sake!' Smith shouted in exasperation.

'I'm twenty years older than any of you.'

'Well, there's that.' Smith nodded consideringly, held out his right hand, said, 'Mr. Jones. Good luck,' brought across his left hand and half-dragged, half-carried the dazed Jones into the cable-car. Smith moved quickly across to the controls, engaged gear all the way, released the handbrake and ran after the moving car.

As they moved out from below the roof of the station, the sound of the assault on the inner door seemed to double in its intensity. In the Schloss Adler, Smith reflected, there would be neither pneumatic chisels nor oxy-acetylene equipment for there could be no conceivable call for either, but, even so, it didn't seem to matter: with all the best will in the world a couple of iron hasps couldn't for long withstand an attack of that nature. Thoughtfully, Smith closed the rear door. Schaffer was seated, his elbows on his knees, his head in his hands. Mary was kneeling on the floor, Jones's head in her lap, looking down at the handsome silvery-haired head. He couldn't see her expression but was dolefully certain that she was even then preparing a homily about the shortcomings of bullies who went around clobbering elderly and defenceless American actors. Almost two minutes passed in complete silence before Carnaby-Jones stirred, and, when he did, Mary herself stirred and looked up at Smith. To his astonishment, she had a half-smile on her face.

'It's all right,' she said. 'I've counted ten. In the circumstances, it was the only argument to use.' She paused and the smile faded. 'I thought you were gone then.'

'You weren't the only one. After this I retire. I've used up a lifetime's luck in the past fifteen minutes. You're not looking so bright yourself.'

'I'm not feeling so bright.' Her face was pale and strained as she braced herself against the wild lurching of the cable-car. 'If you want to know, I'm sea-sick. I don't go much on this form of travel.'

Smith tapped the roof. 'You want to try travelling steerage on one of those,' he said feelingly. 'You'd never complain about

77

first-class travel again. Ah! Pylon number two coming up. Almost half-way.'

'*Only* half-way.' A pause. 'What happens if they break through that door up there?'

'Reverse the gear lever and up we go.'

'Like it or not?'

'Like it or not.'

Carnaby-Jones struggled slowly to a sitting position, gazed uncomprehendingly around him until he realised where he was, rubbed his jaw tenderly and said to Smith: 'That was a dirty trick.'

'It was all of that,' Smith acknowledged. 'I'm sorry.'

'I'm not.' Jones smiled shakily. 'Somehow, I don't really think I'm cut out to be a hero.'

'Neither am I, brother, neither am I,' Schaffer said mournfully. He lifted his head from his hands and looked slowly around. His eyes were still glassy and only partially focusing but a little colour was returning to his right cheek, the one that wasn't masked in blood. 'Our three friends. What became of our three friends?'

'Dead.'

'Dead?' Schaffer groaned and shook his head. 'Tell me about it sometime. But not now.'

'He doesn't know what he's missing,' Smith said unsympathetically. 'The drama of it all escapes him, which is perhaps just as well. Is the door up above still standing or are the hinges or padlocks going? Is someone rushing towards the winch controls – Is there—'

'Stop it!' Mary's voice was sharp, high-pitched and carried overtones of hysteria. 'Stop talking like that!'

'Sorry,' Smith said contritely. He reached out and touched her shoulder. 'Just whistling in the dark, that's all. Here comes the last pylon. Another minute or so and we're home and dry.'

'Home and dry,' Schaffer said bitterly. 'Wait till I have that Savoy Grill menu in my hand. *Then* I'll be home and dry.'

'Some people are always thinking of their stomachs,' Smith

observed. At that moment he was thinking of his own and it didn't feel any too good. No stomach does when it feels as if it has a solid lead ball, a chilled lead ball lodged in it with an icy hand squeezing from the outside. His heart was thumping slowly, heavily, painfully in his chest and he was having difficulty in speaking for all the saliva seemed to have evaporated from his mouth. He became suddenly aware that he was unconsciously leaning backward, bracing himself for the moment when the cable-car jerked to a stand-still then started climbing back up to the Schloss Adler again. I'll count to ten, he said to himself, then if we get that far without being checked, I'll count to nine, and then – And then he caught sight of Mary's face, a dead-white, scared and almost haggard face that made her look fifteen years older than she was, and felt suddenly ashamed of himself. He sat on the bench, and squeezed her shoulder. 'We'll be all right,' he said confidently. All of a sudden he found it easy to speak again. 'Uncle John has just said so, hasn't he? You wait and see.'

She looked up at him, trying to smile. 'Is Uncle John always right?'

'Always,' Smith said firmly.

Twenty seconds passed. Smith rose to his feet, walked to the front of the cable-car and peered down. Though the moon was obscured he could just dimly discern the shape of the lower station. He turned to look at the others. They were all looking at him.

'Not much more than a hundred feet to go,' Smith said. 'I'm going to open that door in a minute. Well, a few seconds. By that time we won't be much more than fifteen feet above the ground. Twenty, at the most. If the car stops, we jump. There's two or three feet of snow down there. Should cushion our fall enough to give an even chance of not breaking anything.'

Schaffer parted his lips to make some suitable remark, thought better of it and returned head to hands in weary silence. Smith opened the leading door, did his best to ignore the icy blast of wind that gusted in through the opening, and looked vertically downwards, realising that he had been over-optimistic in his assessment of the distance between cable-car and ground. The distance was at least fifty feet, a distance sufficient to arouse in even the most optimistic mind dismaying thoughts of fractured femurs and tibias. And then he dismissed the thought, for an even more dismaying factor had now to be taken into consideration: in the far distance could be heard the sound of sirens, in the far distance could be seen the wavering beams of approaching headlamps. Schaffer lifted his head. The muzziness had now left him, even if his sore head had not.

'Enter, left, reinforcements,' he announced. 'This wasn't on the schedule, boss. Radio gone, telephone gone, helicopter gone—'

'Just old-fashioned.' Smith pointed towards the rear window. 'They're using smoke signals.'

'Jeez!' Schaffer stared out the rear windows, his voice awestruck. 'For stone, it sure burns good!'

Schaffer was in no way exaggerating. For stone, it burnt magnificently. The Schloss Adler was well and truly alight, a conflagration in which smoke had suddenly become an inconsiderable and, indeed, a very minor element. It was wreathed in flames, almost lost to sight in flames, towering flames that now reached up almost to the top of the great round tower to the north-east. Perched on its volcanic plug half-way up the mountain-side against the dimly seen back-drop of the unseen heights of the Weisspitze, the blazing castle, its effulgence now beginning to light up the entire valley and quite drowning out the pale light of a moon again showing through, was an incredibly fantastic sight from some equally incredible and fantastic fairy tale.

'One trusts that they are well insured,' Schaffer said. He was on his feet now, peering down towards the lower station. 'How far, boss? And how far down?'

'Thirty feet. Maybe twenty-five. And fifteen feet down.' The lights of the leading cars were passing the still smouldering embers of the station. 'We have it made, Lieutenant Schaffer.'

'We have it made.' Schaffer cursed and staggered as the car jerked to a violent and abrupt stop. 'Almost, that is.'

'All out!' Smith shouted. 'All out!'

'There speaks the eternal shop steward,' Schaffer said. 'Stand back, I've got two good hands.' He brushed by Smith, clutched the door jamb with his left hand, pulled Mary towards him, transferred his grip from waist to wrist and dropped her out through the leading door, lowering her as far as the stretch of his left arm would permit. When he let her go, she had less than three feet to fall. Within three seconds he had done the same with Carnaby-Jones. The cable-car jerked and started to move back up the valley. Schaffer practically bundled Smith out of the car, wincing in pain as he momentarily took all of Smith's two hundred pound weight, then slid out of the doorway himself, hung momentarily from the doorway at the full stretch of his arms, then dropped six feet into the soft yielding snow. He staggered, but maintained balance.

Smith was beside him. He had fished out a plastic explosive from the bag on his back and torn off the friction fuse. He handed the package to Schaffer and said: 'You have a good right arm.'

'I have a good right arm. Horses, no. Baseball, yes.' Schaffer took aim and lobbed the explosive neatly through the doorway of the disappearing cable-car. 'Like that?'

'Like that. Come on.' Smith turned and, catching Mary by the arm while Schaffer hustled Carnaby-Jones along, ran down the side of the lower station and into the shelter of the nearest house bare seconds before a command car, followed by several trucks crammed with soldiers, slid to a skidding halt below the lower station. Soldiers piled out of the trucks, following an officer, clearly identifiable as Colonel Weissner, up the steps into the lower station.

The castle burned more fiercely than ever, a fire obviously totally out of control. Suddenly, there was the sharp crack of an explosion and the ascending cable-car burst into flames. The car, half-way up to the first pylon, swung in great arcs across the valley, its flames fanned by the wind, and climbed steadily upwards into the sky until its flame was lost in the greater flame of the Schloss Adler.

Crouched in the shelter of the house, Schaffer touched Smith's arm. 'Sure you wouldn't like to go and burn down the station as well?'

'Come on,' Smith said. 'The garage.'

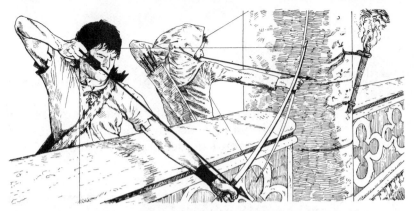

In the Abbey Church

R. L. STEVENSON

Dick Shelton is a staunch Lancastrian during the Wars of the Roses and fallen foul of his guardian, Sir Daniel Brackley, after voicing his suspicions that the latter had murdered his father. Accompanied by Will Lawless, one of a band of local outlaws who are out for Sir Daniel's blood, Dick has just returned secretly to Sir Daniel's house to rescue Joanna Sedley. He is in love with her but she is in Sir Daniel's power and is to be forced to marry a notorious nobleman, Lord Shoreby. Unfortunately, Dick is drawn into a trap in the abbey church; his guard for the night there is the priest, Sir Oliver, whom Dick has known since childhood.

In Shoreby Abbey Church the prayers were kept up all night without cessation, now with the singing of psalms, now with a note or two upon the bell.

Rutter, the spy, was nobly waked. There he lay, meanwhile, as they had arranged him, his dead hands crossed upon his bosom, his dead eyes staring on the roof; and hard by, in the stall, the lad who had slain him waited, in sore disquietude, the coming of the morning.

Once only, in the course of the hours, Sir Oliver leaned across to his captive.

'Richard,' he whispered, 'my son, if ye mean me evil, I will certify, on my soul's welfare, ye design upon an innocent man. Sinful in the eye of Heaven I do declare myself! but sinful as against you I am not neither have been ever.'

'My father,' returned Dick, in the same tone of voice, 'trust me, I design nothing; but as for your innocence, I may not forget that ye cleared yourself but lamely.'

'A man may be innocently guilty,' replied the priest. 'He may be set blindfolded upon a mission, ignorant of its true scope. So it was with me. I did decoy your father to his death; but as Heaven sees us in this sacred place, I knew not what I did.'

'It may be,' returned Dick. 'But see what a strange web ye have woven, that I should be, at this hour, at once your prisoner and your judge; that ye should both threaten my days and deprecate my anger. Methinks, if ye had been all your life a true man and good priest, ye would neither thus fear nor thus detest me. And now to your prayers. I do obey you, since needs must; but I will not be burthened with your company.'

The priest uttered a sigh so heavy that it had almost touched the lad into some sentiment of pity, and he bowed his head upon his hands like a man borne down below a weight of care. He joined no longer in the psalms; but Dick could hear the beads rattle through his fingers and the prayers a-pattering between his teeth.

Yet a little, and the grey of the morning began to struggle through the painted casements of the church, and to put to shame the glimmer of the tapers. The light slowly broadened and brightened, and presently through the south-eastern clerestories a flush of rosy sunlight flickered on the walls. The storm was over; the great clouds had disburdened their snow and fled farther on and the new day was breaking on a merry winter landscape sheathed in white.

A bustle of church officers followed; the bier was carried forth to the deadhouse, and the stains of blood were cleansed from off the tiles, that no such ill-omened spectacle should disgrace the marriage of Lord Shoreby. At the same time, the very ecclesiastics who had been so dismally engaged all night began to put on morning faces, to do honour to the merrier ceremony which was about to follow. And further to announce the coming of the day, the pious of the town began to assemble and fall to prayer before their favourite shrines, or wait their turn at the confessionals.

Favoured by this stir, it was of course easily possible for any man to avoid the vigilance of Sir Daniel's sentries at the door; and presently Dick, looking about him wearily, caught the eye of no less a person than Will Lawless, still in his monk's habit.

The outlaw, at the same moment, recognised his leader, and privily signed to him with hand and eye.

Now, Dick was far from having forgiven the old rogue his most untimely drunkenness, but he had no desire to involve him in his own predicament; and he signalled back to him, as plain as he was able, to begone.

Lawless, as though he had understood, disappeared at once behind a pillar, and Dick breathed again.

What, then, was his dismay to feel himself plucked by the sleeve and to find the old robber installed beside him, upon the next seat, and, to all appearance, plunged in his devotions!

Instantly Sir Oliver arose from his place, and, gliding behind the stalls, made for the soldiers in the aisle. If the priest's suspicions had been so lightly wakened, the harm was already done, and Lawless a prisoner in the church.

'Move not,' whispered Dick. 'We are in the plaguiest pass, thanks, before all things, to thy swinishness of yestereven. When ye saw me here, so strangely seated, where I have neither right nor interest, what a murrain! could ye not smell harm and get ye gone from evil?'

'Nay,' returned Lawless, 'I thought ye had heard from Ellis, and were here on duty.'

'Ellis!' echoed Dick. 'Is Ellis then returned?'

'For sure,' replied the outlaw. 'He came last night, and belted me sore for being in wine – so there ye are avenged, my master.

A furious man is Ellis Duckworth! He hath ridden me hot-spur from Craven to prevent this marriage; and, Master Dick, ye know the way of him – do so he will!'

'Nay, then,' returned Dick, with composure, 'you and I, my poor brother, are dead men; for I sit here a prisoner upon suspicion, and my neck was to answer for this very marriage that he purposeth to mar. I had a fair choice, by the rood! to lose my sweetheart or else lose my life! Well, the cast is thrown – it is to be my life.'

'By the mass,' cried Lawless, half arising, 'I am gone!'

But Dick had his hand at once upon his shoulder.

'Friend Lawless, sit ye still, ' he said. 'An ye have eyes, look yonder at the corner by the chancel arch; see ye not that, even upon the motion of your rising, yon armed men are up and ready to intercept you? Yield ye, friend. Ye were bold aboard ship, when ye thought to die a sea-death; be bold again, now that y' are to die presently upon the gallows.'

'Master Dick,' gasped Lawless, 'the thing hath come upon me somewhat of the suddenest. But give me a moment till I fetch my breath again; and, by the mass, I will be as stout-hearted as yourself.'

'Here is my bold fellow!' returned Dick. 'And yet, Lawless, it goes hard against the grain with me to die; but where whining mendeth nothing, wherefore whine?'

'Nay, that indeed!' chimed Lawless. 'And a fig for death, at worst! It has to be done, my master, soon or late. And hanging in a good quarrel is an easy death, they say, though I could never hear of any that came back to say so.'

And so saying the stout old rascal leaned back in his stall, folded his arms, and began to look about him with the greatest air of insolence and unconcern.

'And for the matter of that,' Dick added, 'it is yet our best chance to keep quiet. We wot not yet what Duckworth purposes; and when all is said, and if the worst befall, we may yet clear our feet of it.'

Now that they ceased talking, they were aware of a very

distant and thin strain of mirthful music which steadily drew nearer, louder and merrier. The bells in the tower began to break forth into a doubling peal, and a greater and greater concourse of people to crowd into the church, shuffling the snow from off their feet, and clapping and blowing in their hands. The western door was flung wide open, showing a glimpse of sunlit, snowy street, and admitting in a great gust the shrewd air of the morning; and in short, it became plain by every sign, that Lord Shoreby desired to be married very early in the day, and that the wedding-train was drawing near.

Some of Lord Shoreby's men now cleared a passage down the middle aisle, forcing the people back with lance-stocks; and just then, outside the portal, the secular musicians could be descried drawing near over the frozen snow, the fifers and trumpeters scarlet in the face with lusty blowing, the drummers and the cymbalists beating as for a wager.

These, as they drew near the door of the sacred building, filed off on either side, and marking time to their own vigorous music, stood stamping in the snow. As they thus opened their ranks, the leaders of this noble bridal train appeared behind and between them; and such was the variety and gaiety of their attire, such the display of silks and velvet, fur and satin, embroidery and lace, that the procession showed forth upon the snow like a flower-bed in a path or a painted window in a wall.

First came the bride, a sorry sight, as pale as winter, clinging to Sir Daniel's arm, and attended, as bridesmaid, by the short young lady who had befriended Dick the night before. Close behind, in the most radiant toilet, followed the bridegroom, halting on a gouty foot, and as he passed the threshold of the sacred building, and doffed his hat, his bald head was seen to be rosy with emotion.

And now came the hour of Ellis Duckworth.

Dick, who sat stunned among contrary emotions, grasping the desk in front of him, beheld a movement in the crowd, people jostling backward, and eyes and arms uplifted. Following these signs, he beheld three or four men with bent bows, leaning from the clerestory gallery. At the same instant they delivered their discharge, and before the clamour and cries of the astounded populace had time to swell fully upon the ear, they had flitted from their perch and disappeared.

The nave was full of swaying heads and voices screaming; the ecclesiastics thronged in terror from their places; the music ceased, and though the bells overhead continued for some seconds to clang upon the air, some wind of the disaster seemed to find its way at last even to the chamber where the ringers were leaping on their ropes, and they also desisted from their merry labours.

Right in the midst of the nave the bridegroom lay stone-dead, pierced by two black arrows. The bride had fainted. Sir Daniel stood, towering above the crowd in his surprise and anger, a clothyard shaft quivering in his left forearm, and his face streaming blood from another which had grazed his brow.

Long before any search could be made for them, the authors of this tragic interruption had clattered down a turnpike stair and decamped by a postern door.

But Dick and Lawless still remained in pawn; they had indeed arisen on the first alarm, and pushed manfully to gain the door; but what with the narrowness of the stalls, and the crowding of terrified priests and choristers, the attempt had been in vain, and they had stoically resumed their places.

And now, pale with horror, Sir Oliver rose to his feet and called upon Sir Daniel, pointing with one hand to Dick.

'Here,' he cried, 'is Richard Shelton – alas the hour! – blood guilty! Seize him! – bid him be seized! For all our lives' sakes, take him and bind him surely! He hath sworn our fall.'

Sir Daniel was blinded by anger – blinded by the hot blood that still streamed across his face.

'Where?' he bellowed. 'Hale him forth! By the cross of Holywood but he shall rue this hour.'

The crowd fell back, and a party of archers invaded the choir, laid rough hands on Dick, dragged him head foremost from the stall, and thrust him by the shoulders down the chancel steps.

The bridegroom lay stone dead pierced by two black arrows

Lawless, on his part, sat as still as a mouse.

Sir Daniel, brushing the blood out of his eyes, stared blinkingly upon his captive.

'Ay,' he said, 'treacherous and insolent, I have thee fast; and by all potent oaths, for every drop of blood that now trickles in mine eyes, I will wring a groan out of thy carcase. Away with him!' he added. 'Here is no place! Off with him to my house. I will number every joint of thy body with a torture.'

But Dick, putting off his captors, uplifted his voice.

'Sanctuary!' he shouted. 'Sanctuary! Ho, there, my fathers! They would drag me from the church!'

'From the church thou hast defiled with murder, boy,' added a tall man, magnificently dressed.

'On what probation?' cried Dick. 'They do accuse me, indeed, of some complicity, but have not proved one tittle. I was, in truth, a suitor for this damsel's hand; and she, I will be bold to say it, repaid my suit with favour. But what then? To love a maid is no offence, I trow – nay, nor to gain her love. In all else, I stand here free from guiltiness.'

There was a murmur of approval among the bystanders, so boldly Dick declared his innocence; but at the same time a throng of accusers arose upon the other side, crying how he had been found last night in Sir Daniel's house, how he wore a sacrilegious disguise; and in the midst of the babel, Sir Oliver indicated Lawless, both by voice and gesture, as accomplice to the fact. He, in his turn, was dragged from his seat and set beside his leader. The feelings of the crowd rose high on either side, and while some dragged the prisoners to and fro to favour their escape, others cursed and struck them with their fists. Dick's ears rang and his brain swam dizzily, like a man struggling in the eddies of a furious river.

But the tall man who had already answered Dick, by a prodigious exercise of voice restored silence and order in the mob.

'Search them,' he said, 'for arms. We may so judge of their intentions.'

Upon Dick they found no weapon but his poniard, and this told in his favour, until one man officiously drew it from its sheath, and found it still uncleansed of the blood of Rutter. At this there was a great shout among Sir Daniel's followers, which the tall man suppressed by a gesture and an imperious glance. But when it came to the turn of Lawless, there was found under his gown a sheaf of arrows identical with those that had been shot.

'How say ye now?' asked the tall man, frowningly, of Dick.

'Sir,' replied Dick, 'I am here in sanctuary, is it not so? Well, sir, I see by your bearing that ye are high in station, and I read in your countenance the marks of piety and justice. To you, then, I will yield me prisoner, and that blithely, foregoing the advantage of this holy place. But rather than to be yielded into the discretion of that man – whom I do here accuse with a loud voice to be the murderer of my natural father and the unjust detainer of my lands and revenues – rather than that, I would beseech you, under favour, with your own gentle hand, to despatch me on the spot. Your own ears have heard him, how before that I was proven guilty he did threaten me with torments. It standeth not with your own honour to deliver me to my sworn enemy and old oppressor, but to try me fairly by the way of law, and, if that I be guilty indeed, to slay me mercifully.'

'My lord,' cried Sir Daniel, 'ye will not hearken to this wolf? His bloody dagger reeks him the lie into his face.'

'Nay, but suffer me, good knight,' returned the tall stranger; 'your own vehemence doth somewhat tell against yourself.'

And here the bride, who had come to herself some minutes past and looked wildly on upon this scene, broke loose from those that held her, and fell upon her knees before the last speaker.

'My Lord of Risingham,' she cried, 'hear me, in justice. I am here in this man's custody by mere force, reft from mine own people. Since that day I had never pity, countenance, nor comfort from the face of man – but from him only – Richard Shelton – whom they now accuse and labour to undo. My lord, if he was yesternight in Sir Daniel's mansion, it was I that brought him there; he came but at my prayer, and thought to do no hurt. While yet Sir Daniel was a good lord to him, he fought with them of the Black Arrow loyally; but when his foul guardian sought his life by practices, and he fled by night, for his soul's sake, out of that bloody house, whither was he to turn – he, helpless and penniless? Or if he be fallen among ill company, whom should ye blame – the lad that was unjustly handled, or the guardian that did abuse his trust?'

And then the short young lady fell on her knees by Joanna's side.

'And I, my good lord and natural uncle,' she added, 'I can bear testimony, on my conscience and before the face of all, that what this maiden saith is true. It was I, unworthy, that did lead the young man in.'

Earl Risingham had heard in silence, and when the voices ceased, he still stood silent for a space. Then he gave Joanna his hand to arise, though it was to be observed that he did not offer the like courtesy to her who had called herself his niece.

'Sir Daniel,' he said, 'here is a right intricate affair, the which, with your good leave, it shall be mine to examine and adjust. Content ye, then: your business is in careful hands; justice shall be done you; and in the meanwhile, get ye incontinently home, and have your hurts attended. The air is shrewd, and I would not ye took cold upon these scratches.'

He made a sign with his hand; it was passed down the nave by obsequious servants, who waited there upon his smallest gesture. Instantly, without the church, a tucket sounded shrill, and through the open portal archers and men-at-arms, uniformly arrayed in the colours and wearing the badge of Lord Risingham, began to file into the church, took Dick and Lawless from those who still detained them, and, closing their files about the prisoners, marched forth again and disappeared.

As they were passing, Joanna held both her hands to Dick and cried him her farewell; and the bridesmaid, nothing downcast by her uncle's evident displeasure, blew him a kiss, with a 'Keep your heart up, liondriver!' that for the first time since the accident called up a smile to the faces of the crowd.

Earl Risingham, although by far the most important person then in Shoreby, was poorly lodged in the house of a private gentleman upon the extreme outskirts of the town. Nothing but the armed men at the doors, and the mounted messengers that kept arriving and departing, announced the temporary residence of a great lord.

Thus it was that, from lack of space, Dick and Lawless were clapped into the same apartment.

'Well spoken, Master Richard,' said the outlaw! 'It was excellently well spoken, and, for my part, I thank you cordially. Here we are in good hands; we shall be justly tried, and some time this evening, decently hanged on the same tree.'

'Indeed, my poor friend, I do believe it,' answered Dick.

'Yet have we a string to our bow,' returned Lawless. 'Ellis Duckworth is a man out of ten thousand; he holdeth you right near his heart, both for your own and for your father's sake; and knowing you guiltless of this fact, he will stir earth and heaven to bear you clear.'

'It may not be,' said Dick. 'What can he do? He hath but a handful. Alack, if it were but tomorrow – could I but keep a certain tryst an hour before noon to-morrow – all were, I think, otherwise. But now there is no help.'

'Well,' concluded Lawless, 'an ye will stand to it for my innocence, I will stand to it for yours, and that stoutly. It shall naught avail us; but an I be to hang, it shall not be for lack of swearing.'

And then, while Dick gave himself over to his reflections, the old rogue curled himself down into a corner, pulled his monkish hood about his face, and composed himself to sleep. Soon he was loudly snoring, so utterly had his long life of hardship and adventure blunted the sense of apprehension.

It was long after noon, and the day was already failing, before the door was opened and Dick taken forth and led up-stairs to where, in a warm cabinet, Earl Risingham sat musing over the fire.

On his captive's entrance he looked up.

'Sir,' he said, 'I knew your father, who was a man of honour, and this inclineth me to be the more lenient; but I may not hide from you that heavy charges lie against your character. Ye do consort with murderers and robbers; upon a clear probation ye have carried war against the king's peace; ye are suspected to have piratically seized upon a ship; ye are found skulking with a counterfeit presentment in your enemy's house; a man is slain that very evening—'

'An it like you, my lord,' Dick interposed, 'I will at once avow my guilt, such as it is. I slew this fellow Rutter; and to the proof' – searching in his bosom – 'here is a letter from his wallet.'

Lord Risingham took the letter, and opened and read it twice.

'Ye have read this?' he inquired.

'I have read it,' answered Dick.

'Are ye for York or Lancaster?' the earl demanded.

'My lord, it was but a little while back that I was asked that question, and knew not how to answer it,' said Dick; 'but having answered once, I will not vary. My lord, I am for York.'

The earl nodded approvingly.

'Honestly replied,' he said. 'But wherefore, then, deliver me this letter?'

'Nay, but against traitors, my lord, are not all sides arrayed?' cried Dick.

'I would they were, young gentleman,' returned the earl; 'and I do at least approve your saying. There is more youth than guile in you, I do perceive; and were not Sir Daniel a mighty man upon our side, I were half tempted to espouse your quarrel. For I have inquired, and it appears that you have been hardly dealt with, and have much excuse. But look ye, sir, I am, before all else, a leader in the queen's interest; and though by nature a just man, as I believe, and leaning even to the excess of mercy, yet must I order my goings for my party's interest, and, to keep Sir Daniel, I would go far about.'

'My lord,' returned Dick, 'ye will think me very bold to counsel you: but do ye count upon Sir Daniel's faith? Methought he had changed sides intolerably often.'

'Nay, it is the way of England. What would ye have?' the earl demanded. 'But ye are unjust to the knight of Tunstall; and as faith goes, in this unfaithful generation, he hath of late been honourably true to us of Lancaster. Even in our last reverses he stood firm.'

'An it please you, then,' said Dick, 'to cast your eye upon this letter, ye might somewhat change your thought of him,' and he handed to the earl Sir Daniel's letter to Lord Wensleydale.

The effect upon the earl's countenance was instant; he lowered like an angry lion, and his hand, with a sudden movement, clutched at his dagger.

'Ye have read this also?' he asked.

'Even so,' said Dick. 'It is your lordship's own estate he offers to Lord Wensleydale.'

'It is my own estate, even as ye say!' returned the earl. 'I am your bedesman for this letter. It hath shown me a fox's hole. Command me, Master Shelton; I will not be backward in gratitude, and to begin with, York or Lancaster, true man or thief, I do now set you at freedom. Go, a Mary's name! But judge it right that I retain and hang your fellow, Lawless. The crime hath been most open, and it were fitting that some open punishment should follow.'

'My lord, I make it my first suit to you to spare him also,' pleaded Dick.

'It is an old condemned rogue, thief, and vagabond, Master Shelton,' said the earl. 'He hath been gallowsripe this score of years. And, whether for one thing or another, whether tomorrow or the day after, where is the great choice?'

'Yet, my lord, it was through love to me that he came hither,' answered Dick, 'and I were churlish and thankless to desert him.'

'Master Shelton, ye are troublesome,' replied the earl, severely. 'It is an evil way to prosper in this world. Howbeit, and to be quit of your importunity, I will once more humour you. Go then, together; but go warily, and get swiftly out of Shoreby town. For this Sir Daniel (whom may the saints confound!) thirsteth most greedily to have your blood.'

'My lord, I do now offer you in words my gratitude, trusting at some brief date to pay you some of it in service,' replied Dick, as he turned from the apartment.

Rogue Male

GEOFFREY HOUSEHOLD

I cannot blame them. After all, one doesn't need a telescopic sight to shoot boar and bear; so that when they came on me watching the terrace at a range of five hundred and fifty yards, it was natural enough that they should jump to conclusions. And they behaved, I think, with discretion. I am not an obvious anarchist or fanatic, and I don't look as if I took any interest in politics; I might perhaps have sat for an agricultural constituency in the south of England, but that hardly counts as politics. I carried a British passport, and if I had been caught walking up to the House instead of watching it I should probably have been asked to lunch. It was a difficult problem for angry men to solve in an afternoon.

They must have wondered whether I had been employed on, as it were, an official mission; but I think they turned that suspicion down. No government – least of all ours – encourages assassination. Or was I a free-lance? That must have seemed very unlikely; anyone can see that I am not the type of avenging angel. Was I, then, innocent of any criminal intent, and exactly what I claimed to be – a sportsman who couldn't resist the temptation to stalk the impossible?

After two or three hours of their questions I could see I had them shaken. They didn't believe me, though they were beginning to understand that a bored and wealthy Englishman

97

who had hunted all commoner game might well find a perverse pleasure in hunting the biggest game on earth. But even if my explanation were true and the hunt were purely formal, it made no difference. I couldn't be allowed to live.

By that time I had, of course, been knocked about very considerably. My nails are growing back but my left eye is still pretty useless. I wasn't a case you could turn loose with apologies. They would probably have given me a picturesque funeral, with huntsmen firing volleys and sounding horns, with all the big-wigs present in fancy dress, and put up a stone obelisk to the memory of a brother sportsman. They do these things well.

As it was, they bungled the job. They took me to the edge of a cliff and put me over, all but my hands. That was cunning. Scrabbling at the rough rock would have accounted – near enough – for the state of my fingers when I was found. I did hang on, of course; for how long I don't know. I cannot see why I wasn't glad to die, seeing that I hadn't a hope of living and the quicker the end the less the suffering. But I was not glad. One always hopes – if a clinging to life can be called hope. I am not too civilised to be influenced by that force which makes a rabbit run when a stoat is after him. The rabbit doesn't hope for anything, I take it. His mind has no conception of the future. But he runs. And so I hung on till I dropped.

I was doubtful whether I had died or not. I have always believed that consciousness remains after physical death (though I have no opinion on how long it lasts), so I thought I was probably dead. I had been such a hell of a time falling; it didn't seem reasonable that I could be alive. And there had been a terrifying instant of pain. I felt as if the back of my thighs and rump had been shorn off, pulled off, scraped off – off, however done. I had parted, obviously and irrevocably, with a lot of my living matter.

My second thought was a longing for death, for it was revolting to imagine myself still alive and of the consistency of mud. There was a pulped substance all around me, in the midst of which I carried on my absurd consciousness. I had supposed that this bog was me; it tasted of blood. Then it occurred to me that this soft extension of my body might really be bog; that anything into which I fell would taste of blood.

I had crashed into a patch of marsh; small, but deep. Now, I think that I am alive – today, that is, for I still hesitate to describe myself as alive with any permanency – because I couldn't see or feel how much damage had been dealt. It was dark, and I was quite numb. I hauled myself out by the tussocks of grass, a creature of mud, bandaged and hidden in mud. A slope of scree rose sharply from the marsh. I had evidently grazed it in my fall. I didn't feel the pain any longer. I could persuade myself that I was no more seriously hurt than when they put me over the cliff; so I determined to move off before they came to find my body.

I had, though I didn't then know it, a good deal of time to play with; they hadn't any intention of finding my body until it was stiff and there were independent witnesses with them. The unfortunate brother sportsman would be accidentally discovered with his corpse undisturbed, and the whole history of his fate perfectly plain on the nasty sloping rock from which he had slipped.

The country at the foot of the cliff was open woodland. I remember nothing except that there were thin shadows and thick shadows. The image in my mind is so vague that they might have been coverts or clouds or waves of the sea. I walked about a mile, I suppose, and chose a thick darkness to faint in. I came to a sort of consciousness several times during the night, but let it slide away. I wasn't returning to this difficult world till dawn.

When it was light, I tried to stand on my feet, but of course I couldn't. I made no second effort. Any movement of the muscles interfered with my nice cake of mud. Whenever a crust fell off I started to bleed. No, I certainly wasn't interfering with the mud.

I knew where there was water. I had never seen that stream, and my certainty of its direction may have been due to a subconscious memory of the map. But I knew where water was, and I made for it. I travelled on my belly, using my elbows for legs and leaving a track behind me like that of a wounded crocodile, all slime and blood. I wans't going into the stream – I wouldn't have washed off that mud for anything in the world; for all I knew, my bowels were only held in by mud – but I was going to the edge.

This was the reasoning of a hunted beast; or rather, it was not reasoning at all. I don't know whether a sedentary townsman's mind would have worked the same way. I think it would, if he had been badly enough hurt. You must be badly hurt to reach the stage of extinction where you stop thinking what you ought to do, and merely do it.

I made the trail look as if I had taken to the stream. I crawled to the edge and drank, and turned myself round in a shallow, a safe two inches deep, where the signs of my wallowing would be washed out. They could track me to the cover where I had lain up for the night, and from there to the water. Where I had gone when I left the water they would have to guess.

Myself I had no doubt where I was going, and the decision must be credited to my useful ancestors. A deer would trot upstream or downstream and leave the water at some point that the hunter's nose or eyes could determine. A monkey would do nothing of the sort; he would confuse his tracks and vanish into a third dimension.

When I had turned round in the shallows, I wriggled back again – back and back along the damned snake's track I had made. It was easy to follow; indeed it looked as definite as a country lane, for my face was only six inches above the ground. Thinking about it now, I wonder that they didn't notice, when they followed me to the stream, that some of the grass was bent the wrong way and that I must have gone back on my tracks. But who the devil would think of that? There aren't any laws on what print a man leaves when he's dragging his belly – and on such a monster of a trail there was no apparent need to look for details.

The outward journey had taken me under a stand of larch, where the earth was soft and free of undergrowth. I had brushed past the trunk of one tree which I now meant to climb. The lowest branch was within two feet of the ground; above that were another and another, sweet-smelling sooty branches as close together as the rungs of a ladder. The muscles of my hands were intact; I had gone beyond worrying about the state of surfaces.

Until I was well above the level of a man's eyes, I did not dare rest boots on branch; they would have left caked prints that no one could miss. I went up the first ten feet in a single burst, knowing that the longer I held on to a branch the less strength remained to reach the next. That half-minute was just a compelling of one hand above the other: two pistons shooting alternately from heaven knows what cylinder of force. My friends have sometimes accused me of taking pride in the maceration of my flesh. They are right. But I did not know that I could persuade myself to such agony as that climb.

The rest was easier, for now I could let my feet bear my weight and pause as long as I wished before each hoist. My legs were not limp; they were immovable. That was no disadvantage. I couldn't fall, wedged in as I was between the little branches of that prolific tree. When I climbed into the narrowing of the cone and the boughs were thicker and smaller and greener, I got jammed. That suited me well enough, so I fainted again. It was luxury, almost sin.

When I became conscious, the tree was swaying in the light wind and smelling of peace. I felt deliciously secure, for I was not looking forward at all; I felt as if I were a parasite on the tree, grown to it. I was not in pain, not hungry, not thirsty, and I was safe. There was nothing in each passing moment of the present that could hurt me. I was dealing exclusively with the present. If I had looked forward I should have known despair, but for a hunted, resting mammal it is no more possible to experience despair than hope.

It must have been the early afternoon when I heard the search-party. As they worked down the slope to the north of my tree I could watch them. The sun was in their eyes, and there was no risk of them spotting my face among the soft green feathers of the larch which I pushed aside. So far as I could tell, my legs were not bleeding; drops falling on the lower branches would be the only immediate sign of my presence. The slight bloodstains from my hands were there to be seen if anyone looked for them, but, on black boughs in the half-lit centre of a tree, not readily to be seen.

Three uniformed police trampled down the hillside: heavy, stolid fellows enjoying the sunshine and good-humouredly following a plain-clothes man who was ranging about on my trail like a dog they had taken for a walk. I recognized him. He was the house detective who had conducted the first part of my examination. He had proposed a really obscene method of dragging the truth out of me, and had actually started it when his colleagues protested. They had no objection to his technique, but they had the sense to see that it might be necessary for my corpse to be found and that it must not be found unreasonably mutilated.

When they came nearer I could hear scraps of their conversation. The policemen were looking for me with decent anxiety. They knew nothing of the truth, and were in doubt whether I had been man or woman, and whether the case had been accident or attempted suicide. They had been notified, I gathered, that a cry or a fall was heard in the night; then unobtrusively guided by the detective, they had found my knapsack and the disturbance in the patch of marsh. Of course I could not work out the situation at the time. I could only receive impressions. I was growing to my tree and aware of immense good nature as I listened to them. Later on, I made sense of their words.

Seeing my reptilian trail disappear into the stand of larch, the house detective perked up and took command. He seemed certain that I should be found under the trees. He shouted to his three companions to run round to the other side in case I should escape, and himself crawled under the low boughs. He nearly gave the show away there, for I was supposed to be eagerly awaiting help; but he wanted to find me himself and alone. If I were alive, it was necessary to finish me off discreetly.

He passed rapidly beneath my tree, and on into the open. I heard him curse when he discovered that I had not stopped in the wood. Then I heard their faint voices as they shouted to one another up and down the stream. That surprised me. I had thought of the stream, naturally, as a morning's march away.

I saw no more of the hunt. A few hours later there was a lot of splashing and excitement down by the water. They must have been dragging the pools for my body. The stream was a shallow mountain torrent, but quite fast enough to roll a man along with it until he was caught by rock or eddy.

In th evening I heard dogs, and felt really frightened. I started to tremble, and knew pain again, aches and stabs and throbbings, all the symphony of pain, all my members fiddling away to the beat of my heart, on it or off it or half a bar behind. I had come back to life, thanks to that healing tree. The dogs might have found me, but their master, whoever he was, never gave them a chance. He wasn't wasting time by putting them on a trail that he could follow himself; he was casting up and down the stream.

When night fell I came down from my tree. I could stand, and, with the aid of two sticks, I could shuffle slowly forwards, flat-footed and stiff-legged. I could think, too. None of my mental activities for the past twenty-four hours might be called thinking. I had allowed my body to take charge. It knew far more about escaping and healing than I did.

I must try to make my behaviour intelligible. This confession – shall I call it? – is written to keep myself from brooding, to get down what happened in the order in which it happened. I am not content with myself. With this pencil and excercise-book I hope to find some clarity. I create a second self, a man of the past by whom the man of the present may be measured. Lest what I write should ever, by accident or intention, become public property, I will not mention who I am. My name is widely known. I have been frequently and unavoidably dishonoured by the banners and praises of the penny press.

Escape Stories

This shooting trip of mine started, I believe, innocently enough. Like most Englishmen, I am not accustomed to enquire very deeply into motives. I dislike and disbelieve in cold-blooded planning, whether it be suggested of me or of anyone else. I remember asking myself when I packed the telescopic sight what the devil I wanted it for; but I just felt that it might come in handy.

It is undoubtedly true that I had been speculating – a curiosity that we all share – upon the methods of guarding a great man, and how they might be circumvented. I had a fortnight's sport in Poland, and then crossed the frontier for more. I began moving rather aimlessly from place to place, and as I found myself getting a little nearer to the House with each night's lodging I became obsessed by this idea of a sporting stalk. I have asked myself once or twice since why I didn't leave the rifle behind. I think the answer is that it wouldn't have been cricket.

Police protection is based upon the assumption that an assassin is a half-crazed idiot with a clumsy, close-range weapon – the bomb, the revolver, or the knife. It is obvious that the type of man who is a really fine shot and experienced in the approaching and killing of big-game would shrink from political or any other kind of murder. He probably hasn't any grievances, and, if he had, the rifle would not occur to him as a means of redressing them. I haven't any grievances myself. One can hardly count the upsetting of one's trivial private life and plans by European disturbances as a grievance. I don't see myself yowling of love like an Italian tenor and poking at the baritone with a stiletto.

A Bond Street rifle, I say, is not a weapon that the bodyguard need consider, for the potential assassin cannot train himself to use it. The secret police, who know all about the political antecedents of anyone disaffected to the régime, are not going to allow such a man to possess a good rifle, to walk about with it, or even to turn himself into a first-class shot. So the assassin is compelled to use a weapon that can be easily concealed.

Now, I argued, here am I with a rifle, with a permit to carry it, with an excuse for possessing it. Let us see whether, as an academic point, such a stalk and such a bag are possible. I went no further than that. I planned nothing. It has always been my habit to let things take their course.

I sent my baggage home by train, and covered the last hundred miles or so on foot, travelling only with a knapsack, my rifle and sight, my maps and my field-glasses. I marched by night. During daylight I lay up in timber or heath. I have never enjoyed anything so much. Whoever has stalked a beast for a couple of miles would understand what a superbly exciting enterprise it was to stalk over a hundred, passing unseen through the main herds of human beings, the outliers, the young males walking unexpectedly upon hillsides. I was killing two birds with one stone; I revived in myself a sense of adventure and – well, I don't see why I wrote two birds. There was only one bird: the fun of the stalk.

I arrived on the ground at dawn and spent the whole day in reconnaissance. It was an alarming day, for the forest surrounding the House was most efficiently patrolled. From tree to tree and gully to gully I prowled over most of the circuit, but only flat on the earth was I really safe. Often I hid my rifle and glasses, thinking that I was certain to be challenged and questioned. I never was. I might have been transparent. I have learned the trick of watching shadows, and standing motionless in such a position that they cut and dapple my outline; still, there were times when even a rhinoceros could have seen me.

Here, at any rate, they had considered the offensive possibilities of the rifle. At all points commanding the terrace and the gardens clearings had been cut; nobody, even at extreme ranges, could shoot from cover. Open spaces, constantly crossed by guards, there were in plenty. I chose the narrowest of them: a ride some fifty feet broad which ran straight through the woods and ended at the edge of a low cliff. From the grass slope above the cliff the terrace and the doors leading on to it were in full sight. I worked out the range as five hundred and fifty yards.

I spent the night on a couch of pine needles, well hidden

under the mother tree, and finished my provisions and slept undisturbed. A little before dawn I climbed a few feet down the cliff and squatted on a ledge where the overhang protected me from anyone who might peer over the brink. A stunted elder, clawing at the gravel with the tips of its top-heavy roots, was safe enough cover from distant eyes looking upwards. In that cramped position my rifle was useless, but I could, and very clearly, see the great man were he to come out and play with the dog or smell a rose or practise gestures on the gardener.

A path ran across the bottom of the ride, just above my head, and continued along the lower edge of the woods. I timed the intervals at which I heard footsteps, and discovered that somebody crossed the ride about every fourteen minutes. As soon as I was certain of that, I came out of hiding and followed. I wanted to understand his exact routine.

He was a young guard of splendid physique, with loyalty written all over him, but he had, I should think, hardly ever been out of an industrial town in his life. He couldn't have seen me if I had been under his feet. He knew perfectly well that he was not alone, for he looked over his shoulder again and again, and stared at the bush or the fold in the ground where I was; but of course he put his sensation down to nervousness or imagination. I treated him with disrespect, but I liked him; he was such a sturdy youth, with one of those fleshy open faces and the right instincts – a boy worth teaching. His eyes when he bagged his first tiger would be enough reward for putting up with a month of his naïve ideas.

After I had been round his beat with him and behind him, I knew for how many minutes, at any given time, I could occupy the grass slope, and by what route I must escape. When at last the great man came out to the terrace, my young friend had just passed. I had ten minutes to play with. I was up at once on to the slope.

I made myself comfortable, and got the three pointers of the sight steady on the V of his waistcoat. He was facing me and winding up his watch. He would never have known what shattered him – if I had meant to fire that is. Just at that moment I felt a slight breeze on my cheek. It had been dead calm till then. I had to allow for the wind. No doubt the great man's disciples would see the hand of the Almighty in that. I should not disagree with them, for providence assuredly takes special care of any lone and magnificent male. Everyone who has stalked a particularly fine head knows that. It's natural enough. The Almighty Himself is always considered to be masculine.

I heard a yell. The next thing I knew was that I was coming round from a severe blow on the back of the head, and my young friend was covering me with his revolver. He had hurled a stone at me and himself after it – immediate, instinctive action far swifter than fiddling with his holster. We stared at each other. I remember complaining incoherently that he was seven minutes early. He looked at me as if I had been the devil in person, with horror, with fear – not fear of me, but fear at the suddenly revealed depravity of this world.

'I turned back,' he said, 'I knew.'

Well, of course he did. I should never have been such a conceited fool as to upset his nerves and his routine by following him about. He had neither heard me nor set eyes on me, but he was aware enough to make his movements irregular.

Together with his commanding officer he took me down to the House, and there, as I have already written, I was questioned by professionals. My captor left the room after disgracing his manhood – or so he thought – by being violently sick. Myself, I was detached. Perhaps I should not call it detachment, for my body is sensitive and there was no interruption or hiatus in its messages to my brain. But training counts.

I hold no brief for the pre-war Spartan training of the English upper class – or middle class as it is now the fashion to call it, leaving the upper to the angels – since in the ordinary affairs of a conventional life it is not of the slightest value to anyone; but it is of use on the admittedly rare occasions when one needs a high degree of physical endurance. I have been through an initiation ceremony on the Rio Javary – the only way I could persuade them to teach me how their men can exercise a slight muscular control over haemorrhage – and I thought it more a disagreeable experience than any proof of maturity. It lasted only a day and a night, whereas the initiation ceremonies of the tribal English continue for the ten years of education. We torture a boy's spirit rather than his body, but all torture is, in the end, directed at the spirit. I was conditioned to endure without making an ass of myself. That is all I mean by detachment.

I suspect that resignation was a lot easier for me than for a real assassin, since I had nothing at all to give away, no confederates, no motive. I couldn't save myself by telling them anything interesting. I had no right to endanger others by irresponsible invention. So I kept on automatically repeating the truth without the slightest hope that it would be believed.

At last someone recognized my name, and my story of a sporting stalk became faintly possible; but, whether it were true or not, it was now more than ever essential that I be discreetly murdered. And that was easy. I had admitted that I had not spent a night under a roof for five days, and that nobody knew where I was. They put all my papers and possessions back into my pockets, drove me fifty miles to the north, and staged the accident.

When I came down from the blessed larch and found that my legs would carry me, I began, I say, to look foreward. It would be supposed either that I was drowned or that I was lying hurt and incapable in some riverside cover where my corpse would eventually be found. The police and the authorities in neighbouring villages would be warned to look out for a moribund stranger, but it was most unlikely that any description of me would have been circularized to other districts. The security officers at the House had no official knowledge of my existence and would share their unofficial knowledge with as few outsiders as possible. It was a convenience to have no existence. Had I stolen a watch instead of stalking the head of a nation my photograph would have been in all the police stations.

If I could walk, if I had new breeches, and if I could pass the danger zone without calling attention to myself, my chance of getting clear out of the country was not negligible. I had my passport, my maps, and my money. I spoke the language well enough to deceive anyone but a highly educated man listening for mistakes. Dear old Holy George – my private nickname for their ambassador in London – insists that I speak a dialect, but to him polished grammar is more important than accent. That's a superstition inseparable from foreign affairs. A well-trained diplomat is supposed to write French, for example, like an angel, but to speak it with the peculiar gutlessness of a Geneva nancy-boy.

I wish I could apologise to Holy George. He had certainly spent some hours of those last twenty-four in answering very confidential cables about me – wiring as respectfully as possible that the bodyguard of his revered master were a pack of bloody fools, and following up with a strong letter to the effect that I was a member of his club and that it was unthinkable I should be mixed up in any such business as was, he could hardly believe seriously, suggested. I fear he must have been reprimanded. The bodyguard were, on the face of it, right.

It was now, I think, Sunday night; it was a Saturday when I was caught, but I am not sure of the lapse of time thereafter. I missed a day somewhere, but whether it was in my tree or on my island I cannot tell.

I knew roughly where I was, and that, to escape from this tumbled world of rock and forest, I should follow any path which ran parallel to the stream. My journey would not have been difficult if I had had crutches, but I could find no pieces of wood of the right height and with an angle to fit under the arm. It was now, I think, Sunday night; it was a Saturday when I at the time I was angry with myself, angry to the point when I wept childish tears of impotence. I couldn't make my hands use enough pressure on a knife, and I couldn't find sticks of the right length and shape. For an hour I raged and cursed at myself. I thought my spirit had altogether broken. It was pardonable. When everything was impossible, it was unreasonable to expect myself to distinguish between the miracle that could be forced to happen and the miracle that could not happen.

Finally, of course, I had to accept a miracle that could be forced; to make myself progress without crutches. With a rough staff in each hand I managed about four miles, shuffling over even ground, and crawling for short distances over obstacles or for long distances whenever my legs became unbearably painful. I remember that common experience of carrying a heavy suitcase farther than it can reasonably be carried; one changes it from arm to arm at shorter and shorter intervals until one can no longer decide whether to continue the pain in the right or change to instant pain in the left. So it was with me in my changes from crawling to walking and back again.

I thanked God for the dawn, for it meant that I need not drive myself any farther. Until I knew exactly where I was, and upon what paths men came and went, I had to hide. I collapsed into a dry ditch and lay there for hours. I heard no sounds except a lark and the crunch of cows tearing at the grass in a neighbouring field.

At last I stood up and had a look at my surroundings. I was near the top of a ridge. Below me and to the left was the wooded valley along which I had come. I had not noticed in the night that I was climbing. Part of my exhaustion had been due to the rising ground.

I shuffled upwards to the skyline. The long curve of a river was spread out at my feet. The near bank was clothed in low bushes through which ran a footpath, appearing and disappearing until it crossed the mouth of my stream by an iron bridge. On the farther bank, a mile upstream, was a country town with a few small factories. Downstream there were pastures on both banks and a small islet in the centre of the river. It was tranquil and safe as any of our hidden English Avons.

I got out the map and checked my position. I was looking at a tributary which, after a course of thirty miles, ran into one of the main rivers of Europe. From this town, a provincial capital, the search for me would be directed, and to it the police, my would-be rescuers, presumably belonged. Nevertheless I had to go there. It was the centre of communications: road, river, and railway. And since I could not walk I had to find some transport to carry me to the frontier.

At intervals the breeze bore to me the faint sound of cries and splashing. I thought someone was being hurt – a morbid fancy, natural enough in the circumstances – but then I realized that the screaming was the collective voice of several women, and that they were bathing. It occurred to me that when commerce and education stopped for lunch men might come to swim at the same place, and I could lay my hands on a pair of trousers.

I waited until I saw the girls cross the iron footbridge on their way back to town, and then hobbled down the ridge – a stony, barren hillside where there were, thank heaven, no fences to cross and no officious small-holder to ask me what I was doing. The bathing-place was plain enough, a semicircle of grass with a clean drop of three feet into the river. Above and below it the bank was covered with a dense growth of willow and alder. I took to my elbows and belly again, and crawled into the thicket. There was already a sort of runway leading into it, which, at the time, I could only assume the Lord had made for my special benefit. I realized afterwards that it had been bored through the bushes by some young fellow who was curious to know the female form and too poor to arrange for it in the ordinary way. I think of him as charitably as I can. From the end of his burrow I had an excellent view of the bushes behind which a modest bather would undress.

My necessary males were not long in coming. Indeed I had a narrow shave, for I heard them yelling and singing their way along the path before I had turned myself round. They were five hefty lads: sons, I should think, of shopkeepers and petty officials. There were two pairs of shorts, two nondescript trousers, and an old pair of riding-breeches. For my build all had the waistbands too roomy and the legs too short, and I couldn't guess which pair would best fit me. It was that, I think, which gave me the brilliant idea of taking them all. To steal one pair of trousers would obviously direct attention to some passing tramp or fugitive; but if all disappeared, the theft would be put down as the practical joke of a comrade. I remember chuckling crazily as I worked my way back to the edge of the bushes.

They undressed in the open, ten yards from the water. That meant there was only one chance for me – to do the job the moment the last man had dived in and before the first came out. It was a mad risk, but I had gone long beyond caring what risks I took.

They dived in within a few seconds of each other, all but one who remained on the bank shadow-boxing with his fat-bottomed, idiotic self until a friend, as fed up with his posing as I was, reached an arm for his ankles and pulled him in. I was out of my observation post on the instant and hunching myself across the grass. I got four pairs; the fifth was too far away. I just had time to slip behind a bramble bush before one of them pulled himself up the bank. He didn't look at the clothes – why should he? – and I crawled downstream with the trousers.

Now what was the one place where they would not look? To climb a second tree was unsafe; young men in high spirits naturally think of trees. As for the bushes, they would trample them down like a herd of buffalo. The best place for me was, I decided, the water. No one would expect a practical joker, presumably fully dressed, to go to such lengths as to sink himself and his friends' breeches in the river. I made for the bank and slid under the willows into a patch of still water full of scum and brushwood. Two of them were swimming quite close, but the boughs trailing in the water protected me well enough from casual glances.

I needn't have taken so much trouble, for the plan succeeded more easily than I dared hope. They dashed up the path, and I heard their voices resounding from the hillside as they yelled for one Willy. When Willy was not to be found, they draped towels round the tails of their shirts and stormed through the thicket. I don't know if they actually looked over the bank where I was. I heard one of them within a yard or two, and ducked. At last, in an evil mood, they took the path for home and Willy. They never doubted for a moment that the culprit was Willy. I hope they didn't believe his denials till he was thoroughly punished. The sort of man whom one instantly accuses of any practical joke that has been played deserves whatever is coming to him.

Together with the trousers I let myself float down to the islet which I had seen from the top of the ridge. I could only use my arms for swimming. My generation never normally learned the crawl, and my old-fashioned frog's leg-stroke was too painful to be possible. However, I managed to keep myself and my soggy raft of trousers well out into the river, and the current did the rest.

The islet was bare, but with enough low vegetation on its shores to cover me, provided I kept close to the edge, from observation by anyone on the high ground where I had lain that morning. There were four notices, neatly spaced, to the effect that it was forbidden to land. I can't conceive why. Perhaps because any idle person in a boat would naturally want to land, and anything that encourages idleness is considered immoral.

I spread out myself, my clothes, and the breeches to dry in the afternoon sun. I did not attempt to examine my body. It was enough that the soaking had separated textile from flesh with no worse result than a gentle oozing of matter.

I remained on the islet for the Monday night and all the following day. Probably I was there for the Tuesday night too. I do not know; as I say, I lost a day somewhere. It was very heaven, for I lay on the sand naked and undisturbed, and allowed the sun to start the work of healing. I was barely conscious most of the time. I would hunch myself into the half-shade of the weeds and rushes and sleep till I grew cold, and I would hunch myself back again and roast and scar my wounds. I had but those two pleasures within attaining, and both were utterly satisfying. I did not want food. I was, I suppose, running a fever, so my lack of appetite was natural. I did suffer from the cold at night, but not severely. I had all the various garments to cover me, and, at any other time, I should have thought the weather too hot and still for easy sleep.

I awoke, feeling clear-headed and ravenously hungry, at the false dawn of what turned out to be Wednesday. I chose the riding-breeches – holding them against my body they seemed roomy enough not to rub my hide – and threw shorts and trousers into the river. I hope that their small change was not too great a loss to the owners. Only one had a wallet, and that, since it stuck out from his hip-pocket, I had managed to slip on top of the rest of his clothes.

I tied two bits of driftwood together with my belt, and put all my possessions on this improvised raft. I found that I could splash with more ease – though the regular motions of swimming were still beyond me – and reached the farther bank, the raft helping, without being carried more than a hundred yards downstream.

On dry land and within a stone's throw of a main road, I had to take stock of my appearance. So far my looks had mattered no more to me than the condition of its fur to an animal; but now I proposed to re-enter the world of men, and the impression I made was vitally important. Only my shoes and stockings were respectable. I couldn't bend to take them off, so the river had cleaned them.

Item: I had to shave off a four days' beard. That was far from being the mere prejudice of an Englishman against appearing in public with his bristles. If a man is clean shaved and has a well-fitting collar and tie – even reasonably dirty – he can get away with a multitude of suspicious circumstances.

Item: Gloves. The ends of my fingers had to be shown while paying money and taking goods, and they were not human.

Item: An Eyeshade. My left eye was in a condition that could not be verified without a mirror. The eyelid had stuck to a mess of what I hoped was only blood.

Item: A Clothes Brush. My tweed coat had no elbows, but it
        might pass provided I brushed off the mud and did not
        turn away from anyone I spoke to.

I had to have these things. Without them I might as well have
given myself up. I had not the will to crawl and hobble night
after night to the frontier, nor the agility to steal enough to eat;
but if I entered so much as a village shop as I was, the proprietor
would promptly escort me to the police or a hospital.

The putting-on of the breeches was an interminable agony.
When at last I had them up, I couldn't fasten the blasted
buttons. I managed three and had to forego the rest for fear of
leaving bloodstains all over the cloth. Shirt buttons were quite
impossible.

I crossed a field and stood for a moment on the empty main
road. It was the hour before dawn, the sky an imperial awning
fringed with blue and gold. The tarred surface of the road was
blue and calm as a canal. Only the trains were alive, dashing
across the flat vale as if striving to reach the mountains before
day. At my disposal, as the map had told me, were river, road,
and railway. I was inclined to favour escape by river. A man
drifting down the current in a boat doesn't have to answer
questions or fill up forms. But again there was the insuperable
handicap of my appearance. I couldn't present myself as I was to
buy a boat, and if I stole one and it were missed, my arrest was
certain at the next village down-river.

On the far side of the road was a farm-cart, backed against the
edge of a field of wheat. I knelt behind it to watch the passers-by.
Men were already stirring, a few peasants in the fields, a few
walkers on the road. From the latter I hoped to obtain help, or at
least, by observing them, an inspiration how to help myself.

There was a workman bound for some small factory in the
town to whom I nearly spoke. He had an honest kindly face – but
so have most of them. I had no reason at all to suppose he would
protect me. Two aimless wanderers went by together. They
looked to be persons who would sympathize, but their faces
were those of scared rabbits. I couldn't trust them. Then there

were several peasants on their way to the fields. I could only pray that they wouldn't enter mine. They would have had some sport with me before handing me over to the police; they seemed that sort. There was a wretched fellow mumbling and weeping, who raised my hopes for a moment. But misery is in some way as sacred as happiness; one doesn't intrude – not, at any rate, if there is a risk that one might merely add to the misery. Then came another factory-worker, and then a tall, stooping man with a fishing rod. He cut across to the river and began to fish not far from where I had landed. He had a melancholy, intellectual face with a deal of strength in it, I decided to have another look at him.

Their tiresome conception of the State has one comforting effect; it creates so many moral lepers that no one of them, if he has a little patience, can long be lonely. The flotsam of the nation is washed together into an unrecognized, nameless, formless secret society. There isn't much that the bits of scum can do to help one another, but at least they can cling and keep silence. And dawn, I think, is the hour when the pariah goes out. Not for him is the scornful morning with its crowds pointing the fingers of their minds at him, nor the evening when all but he may rest and be merry; but the peace before sunrise cannot be taken from him. It is the hour of the outlawed, the persecuted, the damned, for no man was ever born who could not feel some shade of hope if he were in open country with the sun about to rise. I did not formulate these thoughts at the time. I have developed them in the curious and lonely circumstances under which I write. But I give them for what they are worth to account for my intuition in choosing the right face and the fact that there were so many to choose from.

There was no cover on the farther side of the road and precious little on the bank, so that I had to make up my mind about the fisherman as I slowly and silently crossed the field towards him. He was paying more attention to his thoughts than to his rod. By the angle of his float I could see that he had hooked the bottom, but he was quite unaware of it. I walked up behind him and wished him good morning and asked if he had had any luck. He jumped to his feet with the butt of the rod pointed towards me as if to keep me off. I expect he hadn't seen a creature like me in a long time; they haven't any tramps. Even considering me the last word in villains, he thought it best to propitiate me. He apologized for his fishing, and said he didn't think there was anything wrong in it. He did his best to look servile, but his eyes burned with courage.

I held out my hands to him and asked if he knew how that was done. He didn't answer a word, just waited for further information.

'Look here!' I said to him, 'I swear there isn't a soul in this country who knows I am alive except yourself. I want gloves, shaving tackle, and a clothes brush. Don't buy them. Give me old things that have no mark on them by which they could be traced back to you if I am caught. And if you don't mind putting your hand in my inside coat-pocket you will find money.'

'I don't want money,' he said.

His face was absolutely expressionless. He wasn't giving anything away. He might have meant that he wouldn't help a fugitive for all the money in the world, or that he wouldn't take money for helping a fugitive. The next move was up to me.

'Do you speak English?' I asked.

I saw a flicker of interest in his eyes, but he made no sign that he had understood me. I carried on in English. I was completely in his power, so that there was no point in hiding my nationality. I hoped that the foreign tongue might break down his reserve.

'I won't tell you who I am or what I have done,' I said, 'because it is wiser that you shouldn't know. But so long as no one sees us talking together, I don't think you run the slightest risk in helping me.'

'I'll help you,' he answered in English. 'What was it you wanted?'

I repeated my requirements and asked him to throw in an eye-patch and some food if he could manage it. I also told him I was a rich man and he shouldn't hesitate to take any money he might need. He refused – with a very sweet, melancholy smile – but gave me an address in England to which I was to pay what I thought fit if ever I got home.

'Where shall I put the things?' he asked.

'Under the cart over there,' I answered. 'And don't worry. I shall be in the wheat, and I'll take care not to be seen.'

He said good-bye and moved off abruptly. In one stride he had dissociated himself from me completely. He knew by experience that among the proscribed the truest courtesy was to waste no time in courtesy.

The traffic on the road was increasing, and I had to wait some minutes before I could safely cross into the shelter of the wheat. The sun rose and the landscape budded men and business – barges on the river, a battalion out for a route march on the road, and damned, silent bicycles sneaking up every time I raised my head.

The fisherman was back in an hour, but the road was too busy for him to drop a parcel under the cart unseen. He solved the problem by fetching his rod and sitting on the cart while he took it apart and packed it. When he got up he accidentally left the parcel behind.

To get possession of it was the devil of a job, for I could not see what was about to pass until the traffic was nearly opposite me. I knelt in the wheat, bobbing my head up and down like a pious old woman divided between silent prayer and the responses. At last I plucked up courage and reached the cart. A stream of cars went by, but they did not matter; the danger was a pedestrian or a cyclist who might be tempted to stop and talk. I kept my back to the road and pretended to be tinkering with the axle. A woman wished me good morning, and that was the worst fright I had had since they pushed me over the cliff. I answered her surlily and she passed on. To wait for a clear road was exasperating, but I needed a full minute free from possible observation. I couldn't plunge boldly back into the wheat. I had to tread gently, separating the stalks so as not to leave too obvious a track behind me.

At last I knelt in peace and unpacked the parcel which that

blessed fisherman had left for me. There were a bottle of milk well laced with brandy, bread and the best part of a cold chicken. He had thought of everything, even hot shaving-water in a thermos flask.

When I had finished his food I felt equal to looking in the mirror. I was cleaner than I expected; the morning swim was responsible for that. But I didn't recognize myself. It was not the smashed eye which surprised me – that was merely closed, swollen, and ugly. It was the other eye. Glaring back at me from the mirror, deep and enormous, it seemed to belong to someone intensely alive, so much more alive than I felt. My face was all pallors and angles, like that of a Christian martyr in a medieval painting – and I had the added villainy of bristles. I marvelled how such a beastly crop could grow in so poor and spiritual a soil.

I put on my gloves – limp leather, God reward him, and several sizes too large! – then shaved, brushed my clothes, and dressed myself more tidily. My coat and shirt were patterned in shades of brown, and the blood stains, weakened by my swim to the island, hardly showed. When I had cleaned up and adjusted the eyepatch, I came to the conclusion that I aroused pity rather than suspicion. I looked like a poor but educated man, a clerk or schoolmaster, convalescent after some nasty accident. That was evidently the right part to play.

As soon as I was ready I left the wheat, for now I did not care how wide a track I made so long as no one actually saw me emerge. The road was clearer; it had ceased to feed and empty the town, and become an artery in a greater life. Lorries and cars sped by with the leisurely roar of through traffic. Their drivers had no neighbourly feelings towards that mile of road, no damned curiosity about a lonely pedestrian. I covered the mile into town, limping along as best I could and stopping frequently to rest. At need I could walk very slowly and correctly, hanging on each foot, as if waiting for somebody.

I was desperately nervous when first I engaged myself between two lines of houses. There seemed to be so many windows observing me, such crowds on the streets. Looking back on it, I cannot think that I passed more than a score of people, mostly women shopping; but, at the best of times, I have a tendency to agoraphobia. Even in London I avoid crowds at all cost; to push my way through the drift of suburban idlers in Oxford Street is torment to me. The streets of that town were really no more full nor empty than those of my own country town, and normally I should not have been affected; but I seemed to have been out of human society for years.

I cut down to the river by the first turning, and came out on to a paved walk, with flower-beds and a bandstand, where I could stroll at my artificial pace without making myself conspicuous. Ahead, under the bridge, were moored a dozen boats. When I came abreast of them I saw the expected notice of 'Boats for Hire' in a prettily painted cottage. There was a man leaning on the fence meditative and unbuttoned, and obviously digesting his breakfast while mistaking that process for thought.

I wished him good day and asked if I could hire a boat. He looked at me suspiciously and remarked that he had never seen me before, as if that ended the discussion. I explained that I was a schoolmaster recovering from a motor accident and had been ordered by my doctor to spend a week in the open air. He took his pipe out of his mouth and said that he didn't hire boats to strangers. Well, had he one for sale? No, he had not. So there we were. He evidently didn't like the look of me and wasn't going to argue.

A shrill yell came from a bedroom window:

'Sell him the punt, idiot!'

I looked up. A red face and formidable bust were hanging over the window-sill, both quivering with exasperation. I bowed to her with the formality of a village teacher, and she came down.

'Sell him what he wants, dolt!' she ordered.

Her small, screaming voice came most oddly from so huge a bulk. I imagine he had driven her voice higher and higher with impatience until it stuck permanently on its top note.

'I don't know who he is,' insisted her husband with stupid surliness.

'Well, who are you?' she shrieked, as if I had repeatedly refused her the information.

I told my story: how I couldn't yet walk with any ease, and so had thought of spending a holiday in drifting down the river from town to town and realizing a dream of my youth.

'Where's your baggage?' asked that damned boatman.

I patted my pockets, bulging with the thermos flask and shaving tackle. I told him I needed no more than a night-shirt and a tooth-brush.

That set the old girl off again. She skirled like a sucking-pig separated from the litter.

'You expect him to travel with a trunk? He's a proper man, not an ignorant, shameless idler who wastes good money on clubs and uniforms and whores, and would rather go to the river than raise his hand to pull the plug. He shall have his boat! And cheap!'

She stamped down to the waterfront and showed me the punt. It was comfortable, but far too long and clumsy to be handled by a man who couldn't sit to paddle. It wasn't cheap. She asked about double its fair price. Evidently her kindness was not at all disinterested.

There was a twelve-foot dinghy with a red sail, and I enquired if it was for sale. She said it was too expensive for me.

'I shall sell it again wherever I finish the trip,' I answered. 'And I have a little money – compensation for my accident.'

She made her husband step the mast and hoist the sail. How that man hated the pair of us! He announced with gusto that I should certainly drown myself and that his wife could take the blame. A child couldn't have drowned himself. The boat was exactly what I wanted. The sail was hardly more than a toy, but it would be a considerable help with the wind astern, and was not large enough to be a hindrance if I let go the sheet and drifted with the current. I knew that some days must pass before I felt equal to the effort of tacking.

While she raved at her husband, I got out my wallet. I didn't want them to see how much I had, nor to wonder at my fumbling with gloved hands.

'There!' I said, holding out to her a sheaf of notes. 'That's all I can afford. Tell me yes or no.'

I don't know whether it was less or more than she intended to ask, but it was a sight more than the little tub was worth to anyone but me. She looked astonished at my rural simplicity and began to haggle, just for form's sake. I sympathized; I said that no doubt she was right, but that sum was all I could pay for a boat. She took it, of course, and gave me a receipt. In five minutes I was out on the river, and they were wondering, I suppose, why the crazy schoolmaster should kneel on the bottomboards instead of sitting on a thwart, and why he didn't have his coat decently mended.

Of the days and nights that passed on the tributary and the main river there is little to write. I was out of any immediate danger, and content – far more content than I am now, though no less solitary. I didn't exist, and so long as I was not compelled to show my papers there was no reason why I should exist. Patience was all I needed, and easy enough to keep. I recovered my strength as peacefully as if I had been the convalescent I pretended; indeed, thinking myself into the part actually helped me to recover. I nearly believed in my motor accident, my elementary school, my housekeeper, and my favourite pupils about whom I prattled when I fell in with other users of the river or when I took a meal in an obscure riverside tavern.

From nightfall to dawn I moored my boat in silent reaches of the river, choosing high or marshy or thickly wooded banks where no one could burst in upon me with questions. At first I had taken to the ditches and backwaters, but the danger of that amphibian habit was impressed on me when a farmer led his horses down to drink in my temporary harbour, and insisted on regarding me as a suspicious character. Rain was the greatest hardship I had to endure. After a night's soaking I felt the chill of the morning mist. A rubber sheet was unobtainable, but I managed at last to buy a tarpaulin. It kept me dry and uncomfortably warm, but it was heavy, and hard for my hands to fold and unfold. Only the most persistent rain could force me to use it.

I made but sixty miles in the first week. My object was to heal myself rather than hurry. I took no risks and expended no effort. Until the back of my thighs had grown some sturdy scars I had to kneel while sailing or drifting, and lie on my stomach across the thwarts while sleeping. That limited my speed. I could not row.

In the second week I tried to buy an outboard motor, and only just got out of the deal in time. I found that to purchase an engine and petrol I had to sign enough papers to ensure my arrest by every political or administrative body that had heard of me. I must say, they have made the way of the transgressor uncommonly difficult. At the next town, however, there was an old-fashioned yard where I bought a business-like lugsail and had a small foresail fitted into the bargain. Thereafter I carried my own stores, and never put in to town or village. With my new canvas and the aid of the current I could sometimes do forty miles a day, and – what was more important – I could keep out of the way of the barges and tugs that were now treating the river as their own.

All the way down-river I had considered the problem of my final escape from the country, and had arrived at three possible solutions. The first was to keep on sailing and trust to luck. This was obviously very risky, for only a fast motorboat could slip past the patrol craft off the port. I should be turned back, either as a suspicious character or an ignorant idiot who oughtn't to be allowed in a boat – and the chances, indeed, were against my little twelve-foot tub being able to live in the short, breaking seas of the estuary.

The second plan was to embark openly on a passenger vessel – or train, for that matter – and trust that my name and description had never been circularized to the frontier police. This, earlier, I might have tried if I had had the strength; but as my voyage crept into its third week it seemed probable that even the most extensive search for my body would have been abandoned, that it would be assumed I was alive, and that every blessed official was praying for a sight of me and promotion.

My third solution was to hang around the docks for an opportunity of stowing away or stealing a boat or seeing a yacht which belonged to some friend. But this demanded time – and I could neither sleep in a hotel without being invited to show my papers to a lodging-house keeper, nor in the open without showing them to a policeman. Whatever I did, I had to do immediately after arrival at the port.

Now, of course I was thinking stupidly. The way out of the country was laughably easy. A boy who had merely hit a policeman would have thought of it at once. But in my mind I was a convalescent schoolmaster or I was a ghost. I had divested myself of my nationality and forgotten that I could call on the loyalty of my cómpatriots. I had nearly thrown away my British passport on the theory that no papers whatever would be safer than my own. As soon as I came in sight of the wharves, I saw British ships and realized that I had merely to tell a good enough story to the right man to be taken aboard.

Dead Cert

DICK FRANCIS

**When Alan York's best friend and fellow jockey
dies after a fall from his horse, Alan discovers it
was not an accident. But the men involved in
the murder decide that Alan is getting too close
to the truth and try to get rid of him.**

Pete called to me to hurry up and we'd have a celebration drink
together, so I changed quickly and went outside to join him. He
steered me towards the bar next to the Tote building, and we
stopped at the gap, looking in to where Joe had died. There was a
shoulder-high wooden fence across the entrance now, to keep
sensation seekers out. A rusty brown stain on the gravel was all
that was left of Joe.

'A terrible thing, that,' Pete said, as we stepped into the bar.
'What did he say to you before he died?'

'I'll tell you sometime,' I said idly. 'But just now I'm more
interested in where Admiral runs next.' And over our drinks we
talked solely about horses.

Returning to the weighing-room we found two men in belted
raincoats waiting for us near the door. They wore trilby hats and
large shoes, and gave off that indefinable aura of solid menace
which characterizes many plain-clothes policemen.

One of them put his hand inside his coat, drew out a folded
warrant and flipped it in my direction.

'Mr York?'

'Yes.'

'Inspector Wakefield's compliments, and will you come down to the police station to help his inquiries, please.' The 'please' he tacked on as an afterthought.

'Very well,' I said, and asked Pete to see Clem about my kit.

'Sure,' he said.

I walked with the two men across to the gate and through the car park.

'I'll get my car and follow you to the station,' I said.

'There's a police car waiting for us in the road, sir,' said the larger of the two. 'Inspector Wakefield did say to bring you in it, and if you don't mind, sir, I'd rather do as the Inspector says.'

I grinned. If Inspector Wakefield were my boss I'd do as he said, too. 'All right,' I agreed.

Ahead of us the sleek black Wolseley was parked outside the gate, with a uniformed driver standing beside it and another man in a peaked cap in the front passenger's seat.

Away towards my right, in front of the ranks of parked horse-boxes, several of the runners from Admiral's race were being led up and down to get the stiffness out of their limbs before they were loaded up for the journey home. Admiral was among them, with Victor, his lad, walking proudly at his head.

I was telling the man on my right, the smaller of the two, that there was my horse and wasn't he a beauty, when I got a shock which knocked the breath out of me as thoroughly as a kick in the stomach.

To cover myself I dropped my race glasses on to the turf and bent slowly to pick them up, my escort stopping a pace ahead of me to wait. I grasped the strap and slung it over my shoulder, straightening and looking back at the same time to where we had come from. Forty yards of grass separated us from the last row of cars. There was no one about except some distant people going home. I looked at my watch. The last race was just about to begin.

I turned round unhurriedly, letting my eyes travel blankly

126

past the man on my right and on towards Admiral, now going away from me. As usual after a race, he was belted into a rug to avoid cooling down too quickly, and he still wore his bridle. Victor would change that for a head collar when he put him in the horsebox.

Victor's great drawback was his slow wits. Endowed with an instinctive feeling for horses and an inborn skill in looking after them, he had never risen above 'doing his two' in forty years of stable life, and never would. I would have to do without much help from him.

'Victor,' I shouted, and when he turned round I signalled to him to bring Admiral over.

'I just want to make sure the horse's legs are all right,' I explained to the two men. They nodded and waited beside me, the larger one shifting from foot to foot.

I did not dare to take a third look, and in any case I knew I was not mistaken.

The man on my right was wearing the tie I had lost in the horsebox on Maidenhead Thicket.

It was made from a piece of silk which had been specially woven and given to me on my twenty-first birthday by a textile manufacturer who wanted to do business with my father. I had two other ties like it, and a scarf, and the pattern of small red and gold steamships interlaced with the letter Y on a dark green background was unique.

How likely was it that a junior C.I.D. officer should have come honestly by my tie, I asked myself urgently. Farmer Lawson had not found it, and none of his men admitted to having seen it. It was too much of a coincidence to be innocent that it should reappear round the throat of a man who was asking me to step into a car and go for a ride with him.

Here was the attack I had been waiting for, and I had damn nearly walked meekly into the trap. Getting out of it, when it was so nearly sprung, was not going to be easy. The 'police' car was parked across the gateway barely twenty paces ahead, with the driver standing by the bonnet and looking in our direction. The menacing aura of my two tough escorts now revealed itself to be something a great deal more sinister than a manner assumed to deal with crooks. One of them, perhaps, had killed Joe.

If I gave the slightest sign of doubting them, I was sure the three of them would hustle me into the car and drive off in a cloud of dust, leaving only Victor to report doubtfully what he had seen. And that, as far as I was concerned, would be that. It was to be one of those rides from which the passenger did not return.

My plan to present Wakefield with an attempted murderer was no good. One, I could have managed. But not three, and another sitting in the car.

When Victor was within fifteen paces of me I let the strap of my race-glasses slip from my shoulder, down my arm and into my hand. Abruptly, with all my strength, I swung the glasses like a scythe round the legs of the larger man and overbalanced him, tripped the smaller man with the one elementary judo throw I knew, and sprinted for Admiral.

The five seconds it took them to recover from the unexpected assault were enough. As they started after me with set faces I leaped on to Admiral's back, picked up the reins which lay loosely on his neck, and turned him round sharply out of Victor's grasp.

The third man was running towards me from the car. I kicked Admiral into a canter in two strides, swerving round the advancing chauffeur, and set him towards the hedge which formed the boundary of the car park. He cleared it powerfully landing on the grass verge of the road a few yards in front of the black car. The fourth man had the door open and was scrambling out. I looked back quickly.

Victor was standing stock-still with his mouth open. The three men were all running towards the gate with purposeful strides. They had nearly reached it. I had barely time to hope they were not carrying guns, since I presented a large and close target, when I saw the sun glint on something bright in the hand of the man who was wearing my tie. It hardly seemed the moment to stop and discover whether the glint came from a black-handled chef's knife: but I nearly found out the hard way, because he drew back his arm and threw it at me. I flung myself flat on the horse's neck and it missed, and I heard it clatter on to the road beyond.

I urged Admiral straight across the road, ignoring the squeal of brakes from a speeding lorry, and jumped him into the field opposite. The land sloped upwards, so that when I reined-in about halfway up it and turned round to see what was happening, the road and the car park were spread out below like a map. The men were making no attempt to follow. They had moved the Wolseley away from the gate and were now drawing to a halt some yards further along the verge. It looked as if all four were inside the car.

Victor still stood in the car park, scratching his head as he looked up towards me. I could imagine his bewilderment. I wondered how long it would be before he went to tell Pete what had happened.

Once the last race was over the car park would be buzzing with people, and the cars would pour out of the now unobstructed gateway. I thought that then I would be able to return safely to the racecourse without being abducted.

At this point another black car drew up behind the Wolseley, and then another, and several others, until a line of eight or more stretched along the side of the road. There was something rather horribly familiar about the newcomers.

They were Marconicars.

All the drivers climbed out of the taxis and walked along towards the Wolseley. With its low expensive lines and its efficient-looking aerial on top, it still looked every inch a police car; but the reinforcements it had called up dispelled any last doubts it was possible to have about the nature of the 'C.I.D. officers'.

The men stood in a dark group on the road, and I sat on Admiral half-way up the field watching them. They seemed to be in no hurry, but having seen their armoury of bicycle chains, knives, and assorted knuckledusters when they fought the London gang at Plumpton, and with Joe's fate constantly in mind, I had no doubt what would happen if I let them catch me.

I was in a good position. They could not drive the taxis up the field because there was no gate into it from the road, nor could they hope to reach me on foot, and I was still confident that when the race crowd flocked out I could evade the enemy and return to the course.

Two things quickly happened to change the picture.

First, the men began looking and pointing towards the side of the field I was in. Turning my head to the right I saw a car driving downhill on the farther side of the hedge, and realized that there was a road there. Twisting round, I now took note for the first time that a large house with out-buildings and gardens spread extensively across the skyline.

Three of the taxis detached themselves from the line and drove round into the road on my right, stopping at intervals along it. I now had taxi drivers to the right and ahead, and the big house at my back, but I was still not unduly dismayed.

Then yet another Marconicar came dashing up and stopped with a jerk in front of the Wolseley. A stocky man swung open the door and raised himself out of the driver's seat. He strode across the road to the hedge, and stood there pointing up at me with his arm extended. I was still wondering why when I heard the low whine of a bullet passing at the level of my feet. There was no sound of a shot.

As I turned Admiral to gallop off across the field, a bullet hit the ground with a phut in front of me. Either the range was too far for accurate shooting with a gun fitted with a silencer, or... I began to sweat... the marksman was aiming deliberately low, not at me but at Admiral.

It was only an eight or ten acre field, nothing like big enough for safety. I used precious moments to pull the horse up and take a look at the ragged sprawling hedge on the far side of the field. It was threaded half-way up with barbed wire. Over my shoulder I could see the man with the gun running along the road parallel to the course I had just taken. He would soon be within range again.

I took Admiral back a little way, faced him towards the hedge and urged him to jump. He cleared the whole thing, wire and all, without bending so much as a twig. We landed in another field, this time occupied by a herd of cows but again small and much too open to the road. Also, I discovered, trotting along the top boundary, the barbed wire had been laid lavishly in three strong strands all round it. All pastures have a gate, however, and I came to it in the farthest corner. I opened it, guided Admiral through into the next field, and shut it behind me.

This field was fenced with posts and wire only, and it was the extent of the barbed wire which decided me then to put as much space as I could between me and my pursuers in the shortest possible time. If I let the taxi-drivers follow me slowly from field to field I might find myself in a corner that even Admiral could not jump out of.

I was glad the sun was shining, for at least I could tell in which direction I was going. Since I was already headed towards the east, and because it seemed sensible to have a definite destination to aim for, I decided to take Admiral back to his own stable in Pete's yard.

I reckoned I had about twelve miles to cover, and I racked my brains to remember what the country was like in between. I knew the patchwork farmland which I was then grappling with gave way at some point ahead to Forestry Commission plantations. Then there would be a short distance of bare downland before I reached the hollow and the small village where Pete trained. Of the roads which crossed this area I had but the vaguest idea, and on any of them I could be spotted by a cruising Marconicar.

With this thought uncomfortably in mind, I found another by-road ahead. I let myself out on to it through a gate, and was trotting down it, looking for an opening in the neglected growth on the other side, when a squat black car swept round a distant bend and sped uphill towards me. Without giving Admiral a good chance to sight himself I turned him sharply towards the overgrown hedge and kicked his ribs.

It was too high for him, and too unexpected, but he did his best. He leaped straight into the tangle of sagging wire and beech saplings, crashed his way heavily through, and scrambled up almost from his knees on to the higher ground of the next field. It had been ploughed and planted with mangolds and made heavy going, but I urged him into a canter, hearing behind me the screech of brakes forcefully applied. A glance showed me the driver thrusting through the hole Admiral had made, but he did not try to chase me and I realized thankfully that he was not the man with the gun.

All the same, he had his radio. My whereabouts would be known to all the Marconicars within a minute.

I put another field between us and the taxi before pulling up and dismounting to see what damage Admiral had done himself. To my relief there were only a few scratches and one jagged cut on his stifle from which a thread of blood was trickling. I left it to congeal.

Patting his neck and marvelling at how he retained his calm sensible nature in very upsetting circumstances, I grasped the leather roller he wore round his middle, and sprang up again on to his back. The rug he was wearing now gaped in a right-angled tear on one side, but I decided not to take it off as it gave more purchase for my legs than riding him completely bareback.

Three or four fields farther on the arable land began to give way to bracken, and ahead lay the large enclosures of the Forestry Commission.

The trees, mostly conifers, were being grown in large orderly expanses with rough tracks between each section. These acted both as convenient roadways for the foresters and as breaks in case of fire. They occurred about one in each half-mile, and were crossed at intervals by tracks leading in the opposite direction.

I wanted to set a course towards the south-east, but by consulting my watch and the sun in conjunction, found that the tracks ran from almost due north to south, and from east to west.

Fretting at the extra mileage this was going to cost me, I steered Admiral into an eastbound track, took the next turning right to the south, then the next left to the east, and so on, crabwise across the forest.

The sections of trees were of varying ages and stages of growth, and turning again to the south, I found the area on my left was planted with trees only two feet high. This did not specially alarm me until I saw, a hundred yards to my left, a red and white motor coach speeding along apparently through the middle of the plantation.

I pulled Admiral up. Looking carefully I could see the posts and the high wire fence which formed the boundary between the little trees and the road beyond. If I turned east at the next track according to schedule, I would be facing straight down to the road.

The far side of the road looked similar to the section I was in: regular rows of conifers, put there by careful design.

At some point, I knew, I would have to cross a road of some sort. If I retreated back into the part of the forest I had crossed and took no risks, I would have to stay there all night. All the same, I thought, as I cantered Admiral along the southbound track and turned into the east one, I could have wished for more cover just at that moment.

Ahead of me the wire gates to the road were open, but before going through them I stopped and took a look at the other side of the road. Not all the plantations were surrounded by high mesh wire like the one I was in, and opposite only three strands of plain wire threaded through concrete posts barred the way.

The road had to be crossed quickly because where I was I felt as sheltered as a cock pheasant on a snow field. The heads in all the passing cars turned curiously towards me. But I saw nothing which looked like a Marconicar, and waiting only for a gap in the traffic, I clicked my tongue and set Admiral towards the wire fence opposite. His hooves clattered loudly on the tarmac, drummed on the firm verge, and he lifted into the air like a bird. There was no track straight ahead, only some fairly sparsely growing tall pines, and as Admiral landed I reined him in to a gentle trot before beginning to thread a way through them.

Coming eventually to another track I checked again with my watch and the sun to make sure it was still running from east to west, which it was, and set off along it at a good pace. The going underfoot was perfect, dry and springy with loam and pine needles, and Admiral, though he had completed a three mile race and covered several miles of an unorthodox cross-country course, showed no signs of flagging.

We made two more turns and the sky began to cloud over, dulling the brilliant spring afternoon; but it was not the fading of beauty which bothered me so much as the fact that you cannot use a wrist watch as a compass unless the sun is shining. I would have to be careful not to get lost.

Just ahead, to my right, a small grass-grown hill rose sharply to its little rounded summit, the conifer forest flowing round its edges like sea round a rock. I had now left the bigger trees and was cantering through sections of young feathery pines only slightly taller than the top of my head, and I could see the hill quite clearly. A man, a black distant silhouetted man, was standing on the top, waving his arms.

I did not connect him with myself at all because I thought I had slipped my pursuers, so that what happened next had the full shock of a totally unexpected disaster.

From a track to the right, which I had not yet reached and could not see, a sleek black shape rolled out across my path and stopped, blocking the whole width of the track. It was the Wolseley.

The young pines on each side of me were too thick and low-growing to be penetrated. I flung a look over my shoulder. A squat black Marconicar was bumping up the track behind me.

I was so close to the Wolseley that I could see one of the men looking out of the rear window with a gloating grin on his face, and I decided then that even if I broke Admiral's neck and my own in trying to escape, it would be a great deal better than tamely giving in.

There was scarcely a pause between the arrival of the Wolseley and my legs squeezing tight into Admiral's sides.

I had no reason to suppose he would do it. A horse can bare just so much and no more. He had had a hard day already. He might be the best hunter/chaser in England, but . . . The thoughts flickered through my brain in a second and were gone. I concentrated wholly, desperately, on getting Admiral to jump.

He scarcely faltered. He put in a short stride and a long one, gathered the immense power of his hindquarters beneath him, and thrust himself into the air. Undeterred even by the opening doors and the threatening shouts of the men scrambling out of the Wolseley, he jumped clear over its gleaming black bonnet. He did not even scratch the paint.

I nearly came off when we landed. Admiral stumbled, and I slipped off the rug round on to his shoulder, clinging literally for dear life to the leather roller with one hand and Admiral's plaited mane with the other. The reins hung down, swaying perilously near his galloping feet, and I was afraid he would put his foot through them and trip. I still had one leg half across his rump, and, bumping heavily against his side, I hauled myself inch by inch on to his back. A warning twinge in my shoulder told me my newly-mended collar-bone could not be relied upon for too much of this, but leaning along his neck and holding on with all my strength, I reached the reins, gathered them up, and finally succeeded in reducing Admiral to a less headlong pace.

When I got my breath back I looked to see if the Wolseley was following, but it was so far behind that I was not sure whether it was moving or not. I could not spare time to stop and find out.

I realized that I had underestimated the Marconicars, and that it was only thanks to Admiral's splendid courage that I was still free. They had had an advantage in knowing the lie of the land, and had used the little hill as a spotting point. I suspected that its summit commanded quite a large area, and that as soon as I had entered the young pines I had been seen.

I was forced to admit that they had guessed which direction I would take and had circled round in front of me. And that being so, they probably knew I had been making for Pete's stable. If I went on I should find them in my way again, with perhaps as little warning and less chance of escape.

I had left the hill behind me, and turned right again on the next track, seeing in the distance a section of taller trees. The horse cantered along tirelessly, but he could not keep it up for ever. I had to reach shelter as quickly as I could, out of sight of the man still standing on the hill-top, and out of the danger of being ambushed on another of the straight and suddenly uninviting tracks. Once we were hidden in the big trees, I promised Admiral, he should have a rest.

The light was dim under the tall pines. They had been allowed to grow close together to encourage their bare trunks to height, and the crowns of foliage far above were matted together like a roof, shutting out most of the daylight. I was glad for the obscurity. I slowed Admiral to a walk and dismounted as we entered the trees, and we went quietly and deeply into them. It was like walking through a forest of telegraph poles. Which of course, I thought fleetingly, perhaps they were destined to be.

The forest felt like home, even though it was different from those I was schooled in. It was very quiet, very dark. No birds at all. No animals. The horse and I went steadily on, silent on the thick pine needles, relying on instinct to keep us on a straight course.

I did not find our situation particularly encouraging. Whichever way I went in this extensive plantation I would have to come to a road in the end, and within three or four square miles the Marconicars knew exactly where I was. They had only to stand round the forest like hounds waiting for the fox to break cover, then it would be view tally-ho over the radio intercoms and the hunt would be on again.

There was a track ahead. A narrow one. I tied the reins round a tree and went forward alone. Standing still on the edge of the track and giving, I hoped, a good imitation of a tree trunk in my tweed suit, I slowly turned my head both ways. The daylight was much stronger on the track owing to the gap in the trees overhead, and I could see quite clearly for several hundred yards. There was no one in sight.

I went back for Admiral, made a final check, and led him across the track. There was no alarm. We walked steadily on. Admiral had begun to sweat long ago and had worked up a lather after our dash away from the Wolseley, damping large patches of the rug. Now that he was cooling down it was not good for him to keep it on, but I hadn't a dry one to give him. I decided that a damp rug was better than no rug, and trudged on.

Eventually I began to hear the hum of traffic and the occasional toot of a horn, and as soon as I could see the road in the distance I tied Admiral to a tree and went on alone again.

The end of the plantation was marked by a fence made of only two strands of stout wire, looking as if it were designed mainly to prevent picnickers driving their cars farther in than the verge. I chose a tree as near to the fence as I could get, dropped down on to my belly behind it, and wriggled forward until I could look along the road. There was only sporadic traffic on it.

On the far side of the road there were no plantations, and no fence either. It was unorganized woodland, a mixture of trees, rhododendrons, and briars. Perfect cover, if I could reach it.

A heavy lorry ground past five feet from my nose, emitting a choking cloud of diesel fumes. I put my face down into the pine needles and coughed. Two saloon cars sped by in the other direction, one trying to pass the other, followed by a single-decker country bus full of carefree people taking home their Tuesday afternoon's shopping. A pair of schoolgirls in green uniform cycled past without noticing me, and when their high twittering voices had faded into the distance and the road was empty, I put my hands under my chest to heave myself up and go back for Admiral.

At that moment two Marconicars came into sight round a bend. I dropped my face down again and lay absolutely still. They drove past my head slowly, and though I did not look at them, I guessed they must be staring keenly into the forest. I hoped wholeheartedly that I had left Admiral far enough back to be invisible, and that he would not make a noise.

The Marconicars swerved across the road and pulled up on the opposite verge barely twenty-five yards away. The drivers got out of the taxis and slammed the doors. I risked a glance at them. They were lighting cigarettes, leaning casually against the taxis, and chatting. I could hear the mumble of their voices, but not what they were saying.

They had not seen me, or Admiral. Yet. But they seemed to be in no hurry to move on. I glanced at my watch. It was six o'clock. An hour and a half since I had jumped off the racecourse. More important, there was only one hour of full daylight left. When it grew dark my mobility on Admiral would end and we should have to spend the night in the forest, as I could not get him to jump a fence if he could not see it.

There was a sudden clattering noise from one of the taxis. A driver put his hand through the window and brought out a hand microphone attached to a cord. He spoke into it distinctly, and this time I could make out what he said.

'Yeah, we got the road covered. No, he ain't crossed it yet.' There was some more clattering on the taxi radio, and the driver answered, 'Yeah, I'm sure. I'll let you know the second we see him.' He put the microphone back in the taxi.

I began to get the glimmerings of an idea of how to use the manhunt I had caused.

But first things first, I thought; and slowly I started to slither backwards through the trees, pressing close to the ground and keeping my face down. I had left Admiral a good way inside the forest, and I was not certain that the taxi drivers could not see him. It was uncomfortable travelling on my stomach, but I knew if I stood up the drivers would see me moving among the bare tree trunks. When finally I got to my feet my suit was filthy peat brown, clogged with prickling pine needles. I brushed off the dirt as best I could, went over to Admiral and untied his reins.

Out in the daylight on the road I could still catch glimpses, between the tree trunks, of the two taxis and their drivers, but knowing that they could not see me, I set off towards the west keeping parallel with the road and at some distance from it. It was, I judged, a little more than a quarter of a mile before I saw another Marconicar parked at the side of the road. I turned back and, as I went along, began to collect an armful of small dead branches. About half way between the parked taxis, where they were all out of my sight, I took Admiral right up to the wire fence to give him a look at it. Although extremely simple in construction, it was difficult to see in the shade of the trees. I set the dead branches up on end in a row to make it appear more solid; then jumped on to Admiral's back, and taking him back a few paces, faced him towards the fence and waited for a heavy vehicle to come along. In still air the sound of hooves on tarmacadam would carry clearly, and I did not want the taxi drivers round the nearby bends to hear me crossing the road. The longer they believed I was still in the pine forest, the better. But how long the taxis would *remain* parked I did not know, and the palms of my hands grew damp with tension.

A motor bike sped past, and I stayed still with an effort; but then, obligingly, a big van loaded with empty milk bottles came rattling round the bend on my right. It could not have been better. As it went past me I trotted Admiral forward. He made nothing of the dead-wood patch of fence, popped over on to the grass verge, took three loping strides over the tarmac, and in an instant was safely in the scrub on the far side. The milk lorry rattled out of sight.

I pulled up behind the first rhododendron, dismounted, and peered round it.

I had not been a second too soon. One of the Marconicars was rolling slowly along in the wake of the milk lorry, and the driver's head was turned towards the forest I had left.

If one driver believed me still there, they all did. I walked Admiral away from the road until it was safe to mount, then jumped on to his back and broke him into a slow trot. The ground now was unevenly moulded into little hillocks and hollows and overgrown with brambles, small conifers, and the brown remains of last year's bracken, so I let the horse pick his own footing to a great extent while I worked out what I was going to do. After a little way he slowed to a walk and I left him to it, because if his limbs felt as heavy and tired as mine he was entitled to crawl.

As nearly as I could judge I travelled west, back the way I had come. If there is one thing you can be sure of in England, it is that a straight line in any direction will bring you to a road without much delay, and I had covered perhaps a mile when I came to the next one. Without going too close I followed it to the north.

I was hunting a prey myself, now. A taxi, detached from the herd.

Admiral was picking his way silently across a bare patch of leaf-moulded earth when I suddenly heard the now familiar clatter of a Marconicar radio, and the answering voice of its driver. I pulled up in two strides, dismounted, and tied Admiral to a nearby young tree. Then I climbed up into the branches.

Some way ahead I saw a white four-fingered signpost, and beside it stood a Marconicar, of which only the roof and the top half of the windows were visible. The rest was hidden from me by the rhododendrons, trees, and undergrowth which crowded the ground ahead. My old friend the pine forest rose in a dark green blur away to the right.

I climbed down from the tree and felt in my pocket for the roll of pennies. I also found two lumps of sugar, which I fed to Admiral. He blew down his nostrils and nuzzled my hand, and I patted his neck gently and blessed Scilla for giving him to me.

With so much good cover it was easy enough to approach the cross-roads without being seen, but when, from the inside of an old rhododendron, I at length had a clear view of the taxi, the driver was not in it. He was a youngish sallow-faced man in a bright blue suit, and he was standing bareheaded in the middle of the cross-roads with his feet well apart, jingling some coins in his pocket. He inspected all four directions, saw nothing, and yawned.

I climbed up into the branches

The radio clattered again, but the driver took no notice. I had intended to creep up to his taxi and knock him out before he could broadcast that I was there; but now I waited, and cursed him, and he stood still and blew his nose.

Suddenly he began to walk purposefully in my direction.

For an instant I thought he had seen me, but he had not. He wheeled round a large patch of brambles close in front of me, turned his back towards my hiding place, and began to relieve himself. It seemed hardly fair to attack a man at such a moment, and I know I was smiling as I stepped out of the rhododendron, but it was an opportunity not to be missed. I took three quick steps and swung, and the sock-wrapped roll of pennies connected solidly with the back of his head. He collapsed without a sound.

I put my wrist under his shoulders and dragged him back to where I had left Admiral. Working as quickly as I could I ripped all the brown binding off the edge of the horse rug and tested it for strength. It seemed strong enough. Fishing my penknife out of my trouser pocket I cut the binding into four pieces and tied together the driver's ankles and knees with two of them. Then I dragged him closer to the tree and tied his wrists behind him. The fourth piece of binding knotted him securely to the trunk.

I patted his pockets. His only weapon was a spiked metal knuckleduster, which I transferred to my own jacket. He began to wake up. His gaze wandered fuzzily from me to Admiral and back again, and then his mouth opened with a gasp as he realized who I was.

He was not a big man in stature, nor, I now discovered, in courage. The sight of the horse looming so close above him seemed to worry him more than his trussed condition or the bump on the head.

'He'll tread on me,' he yelled, fright drawing back his lips to show a nicotine-stained set of cheap artificial teeth.

'He's very particular what he walks on,' I said.

'Take him away. Take him away,' he shouted. Admiral began to move restlessly at the noise.

Dead Cert

'Be quiet and he won't harm you,' I said sharply to the driver, but he took no notice and shouted again. I stuffed my handkerchief unceremoniously into his mouth until his eyes bulged.

'Now shut up,' I said. 'If you keep quiet he won't harm you. If you screech you'll frighten him and he might lash out at you. Do you understand?'

He nodded. I took out the handkerchief, and he began to swear vindictively, but fairly quietly.

I soothed Admiral and lengthened his tether so that he could get his head down to a patch of grass. He began munching peacefully.

'What is your name?' I asked the taxi driver.

He spat and said nothing.

I asked him again, and he said, 'What the ruddy hell has it got to do with you?'

I needed particularly to know his name and I was in a hurry.

With no feelings of compunction I took hold of Admiral's reins and turned him round so that the driver had a good close view of a massive pair of hindquarters. My captive's newfound truculence vanished in a flash. He opened his mouth to yell.

'Don't,' I said. 'Remember he'll kick you if you make a noise. Now, what is your name?'

'John Smith.'

'Try again,' I said, backing Admiral a pace nearer.

The taxi-driver gave in completely, his mouth trembling and sweat breaking out on his forehead.

'Blake.' He stumbled on the word.

'First name?'

'Corny. It's a nickname, sort of.' His eyes flickered fearfully between me and Admiral's hind legs.

I asked him several questions about the working of the radio, keeping the horse handy. When I had learned all I wanted I untied the reins from the tree and fastened them to a sapling a few feet away, so that when it grew dark the horse would not accidentally tread on the taxi-driver.

143

Before leaving them I gave Blake a final warning. 'Don't start yelling for help. For one thing there's no one to hear you, and for another, you'll upset the horse. He's a thoroughbred, which means nervous, from your point of view. If you frighten him by yelling he's strong enough to break his reins and lash out at you. Shut up and he'll stay tied up. Get it?' I knew if Admiral broke his reins he would not stop to attack the man, but luckily, Blake did not. He nodded, his body sagging with fear and frustration.

'I won't forget you're here,' I said. 'You won't have to stay here all night. Not that I care about you, but the horse needs to be in a stable.'

Admiral had his head down to the grass. I gave his rump a pat, made sure the knots were still tight on the demoralized driver, and picked my way quickly through the bushes to the taxi.

The signpost was important, for I would have to come back and find it in the dark in miles of haphazard woodland. I wrote down all the names and mileages on all of its four arms, just to make sure. Then I got into the taxi and sat in the driver's seat.

Inside the taxi one could hear the radio as a voice and not as a clatter. The receiver was permanently tuned in so that each driver could hear all messages and replies going from taxis to base and base to taxis.

A man was saying, 'Sid, here. No sign of him. I've got a good mile and a half of the road in view from up here, nearly the whole side of that wood he's in. I'll swear he hasn't got across here. The traffic's too thick for him to do it quickly. I'm sure to see him if he tries it.' Sid's voice came out of the radio small and tinny, like a voice on the telephone, and he spoke casually, as if he were looking for a lost dog.

While he spoke I started the engine, sorted out the gears, and drove off along the road going south. The daylight was just beginning to fade. Half an hour of twilight, I calculated, and perhaps another ten minutes of dusk. I put my foot down on the accelerator.

Escape to Nowhere

FRANCIS S. JONES

Francis Jones is an English soldier who has been captured in Greece during the Second World War. When the story opens he and his fellow prisoners are being marched to a new prison.

Two o'clock in the morning is a God-forsaken hour. It's a time when all honest men should be asleep, with consciences clear and sins temporarily forgotten. There's only one place for it. That's bed.

I wished I was there. It was like a bad dream trudging up and down the Grecian hillsides with guards holding a trigger-brief on every move. What made it worse was knowing there wasn't anything I could do about it. I wasn't sure I wanted to do anything just then. The three Australians lower down the road, with their backs shattered, had put a damper on everyone's enthusiasm for escaping.

I did have one consolation. Barlow was safe. He'd got away as he said he would, which made us one up and one to go. Right now Barlow was somewhere in the Central Peloponnesus. Probably he was snoring his head off. Six weeks had passed since, but the nervous tension still mounted in me every time I thought of that break. When the train chugged into one of the last tunnels before Corinth, Barlow had gathered his kit and edged to the side of the truck. Just before we plunged into the smoky blackness he nudged me. 'This one'll do,' he said. 'You coming?' I heard one bump as his kit hit the ground, and then another as he leapt out of the truck himself. The Germans never missed him. If I'd had more guts I'd have gone myself.

But that was all of six weeks ago. Now we were on the move again, still one up and still one to go: and this time it wasn't going to be so easy. I had more courage screwed up, but I was going to need it. Six weeks at Corinth had educated the Germans. My pal's voice came back to reassure me: 'You'll do it, son,' it said, confidently. 'Just watch your chance. It'll come. And remember, it's not as risky as it looks. There's only one thing. When you *do* move off, for Christ's sake move fast.'

For a moment or two I felt more cheerful. After all, this was Greece, not Germany. All I had to do was dodge the column, and once clear I was safe. And if it comes to that, I thought, what better time than now? It's dark and we're dog-tired, but there's more than a grain of comfort in that. The guards will be dog-tired too. I took a quick glance up and down the column.

The big German walking just ahead seemed to sense the decision. He snapped out of his lethargy, surveyed the column of prisoners in sudden alertness, and hitched up the strap of his Schmeiser. Fat bullets in the magazine winked at me and my resolve weakened. I felt my knees going queer. A sudden vision came of three khaki figures sprawled grotesquely at the side of the road. I shuddered. Those Aussies had also gambled on the guards being too sleepy to shoot.

It was nine hours and twenty-odd miles later before the chance came. By then it was midday, and a Greek sun was sending heat-hazes rippling off the road. Everyone was grey with fatigue. Even the guards were parched with thirst, but the column stumbled on. We were nearing the last village before the repaired railway line. There were only two miles left, with every yard in dead flat country.

The commotion began farther up the line. I saw the front men surging around a roadside pump, filling bottles, pushing their heads underneath, taking huge gulps and sluicing layers of grey dust off their faces. I walked quicker in sudden, fierce exaltation.

The first part couldn't have worked out better. Men drifted away from the pump and straggled up the road in ones and twos. The foremost guards were halting them just around the bend. The other Germans were either filling water bottles or watching the crowd still fighting to get at the pump. Momentarily, the vigilance slackened. Ahead of me, a clear fifty yards of road lay unpatrolled. I took one look behind and turned sharp right. Nobody took any notice. My knees wobbled a bit as I got down by a pile of wood, but that was allowable. It was those three Aussies again. One of them had stopped and put up his hands, but it hadn't influenced the Germans.

Guttural voices were reassembling the column when the real ordeal began. Footsteps sounded at the side of the house and I waited in a tense agony of expectation: but it wasn't a guard. An old crone appeared, saw me, and began screeching at the top of her voice. From her gestures I gathered she was warning me there were Germans about. In greater anguish than before, I implored her to be quiet. 'Shut up, you old fool!' I hissed. 'Pipe down for Christ's sake. You'll have me shot. Go on, beat it! Don't stand there gawping. Beat it! Shove off!' Fragments of Arabic gushed under the strain. 'Imshi!' I urged. 'Yellah!'

The old woman stood her ground, not understanding. I dug feverishly in my kitbag and found a coloured scarf. 'Look,' I pleaded. 'Here's a present for you. Now for the love of God, beat it! Get the hell outa here!'

A moron couldn't have failed to grasp the idea. The old lady took the scarf, looked at it and walked away. I breathed again. A moment later she was back, this time with a swarthy middle-aged man who knew his own mind. He made his point crystal clear. Either I went or he called the guards. One look at that beetling brow ruled out scarves, and very slowly I got up. It looked like this was it. I set off across the flat field. There was no point in waiting for a bullet.

Both ends of the long file came into sight. I was only thirty yards from the column of prisoners, and harsh German voices tortured my ears; but I didn't run. A running man is a mark miles away. It could be any time now. . . .

The file stretched interminably. Seconds passed, each of them an age. I was too tense even to pray, but the expected shouts and rifle cracks didn't happen. Suddenly the ground began to dip. In another few seconds I was out of sight, and out of range. I walked into the wide stream ahead and on the far bank, dived into a clump of bushes and hugged the roots. A moment or two later the tension snapped. I'd done it. I was free, and on the first step of a retreat to our own lines.

From the top of the bank, the railway station didn't seem much more than a mile distant. The column was now clear of the village, and once again close-packed. I could see guards strung out on either side of the marching men. For those chaps, Germany lay ahead, with perhaps years of captivity. For me – well, that depended.

But it was a warm day, and for the moment the future could look after itself. The present was good enough. It was Friday, the 13th June, 1941, the only combination of Friday and the 13th in the whole year. It seemed that omens would be nothing to go by on this venture.

As the last of the column breasted a small hill and disappeared from sight, I began thinking about getting back to Egypt. It shouldn't be too hard, I decided. I'd been over the route a hundred times during those six weeks at Corinth, and if I had no other advantage, at least the geography was familiar. Turkey was the best way out. I opened a pencilled map and took another look at the cluster of Aegean islands that marked the route. They were all there – Andros, Tinos, Mykonos, Nikaria, Samos – all neatly bridging the gap between Greece and Smyrna. There was one wide stretch in the middle, but with any kind of a boat it should still be fairly easy. With real luck, I might find a caique travelling straight to Smyrna.

A voice interrupted the chain of thought. It spoke English that had a strong American flavour. 'Where've you come from?'

it demanded. I looked up and saw an elderly Greek not more than a yard away. He must have come through the bushes like a cat. I pointed towards the railway station. 'I've just got away from that lot,' I said. 'And who are you, and where d'you learn English?' The Greek smiled. 'Been in the States twenty years, son,' he said grinning, 'but that's a while back. You'll be hungry, I guess.'

I was, but just now there was something more important than food. A man doesn't jeopardise his freedom for a full belly. 'I'd like to get out of uniform,' I said. The Greek smiled again. 'Sure,' he agreed. 'You stay right here. I'll be back in ten minutes. And my name's Giorgos.'

I moved to another spot when he left, to be on the safe side. But it wasn't necessary. Giorgos came back alone, and dumped a parcel at my feet. 'There's a suit here might fit you,' he said, 'although you're bigger than I am. And you needn't be scared. I won't turn you in. Didn't the Greeks fight against the Germans?'

I felt a bit ashamed at that reminder, but Giorgos laughed at my confusion. 'Try the suit on,' he suggested. I did. It was tight under the arms, and the top trouser buttons were inches out, but they were minor points. It was civilian wear, not khaki, which was all that mattered. I clapped the old man on the shoulder. 'It'll do fine,' I said. 'I wouldn't ask for better. And I'm very grateful to you.' That part was true enough.

After dark Giorgos came back again, and led me through a quietened village to his house. By this time the rest of 'B' Company were probably nearing Yugoslavia. The sharp night air seemed to emphasise my freedom, and I felt sympathy for them. Sixty men in one cattle truck, with no sanitation, no food, and precious little water, isn't the best way of travelling. So far as I knew, Barlow and I were the only ones who were missing.

The stone house was full of people. Giorgos had gathered the clan together, and as soon as we went in a dozen Greeks began pumping my hand and slapping me on the back. The English were welcome in Greece. The old man restored order, and sat me at the low table. The others crowded round, pressing all manner of strange foods on me, and toasting the Anglo-Greek alliance in lashings of red wine. Giorgos interpreted: 'They're glad you escaped,' he said. 'They don't like Germans any more than you do. But they want to know what you plans are. Where will you make for?'

I took another pull at the wine. It was good stuff. 'Egypt,' I said, 'as quick as I can.'

'How will you get there?'

I shrugged my shoulders. I'd like to know the answer to that one, too. 'By boat, probably,' I told him. 'Via the islands. But I might go to Athens and get on a caique. There'll be plenty going to Turkey from there even now. It'll be some time before the Germans start checking up. I'm not sure yet. I'll think about it to-morrow.'

A criss-cross of voluble Greek followed, and then the old man spoke up again. 'They say Athens is best,' he summarised, 'but it's a big place. D'you know anyone there?'

This put me on firmer ground. 'Yes,' I said. 'There's a man in Kephissia I know well. Very well. He's like a blood brother. If I can get to Athens, I'll be all right.' That seemed to convince the Greeks. We had another round of handshaking and good wishes, and then they left. Women stretched blankets on the wooden floor. I took my boots off and was asleep in an instant.

Next morning I gave Giorgos my uniform, all my kit, and what money I had as a token of thanks. In turn he presented me with a cartwheel loaf and a flask of wine: and as the sun topped the nearby hills, I set off for Athens and Liberty. I felt fine. The morning sunshine seemed to bring Cairo and Shepheard's Hotel all the nearer. Corinth, tightly-jammed cattle trucks, even the unhappy men of 'B' Company, were fast becoming memories. I was free as a bird. Somewhere down South, my pal was free too. Maybe I'd find him again before long.

Athens had been an obvious choice. It was about 200 miles away, and at least eight days' walk. That was along the main roads, where it would be policy to keep a weather eye open: but it was still the best bet. I didn't know just one Greek there, as I'd said. I knew six. Of those six, Rosebud and Pedro alone should be able to 'fix' me a caique.

The tracks were easy enough to follow. I kept to those which ran parallel with the road, and at first made surprising progress. On the first day I covered about 30 miles. On the second I walked 25: but on the third, my good luck deserted me. I doubt if I walked five miles that day. An increasing stiffness was seizing my legs, and as the day wore on, it got worse. Soon after I started, the former brisk pace began to slow down. By mid-day, it wasn't a pace any longer. It was a crawl. I began to get alarmed. Two days' march shouldn't knock me up like this; but it was doing. At dusk I gave up the Athens trip altogether. I couldn't go on. It was painful now even to walk.

The sudden lameness was probably an after-effect of the Corinth camp. The Germans had packed us in like sardines – five thousand men into a barracks built for eight hundred. The Luftwaffe had already blasted whatever sanitary system the place originally had, but that didn't count. There was no water, except from a few deep wells, but apparently that didn't matter either. In we went, and before long the inevitable happened. Dysentery ran riot through the camp. Diphtheria followed on its heels, but the medical staff pleaded in vain. Red Cross officials came and promptly condemned the place. The German authorities weren't so quick off the mark, but when they did come, even they agreed it was unhealthy. That was considerable understatement. By this time prisoners were dying rapidly.

The plague hit me without warning. In the space of ten minutes I was unconscious. The hospital was full, so I stayed unconscious on the stone floor for three days. Someone pushed a kit bag under my head, and another Samaritan covered me with a great-coat. Apart from that, nobody did anything. They couldn't. Live or die, I was fighting this battle on my own. Probably the only person interested was the chap who used my rations to ensure his own health.

I came to about noon on the fourth day. In an hour or two I

was up and about: by the evening I was weak, but quite better. Why and how remain mysteries; but I do remember getting mad at the cook-sergeant's refusal to refund the missing rations.

Very likely the present paralysis dated from that illness. It was getting worse too, which frightened me; and realising I'd have to rest a few weeks I headed away from the main road towards the hills. The Greeks were souls of kindness and generosity. They fed me with all kinds of delicacies, massaged the numbed legs, asked hundreds of questions I wished I could have understood, and in short, did their best. Some wanted me to stay with them, but I said 'No' to those offers. It was too near the road yet for safety.

I pushed on. On the flat I went slowly. When the tracks began to climb, I went slower still, and the pace kept slackening until a village carpenter made me a pair of crutches. They were a big help. My arms were strong, even if my legs were three-quarters dead. On the fifth day I was numb from the waist down, and had to use the crutches to hoist myself up: but I was getting used to the idea. That night I slept between sheets in a schoolmaster's house, and dreamt I was home. In the morning I found I couldn't see. My eyes were stuck together with some kind of discharge, and had to be bathed before they would open. It seemed I'd got conjunctivitis as well.

This more or less put the top hat on things. It was bad enough being a cripple, but up to now I could at least see where I was going. I pressed on despite the double difficulty. Before I could accept any lodging offers, I had to be out of reach of German patrols; as much for the villagers' sakes as for my own.

I was beginning to understand some of the weird language these people spoke. 'Penas?' meant 'Are you hungry?' and was fired at me a dozen times a day. It was easy. All I had to say was 'Penow,' and out came a feast. I liked 'Penas.' 'Ap po poo eiste?' which meant 'Where've you come from?' was harder. I could get as far as 'Ichmalotus—Anglia'—'Prisoner—England,' but after that I stuck and had to rely on arm waving. The positive and negative bothered me too. If I wanted to indicate 'Yes' I had to shake my head and say 'Nay'. For 'No,' the drill was to wag the head up and down, and say 'Oiche'. It was confusing, but I got into it.

I stayed with the schoolmaster for two days, mostly because there was no choice. I could neither see nor walk during that time. I would have stayed longer still, but on the third day word came that the Germans were searching villages lower down. They knew some prisoners had escaped. They also knew that a good many more had never been captured, and from what we heard, the searching seemed to be thorough. I had been expecting something like this. The schoolmaster, who spoke French, told me the news, and agreed the best course was to get moving again. His wife gave me half a loaf and a packet of olives, and wept as I hobbled away. I could have wept, too, in annoyance. I didn't want to go. I wasn't nearly fit enough to travel, and what was more, those blasted Huns were chasing me from the best house I'd yet been in.

I plodded on for another three days. Each morning I had to prise my eyes open with finger and thumb, and then wait for a sympathetic Greek to bring the bathing water. I was well up in the hills now. The tracks were poor, and growing fainter, and the district seemed safe enough from patrols. I felt more cheerful. My eyes were all right as soon as I got them opened and bathed, and vision wasn't affected. As regards the paralysis, well, I'd stopped worrying about it. It would be hard put to get worse than it was. I swung along between the crutches and reached Dremissa in fairly good shape. It was a village about 4,500 feet up in the Parnassus Mountains.

Dimitrion Theodoron stopped me. He had been watching me struggling along the track for over an hour, but he'd let it rest at that. I was coming his way, and these days it didn't pay to be inquisitive with strangers.

The crutches reassured him, but he was still cautious. He pushed his hat back and looked at me for a while. Then the usual preliminaries began. 'Ap po poo eiste?' he asked: but I wasn't feeling strong enough for Greek. 'I'm an English soldier,' I said.

'Escaped a week ago. I'd like a drink of water.' I put a thumb to my mouth and tilted my head back. 'Nero, chum,' I explained, 'Water. Nero.'

The Greek's interest quickened. This time he spoke in English. 'What's wrong with you?' he asked. 'You look bad.'

'I am bad,' I assured him. 'You'd be bad too if you were me. And now how about that water?'

Dimitrion ignored the request. 'You've done well to get this far,' he pointed out. 'We're a long way from the road here. Where did you escape?'

I waved backwards. 'Larissa, I think. There's a river there.'

Dimitrion thought again. 'Have you seen any Germans since?' he asked. 'I hear they're hunting you fellows.'

It struck me that this conversation wasn't getting us anywhere. What I wanted was a bed for the night, not a discussion on Huns or my health. I might as well carry on. 'No, I've seen no Germans,' I said. 'I don't think they'll get this far. You're safe enough. Cheerio.' I turned away, but the Greek jumped after me.

'Hey!' he shouted, suddenly becoming human. 'You can't go like that! God damn it, man, you'll be out all night. You come home with me and we'll eat.'

This was more like it. Once I got sitting down, I would hardly be asked to leave before morning: and sleeping out wasn't my idea of comfort. I'd been trying it the last two nights. But I needn't have worried. I wasn't to know then, but this was Journey's End for a while. At least until I was fit again.

Dimitrion helped me along the cobbled lane towards the village, and stopped at one of the nearer houses. A boy of about seven saw us coming and promptly vanished inside. He reappeared with a pleasant-looking woman who glanced at me, first in alarm, and then more in pity as she saw the crutches. She took a few steps towards us.

'This is Maria,' said Dimitrion. 'My wife.' He patted the lad's head. 'And here's Cristos. He's a chip off the old block. Now let's go in.'

Maria was a sensible woman. She got out a bowl of water, and began bathing my eyes as soon as her husband had manoeuvred me on to a stool. The lad vanished again, but after a minute or so he was back, this time with a glass of goat's milk. I smiled at him and took a long drink.

Over the meal Dimitrion told Maria who I was and what had happened to me. Then he told me about himself. I gathered he had been born in Dremissa – in this very house, to be exact – but had left for America when he was sixteen. He stayed there twenty-four years, changed his name to Jim Thompson and, like most Greeks, did well. Very well. At one time two restaurants bore the name 'James Thompson,' and a dozen men were pedalling his ice cream carts all over Chicago. I took another glance at the sparsely furnished room and felt a bit doubtful about that one.

'Then what in the world brought you back?' I asked.

Jim grinned. 'I didn't expect you'd believe me,' he said, 'but it's true. A good many of us came back. I suppose you've met some of them?'

He was right there. I had. One or two of the older Greeks did speak English, but so far I'd not bothered to be inquisitive. 'Well why did you come back?' I persisted.

Jim smiled again. He didn't exhaust conversation too quickly. 'The '29 crash,' he said ruefully. 'Ruined every Goddam one of us. Fellows were shooting 'emselves left and right. I took a boat home instead.'

'But what made you stay here?' I was going to get to the bottom of this.

This time Jim laughed outright, and explained the question to his wife. She laughed too. 'I met Maria,' he said chuckling. 'And just when I've got her persuaded to go back to the States, along comes Cristos. I guess we've never made it since.' Maria showed her white teeth in a wide grin. Little Cristos, not understanding anything, but wide-eyed with the novelty of a stranger, and not wanting to be left out of the joke, thumped the table in delight. I decided I liked this family.

Later on, Jim suggested I stayed with him until I was fit again.

I didn't argue. 'You can stay till the war's over, if you like,' he added. 'It's quite safe. As you said, we're too far from the road for patrols, and there'll be three feet of snow when winter comes. That should stop them. It stops us going anywhere. What d'you say?'

I didn't have to ponder for long. 'I'll stay,' I said. 'My legs are not too good. I don't suppose I'd get much farther if I did leave you. I'll stay till I'm better, anyway. Then we'll see. And it's damn decent of you. Thank you.' That little speech made me embarrassed. It sounded an almost casual answer to the princely offer Jim was making: but he wasn't looking for thanks.

I spent my first week in Dremissa wrapped in blankets and recuperating on the wooden floor. The Theodorons' daily life went on as usual. It was a Spartan life, but there was no lack of variety in it. The house had only two rooms, one above, level with the path, and one below. Jim and his family lived, ate and slept in the top room. Underneath was a mule (ex-army), an aged donkey named Jericho, a hen, three chicks, and a mountainous heap of odds and ends. Originally there had been nine chicks, but the stray cats had so far got six of them. Maria guarded the survivors as if they were her own children. The mere sight of her was enough to send any cat in the village racing for its life. Through cracks in the floorboards I could see the old hen cluck-clucking around, with the chicks hard on her heels. Periodically Maria did a sentry turn on the wooden verandah, and now and again Cristos let out a yell and hurled stones at possible marauders. Life didn't get much chance to grow stagnant.

The bugs worried me at first. Every house in the hills is full of them. The climate, the design of the houses, and their owners' tolerance, make them inevitable. And Greek bugs are big and bite hard. The first night I was nearly eaten alive. After that I slept on the verandah, where it was colder. The few that still troubled me walked a long way to do it.

Time passed quickly. The conjunctivitis cleared up in a week, and soon after, a little strength began trickling back into the numbed legs; but it was a slow job. A month had passed before I could use a stick in place of crutches. Another went by before I could throw the stick away. I was slow and clumsy even then, but I kept improving. 'Maybe another month,' I thought, 'and I'll be fit. Then we'll see about the trip to Athens.'

In the meantime I studied Greek. The proposed trip to Athens made it more or less essential, but the knowledge didn't come easily. Greek has more complications to the square inch than any language bar Chinese. Like Chinese, it is written in code, presumably to keep students at a distance. It was hard going.

Cristos gave me the first lessons. We opened his school primer and did *alpha beta gamma delta* all the way to *omega*. The lad was hazy himself about some of the harder letters like *psi* and *epsilon*, but we persevered. He had the right pronunciation, which was what I wanted. When we finally closed his book, there was a double sigh of relief: but we were both a good deal wiser.

As soon as Cristos reached his limit I transferred to a couple of adult tutors. One was Tyki, an Athenian undergraduate and son of the village Papas. The other was Costas, the schoolmaster. They were both eager to help. Both understood French, too, which made things easier, and all told, I put in about five or six hours' study a day. About half the time was spent in teaching them English, which was fair exchange, but I made the best progress. That was mainly because a dozen or so amateur teachers pounced on me at all hours of the day and insisted on putting me through my paces. It was a wearing business, but good for the vocabulary.

There had been no sign of Axis troops during these two months. It didn't surprise me. Dremissa was almost inaccessible, and in the July and August of '41, both Germans and Italians had other things to think about. Russia was being overrun by the Wehrmacht, Crete had fallen, and the Libyan see-saw was in full swing. Almost every day saw some tremendous event, but only the vaguest whispers reached us. We were too secluded, too cut-off, for important news to filter through.

And because none came, I let the war look after itself, concentrated on Greek and getting well, and thought only about people I knew. By now, the rest of 'B' Company were probably getting accustomed to barbed wire: those who had missed the draft would either be sunning themselves in Alexandria or moving up into the 'blue', and my friends in Athens would be getting familiar with German method the hard way. As for Barlow, God alone knew where he was. I could only hope he had found as sweet a billet.

The Riddle of the Sands

ERSKINE CHILDERS

**After inviting Carruthers to come sailing in the
Baltic, Arthur Davies eventually tells him of an
adventure he had a few weeks before.**

'You know what I was saying about the Frisian Islands the other
day. A thing happened there which I never told you, when you
were asking about my cruise.'

'It began near Norderney,' I put in.

'How did you guess that?' he asked.

'You're a bad hand at duplicity,' I replied. 'Go on.'

'Well, you're quite right, it was there, on September 9. I told
you the sort of thing I was doing at that time, but I don't think I
said that I had made inquiries from one or two people about
duck-shooting, and had been told by some fishermen at Borkum
that there was a big sailing-yacht in those waters, whose owner,
a German of the name of Dollmann, shot a good deal, and might
give me some tips. Well, I found this yacht one evening,
knowing it must be her from the description I had. She was what
is called a 'barge-yacht,' of fifty or sixty tons, built for shallow
water on the lines of a Dutch galliot, with leeboards and those
queer round bows and square stern. She's something like those
galliots anchored near us now. You sometimes see the same sort

of yacht in English waters, only there they copy the Thames barges. She looked a clipper of her sort and very smart; varnished all over and shining like gold. I came on her about sunset after a long day of exploring round the Ems estuary. She was lying in—'

'Wait a bit, let's have the chart,' I interrupted.

Davies found it and spread it on the table between us, first pushing back the cloth and the breakfast things to one end, where they lay in a slovenly litter. This was one of the only two occasions on which I ever saw him postpone the rite of washing up, and it spoke volumes for the urgency of the matter in hand.

'Here it is,' said Davies, and I looked with a new and strange interest at the long string of the slender islands, the parallel line of coast, and the confusion of shoals, banks, and channels which lay between. Here's Norderney, you see. By the way, there's a harbour there at the west end of the island, the only real harbour on the whole line of islands, Dutch or German, except at Terschelling. There's quite a big town there too, a watering place, where Germans go for sea-bathing in the summer. Well, the *Medusa,* that was her name, was lying in the Riff Gat roadstead, flying the German ensign, and I anchored for the night pretty near her. I meant to visit her owner later on, but I very nearly changed my mind, as I always feel rather a fool on smart yachts, and my German isn't very good. However, I thought I might as well; so, after dinner, when it was dark, I sculled over in the dinghy, hailed a sailor on deck, said what I was, and asked if I could see the owner. The sailor was a surly sort of chap, and there was a good long delay while I waited on deck, feeling more and more uncomfortable. Presently a steward came up and showed me down the companion and into the saloon which, after *this,* looked – well, horribly gorgeous – you know what I mean, plush lounges, silk cushions, and that sort of thing. Dinner seemed to be just over, and wine and fruit were on the table. Herr Dollmann was there at his coffee. I introduced myself somehow—'

'Stop a moment,' I said; 'what was he like?'

'Oh, a tall, thin chap, in evening dress; about fifty I suppose, with greyish hair and a short beard. I'm not good at describing people. He had a high bulging forehead and there was something about him – but I think I'd better tell you the bare facts first. I can't say he seemed pleased to see me, and he couldn't speak English, and, in fact, I felt infernally awkward. Still, I had an object in coming, and as I was there I thought I might as well gain it.'

The notion of Davies in his Norfolk jacket and rusty flannels haranguing a frigid German in evening dress in a 'gorgeous' saloon tickled my fancy greatly.

'He seemed very much astonished to see me; had evidently seen the *Dulcibella* arrive and had wondered what she was. I began as soon as I could about the ducks, but he shut me up at once, said I could do nothing hereabouts. I put it down to sportsman's jealousy – you know what that is. But I saw I had come to the wrong shop, and was just going to back out and end this unpleasant interview, when he thawed a bit, offered me some wine, and began talking in quite a friendly way, taking a great interest in my cruise and my plans for the future. In the end we sat up quite late, though I never felt really at my ease. He seemed to be taking stock of me all the time, as though I were some new animal.' (How I sympathized with that German!) 'We parted civilly enough, and I rowed back and turned in, meaning to potter on eastwards early next day.

'But I was knocked up at dawn by a sailor with a message from Dollmann asking if he could come to breakfast with me. I was rather flabbergasted, but didn't like to be rude, so I said "Yes." Well, he came, and I returned the call – and – well, the end of it was that I stayed at anchor there for three days.'

This was rather abrupt.

'How did you spend the time?' I asked. Stopping three days anywhere was an unusual event for him, as I knew from his log.

'Oh, I lunched or dined with him once or twice – with *them*, I ought to say,' he added hurriedly. 'His daughter was with him. She didn't appear the evening I first called.'

'And what was she like?' I asked promptly, before he could hurry on.

'Oh, she seemed a very nice girl,' was the guarded reply, delivered with particular unconcern, 'and – the end of it was that I and the *Medusa* sailed away in company. I must tell you how it came about, just in a few words for the present.

'It was his suggestion. He said he had to sail to Hamburg, and proposed that I should go with him in the *Dulcibella* as far as the Elbe, and then, if I liked, I could take the ship canal at Brunsbüttel through to Kiel and the Baltic. I had no very fixed plans of my own, though I had meant to go on exploring eastwards between the islands and the coast, and so reach the Elbe in a much slower way. He dissuaded me from this, sticking to it that I should have no chance of ducks, and urging other reasons. Anyway, we settled to sail in company direct to Cuxhaven, in the Elbe. With a fair wind and an early start it should be only one day's sail of about sixty miles.

'The plan only came to a head on the evening of the third day, the 12th of September.

'I told you, I think, that the weather had broken after a long spell of heat. That very day it had been blowing pretty hard from the west, and the glass was falling still. I said, of course, that I couldn't go with him if the weather was too bad, but he prophesied a good day, said it was an easy sail, and altogether put me on my mettle. You can guess how it was. Perhaps I had talked about single-handed cruising as though it were easier than it was, though I never meant it in a boasting way, for I hate that sort of thing, and besides there *is* no danger if you're careful—'

'Oh, go on,' I said.

'Anyway, we went next morning at six. It was a dirty-looking day, wind W.N.W., but his sails were going up and mine followed. I took two reefs in and we sailed out into the open and steered E.N.E. along the coast for the Outer Elbe Lightship about fifty knots off. Here it all is, you see.' (He showed me the course on the chart.) 'The trip was nothing for his boat, of course, a safe, powerful old tub, forging through the sea as steady as a house. I kept up with her easily at first. My hands were pretty full, for there was a hard wind on my quarter and a troublesome sea; but as long as nothing worse came I knew I should be all right, though I also knew that I was a fool to have come.

'All went well till we were off Wangeroog, the last of the islands – *here* – and then it began to blow really hard. I had half a mind to chuck it and cut in to the Jade River, *down there*: but I hadn't the face to, so I hove to and took in my last reef.' (Simple words, simply uttered; but I had seen the operation in calm water and shuddered at the present picture.) 'We had been about level till then, but with my shortened canvas I fell behind. Not that that mattered in the least. I knew my course, had read up my tides, and, thick as the weather was, I had no doubt of being able to pick up the lightship. No change of plan was possible now. The Weser estuary was on my starboard hand, but the whole place was a lee-shore and a mass of unknown banks – just look at them. I ran on, the *Dulcibella* doing her level best, but we had some narrow shaves of being pooped. I was about *here*, say six miles south-west of the lightship, when I suddenly saw that the *Medusa* had hove to right ahead, as though waiting till I came up. She wore round again on the course as I drew level, and we were alongside for a bit. Dollmann lashed the wheel, leaned over her quarter, and shouted, very slowly and distinctly so that I could understand: 'Follow me – sea too bad for you outside – short cut through sands – save six miles.'

'It was taking me all my time to manage the tiller, but I knew what he meant at once, for I had been over the chart carefully the night before. You see the whole bay between Wangeroog and the Elbe is encumbered with sand. A great jagged chunk of it runs out from Cuxhaven in a north-westerly direction for fifteen miles or so, ending in a pointed spit called the *Scharhorn*. To reach the Elbe from the west you have to go right outside this, round the lightship, which is off the Scharhorn, and double back. Of course, that's what all big vessels do. But, as you see, these sands are intersected here and there by channels, very shallow and winding, exactly like those behind the Frisian Islands. Now look at this one, which cuts right through the big chunk of sand and comes out near Cuxhaven. The *Telte* it's called. It's miles wide, you see, at the entrance, but later on it is split into two by the Hohenhörn bank; then it gets shallow and very complicated, and ends as a mere tidal driblet with another name. It's just the sort of channel I should like to worry into on a fine day or with an off-shore wind. Alone, in thick weather and a heavy sea, it would have been folly to attempt it, except as a desperate resource. But, as I said, I knew at once that Dollmann was proposing to run for it and guide me in.

'I didn't like the idea, because I like doing things for myself, and, silly as it sounds, I believe I resented being told the sea was too bad for me, which it certainly was. Yet the short cut did save several miles and a devil of a tumble off the Scharhorn, where two tides meet. I had complete faith in Dollmann, and I suppose I decided that I should be a fool not to take a good chance. I hesitated, I know; but in the end I nodded and held up my arm as she forged ahead again. Soon after she shifted her course and I followed. You asked me once if I ever took a pilot. That was the only time.'

He spoke with bitter gravity, flung himself back and felt his pocket for his pipe. It was not meant for a dramatic pause, but it certainly was one. I had just a glimpse of still another Davies – a Davies five years older, throbbing with deep emotions, scorn, passion, and stubborn purpose; a being above my plane, of sterner stuff, wider scope. Intense as my interest had become, I waited almost timidly while he mechanically rammed tobacco into his pipe and struck ineffectual matches. I felt that whatever the riddle to be solved, it was no mean one. He repressed himself with an effort, half rose and made his circular glance at the clock, barometer and skylight, and then resumed.

'We soon came to what I knew must be the beginning of the Telte channel. All round you could hear the breakers on the sands, though it was too thick to see them yet. As the water

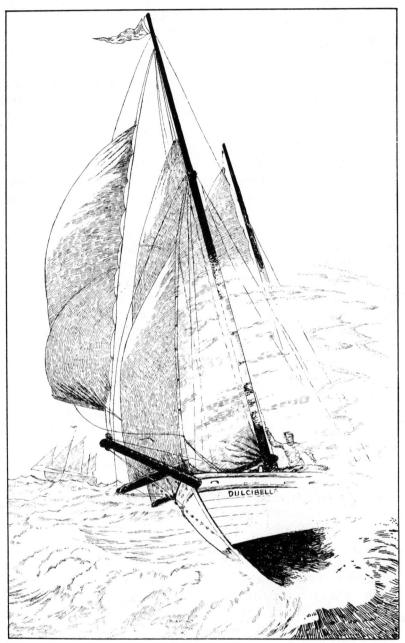

'I ran on, the Dulcibella doing her level best, but we had some narrow shaves'

shoaled, the sea of course got shorter and steeper. There was more wind – a whole gale I should say.

'I kept dead in the wake of the *Medusa*, but to my disgust I found she was gaining on me very fast. Of course I had taken for granted, when he said he would lead me in, that he would slow down and keep close to me. He could easily have done so by getting his men up to check his sheets or drop his peak. Instead of that he was busting on for all he was worth. Once, in a rain-squall, I lost sight of him altogether, got him faintly again, but had enough to do with my own tiller not to want to be peering through the scud after a runaway pilot. It was all right so far, but we were fast approaching the worst part of the whole passage, where the Hohenhörn bank blocks the road and the channel divides. I don't know what it looks like to you on the chart – perhaps fairly simple, because you can follow the twists of the channels, as on a ground-plan; but a stranger coming to a place like that (where there are no buoys, mind you) can tell nothing certain by the eye, unless perhaps at dead low water, when the banks are high and dry, and in very clear weather; he must trust to the lead and compass and feel his way step by step. I knew perfectly well that what I should soon see would be a wall of surf stretching right across and on both sides. To *feel* one's way in that sort of weather is impossible. You must *know* your way, or else have a pilot. I had one, but he was playing his own game.

'With a second hand on board to steer while I conned I should have felt less of an ass. As it was, I knew I ought to be facing the music in the offing, and cursed myself for having broken my rule and gone blundering into this confounded short cut. It was giving myself away, doing just the very thing that you can't do in single-handed sailing.

'By the time I realized the danger it was far too late to turn and hammer out to the open. I was deep in the bottle-neck bight of the sands, jammed on a lee-shore, and a strong flood tide sweeping me on. That tide, by the way, gave just the ghost of a chance. I had the hours in my head, and knew it was about two-thirds flood with two hours more of rising water. That meant the banks would all be covering when I reached them, and harder than ever to locate; but it also meant that I *might* float right over the worst of them if I hit off a lucky place.' Davies thumped the table in disgust. 'Pah! It makes me sick to think of having to trust to an accident like that, like a lubberly Cockney out for a boosy Bank Holiday sail.

'Well, just as I foresaw, the wall of surf appeared clean across the horizon, and curling back to shut me in, booming like thunder. When I last saw the *Medusa* she seemed to be charging it like a horse at a fence, and I took a rough bearing of her position by a hurried glance at the compass. At that very moment I *thought* she seemed to luff and show some of her broadside; but a squall blotted her out and gave me hell with the tiller. After that she was lost in the white mist that hung over the line of breakers. I kept on my bearing as well as I could, but I was already out of the channel. I knew that by the look of the water, and as we neared the bank I saw it was all awash and without the vestige of an opening. I wasn't going to chuck her on to it without an effort; so, more by instinct than with any particular hope, I put the helm down, meaning to work her along the edge on the chance of spotting a way over. She was buried at once by the beam sea, and the jib flew to blazes; but the reefed stays'l stood, she recovered gamely, and I held on, though I knew it could only be for a few minutes as the centre-plate was up and she made frightful leeway towards the bank.

'I was half blinded by scud, but suddenly I noticed what looked like a gap, behind a spit which curled out right ahead. I luffed still more to clear this spit, but she couldn't weather it. Before you could say knife she was driving across it, bumped heavily, bucked forward again, bumped again, and – ripped on in deeper water! I can't describe the next few minutes. I was in some sort of channel, but a very narrow one, and the sea broke everywhere. I hadn't proper command either; for the rudder had crocked up somehow at the last bump. I was like a drunken man running for his life down a dark alley, barking himself at every corner. It couldn't last long, and finally we went crash on to something and stopped there, grinding and banging. So ended that little trip under a pilot.

'Well, it was like this – there was really no danger' – I opened my eyes at the characteristic phrase. 'I mean, that lucky stumble into a channel was my salvation. Since then I had struggled through a mile of sands, all of which lay behind me like a breakwater against the gale. They were covered, of course, and seething like soapsuds; but the force of the sea was deadened. The *Dulce* was bumping, but not too heavily. It was nearing high tide, and at half ebb she would be high and dry.

'In the ordinary way I should have run out a kedge with the dinghy, and at the next high water sailed farther in and anchored where I could lie afloat. The trouble was now that my hand was hurt and my dinghy stove in, not to mention the rudder business. It was the first bump on the outer edge that did the damage. There was a heavy swell there, and when we struck, the dinghy, which was towing astern, came home on her painter and down with a crash on the yacht's weather quarter. I stuck out one hand to ward it off and got it nipped on the gunwale. She was badly stove in and useless, so I couldn't run out the kedge' – (this was Greek to me, but I let him go on) – 'and for the present my hand was too painful even to stow the boom and sails which were whipping and racketing about anyhow. There was the rudder too to be mended; and we were several miles from the nearest land. Of course, if the wind fell, it was all easy enough; but if it held or increased it was a poor look-out. There's a limit to strain of that sort – and other things might have happened.

'In fact, it was precious lucky that Bartels turned up. His galliot was at anchor a mile away, up a branch of the channel. In a clear between squalls he saw us and, like a brick, rowed his boat out – he and his boy, and a devil of a pull they must have had. I was glad enough to see them – no, that's not true; I was in such a fury of disgust and shame that I believe I should have been idiot enough to say I didn't want help, if he hadn't just nipped on board and started work. He's a terror to work, that little mouse of a chap. In half an hour we had stowed the sails, unshackled the big anchor, run out fifty fathoms of warp and hauled her off there and then into deep water. Then they towed her up the channel – it was dead to leeward and an easy job – and berthed her near their own vessel. It was dark by that time, so I gave them a drink, and said goodnight. It blew a howling gale that night, but the place was safe enough, with good ground-tackle.

'The whole affair was over; and after supper I thought hard about it all.'

The Open Window

GEORGETTE ELGEY

Georgette, her mother and grandmother are escaping from Paris to the unoccupied zone of France during the Second World War; life has become dangerous for them since being denounced for their Jewish origins. In spite of surveillance by the authorities, Georgette's mother has somehow managed to obtain the necessary passes for the train journey, but their troubles are not over yet.

We climbed back into the train. Again people helped to carry our luggage and put it up in the racks. Now everyone was back in the train. Barely half an hour had passed since our arrival at Orthez. The stop at Orthez is never very long, we had been told. On the empy platform the station-master was waving his flag. The train began to move. Yes, the train was moving. . . .

What followed took less than a minute – no, seconds only. My grandmother and my mother were sitting opposite one another in the window seats; I was beside my mother. The train was under way. Glancing out of the window, my mother said to me, 'Look what a hurry that German's in!' A soldier on a bicycle came hurtling onto the platform, leapt off his machine, sending it clattering to the ground, dashed for the loud speaker, and shouted, 'The train is not to leave! The train is not to leave!' A squeal of brakes, a shudder, and the train was stationary. Over the loud speaker: 'Madame Gustave Léon and her family travelling from Paris to Les Eaux-Bonnes are to get off the train immediately.'

My mother and my grandmother got to their feet at once without even consulting one another. What else could they do? I followed their example. My sole impression of that moment has to do with the faces of the other passengers. I saw expressed on their features and felt almost as a physical sensation their relief – and also their sympathy. The announcement had not been for them, and they could breathe again; at the same time they felt sorry for us.

We alighted. I have forgotten whether the Germans boarded the train to take our luggage off or whether the people in our compartment passed everything through the window; what I am sure of is that hardly had we set foot on the platform when, with shouts and some brutality, the Germans separated us. They put my grandmother and my mother in different rooms and told me to wait on a bench on the platform. I saw them collect our cases; above all I saw the train pull out.

It was very warm. I had put on a chestnut-coloured woollen costume for the journey. It was decorated with studs and I thought it extremely pretty. My mother had bought it for me for Easter at 'Old England' in the Boulevard des Capucines. I regretted not having chosen something lighter to wear. I must have been terribly frightened, even desperate, but my memory holds no record of such feelings. What was uppermost in my mind at the time was firstly the shock of it all and secondly an obsession with conducting myself correctly. I did not want the Germans to see my fear. It was not something I worked out for myself; it had nothing to do with pride or courage; it was simply the way I reacted. I do not believe one is in any way responsible – certainly not at thirteen – for the attitude one adopts in the face of disaster. I should be no more embarrassed today had I burst into tears.

Escape Stories

I have no idea how the hours passed. I know that I thought a great deal (and it struck me as silly at the time) about *Memoirs of a Donkey*, saying to myself that we were in the same situation as Cadichon's abductors when the police separate them in order to prevent any communication between them.[1] Likening my grandmother to one of the Comtesse de Ségur's scoundrels made me want to laugh, so I clung to the thought of Cadichon.

I also thought about the Jesuit father who had given me religious instruction, and, curiously enough, rather than saying my prayers, I said to myself, 'Let's hope he's praying for us'. His intercession must have struck me as peculiarly effective – better than appealing direct! I have forgotten exactly how long I spent alone on that bench. I remember that another train went through. The Germans had started to search our luggage properly. Several times I heard outraged howls. The fact is, we must have been out of our minds. All gold, even the property of 'Aryans', was supposed to have been declared to and confiscated by the occupying authorities. Needless to say, importing gold to the unoccupied zone was a 'crime punishable under martial law'.

That said, I must tell a little more family history. My grandmother and her husband had been deeply in love and extremely close. Letters my grandfather wrote his wife after twenty years of marriage, at the most dreadful moment of his professional career – it was the time of the Courrières disaster[2] – led me to believe that their love was no mere family legend. My grandfather died suddenly in 1916 – in London, where he had been head of a Franco-British mission. Since then my grandmother had carried with her everywhere the wallet her husband had had in his pocket on the day of his death.

---

[1] *Mémoires d'un Ane* is a children's story – still popular today – published by the Comtesse de Ségur in 1860. Cadichon is the donkey hero. (*Tr.*)
[2] An appalling mining disaster at Courrières near Béthune in northern France in 1906 caused 1,100 deaths. (*Tr.*)

The Open Window

The Germans opened it. They found four gold coins – English, to make matters worse – and a diplomatic passport accrediting my grandfather to His Majesty's Government. The fact that the document dated from 1916 made no difference: the Germans howled with mingled horror and delight. Rarely had these petty officials – with the Wehrmacht fighting in Russia and Africa and sitting in Paris, there was little glory attached to being stationed at Orthez – had such a fine catch to get their teeth into!

After a time – this must have been late morning – a German came to fetch me for interrogation. Before leaving Paris we had not discussed what line we should take in such an eventuality. All I knew was that I must swear to all and sundry that my family was not Jewish. I can still see those Germans waiting for me in their office on Orthez railway station – those two customs officers. One of them seemed old to me. He lacked the slender physique of the master race and he must have been about forty. The other, a much younger man, has stuck in my mind as the caricature of the SS man. Was he SS? It seems unlikely. He was tall, slim, and nasty. There was an interpreter too – also German.

The first thing they asked me was whether I spoke German. At that time I did. I was brought up by an English governess and I learned English at the same time as I learned French. I had German lessons from the age of eight and became quite fluent in the language, though I have totally and deliberately forgotten it since. After Orthez I dropped German at school and my German today is confined to the beginning of *Die Lorelei*.

So my interrogation took place half in German and half in French. The German shouted; he was so sure of his ground that he can really have had little interest in what I said. He quickly put the question I had been expecting: 'Are you Jewish?' Or rather he yelled, 'You're Jewish.' I swore that I was Catholic, which was true, and that no one in my family was Jewish, which was not true. The German then said, 'You say you're not Jewish, your grandmother says she's not Jewish, your mother says she's not Jewish, but your friends – they know you're Jewish. The—know you're Jewish.' And he threw at me the name of the Jewish doctor's family whom my mother had been helping out with food.

'We are not Jewish,' I answered.

'Where did your mother get her passes?' the German asked me.

'At the Kommandantur in the Rue Galilée,' I said without hesitation. It was the only Kommandantur I knew of that issued *Ausweise*, though in fact there were several in the capital. The answer came to me automatically. Whether it was the outcome of chance, simple probability, or a manifestation of providence I cannot say, but to the same question my mother had given the identical answer, and with as little hesitation. We knew nothing of the origin of our passes and had inevitably, since our arrest, been terrified that they were forgeries. My grandmother did not have to answer the question because that mistress of herself and of her world, a woman of more than ordinary intelligence and enormous presence of mind, had decided as soon as she was separated from us to play on her age. Feigning senility, she failed to understand a word they said to her. The Germans very quickly gave up trying to interrogate her at all. They did not tell her as they told my mother and me that certain friends of ours – and they always mentioned one and the same name – knew that we were Jews.

If my grandmother quite simply refused to talk, such was not at all my mother's approach. She became furiously indignant at the accusations levelled against us and demanded that our interrogators get in touch with Paris, where they would receive proof of the authenticity of our identity cards.

There was one very distressing moment as far as I was concerned. My interrogation was over, I seem to remember, or nearly over. I think it must have been over because in my memory the scene takes place in the room in which I had been interrogated and the officer who had asked the questions was no longer at his desk. However, the young SS man (who was probably not one at all) was there, and so was the interpreter. A young 'mouse' (as women auxiliaries in the German army were called) came in. She seemed very young to me, which suggests she must have been, because at that age one tends to regard all adults as being very old. There was something to do with the table, as I recall the scene; I cannot remember whether she sat on it or whether that was where they had placed me. At any rate she was opposite me, and she began to abuse me, calling me a 'filthy little Jewess' and spitting in my face. I had but one thought in my head: to pretend that nothing was happening.

I was not physically maltreated. There was just this one brief, violent incident. She told me that in Germany they would soon put me in my place, and she turned to the young SS man. Clearly she was trying to impress him with her wit. I suppose she was in love with him. The interpreter said nothing. The SS man smiled but – perhaps deep down he was not so 'SS' after all – put an end to the performance by taking his admirer away.

This interlude, as it were, shook me rigid. Even while the German girl was insulting me I was wondering, .'How can anyone be so beastly to a child who's done nothing to you?' Until that moment I had always thought grown-ups were there to protect me. I could not understand what was happening to me. I believe in fact that my apparent impassivity was due to a profound amazement.

The interpreter sent me out. I sat down again on my bench. I did not think about what was going to happen. I was sure I should never see my family again, but what fate might have in store for me I did not even wonder. Lack of imagination can sometimes be a blessing.

A while later my mother was sitting on the bench beside me.

My grandmother must have been kept inside, or was she on another bench farther down the platform? We were not allowed to talk. My mother had seen to it that I received a good education; with her I had never had a conversation on a general subject except on the certainty of the British eventually winning the war. She frequently gave me advice of a moral nature, but invariably in connection with a particular case or a particular person: one must be especially nice to such and such an old friend because she was ill and had no family. She would never lay down a principle for its own sake, outside a specific context. That day, however, once when the German sentry was not looking, my mother said to me, 'You must never forget what your grandfather taught me: the most important thing in life is to cause others as little hurt as possible. . . .' I was convinced they were the last words I should ever hear my mother speak, especially since the German saw her whispering and made me go and sit farther away. I looked at my grandmother – so she must have been out on the platform too – and noticed that her hands were bare. . . . Mamie, as her grandchildren called her, used to wear a great many rings: her engagement ring and the rings she had received for the births of her children. She was no longer wearing them. As a small girl I used to love to climb into her lap and play with those rings, or with the large – and very turn-of-the-century – pendant she always wore around her neck. Seeing her without her jewellery made me want to cry. It was at that moment, I think, that I came closest to tears.

We were still on the station platform. A railwayman went by from time to time – the station-master, I suppose. He gave me a kindly smile.

We sensed that the Germans were waiting for something. It must have been seven in the morning when we got off the train. Now it must be half past four or five. The interrogations completed, the luggage searched – fortunately it had not occurred to them to go through our clothing: my grandmother was carrying a number of gold dollars, which my mother had sewn individually into her coat – our continued presence on those benches was meaningless.

A car drove up. It stopped on the other side of the rails, a man in civilian clothes got out, and the German officers all went across to meet him, one of them carrying our passes and identity cards. They held a discussion on the spot, fifty or a hundred yards from where I was sitting. It was clear they were not in agreement. They argued for a good five or ten minutes, then the man in civilian clothes left the group and came over to me. His French was not very good, and no doubt they had told him I knew German. He had our passes in his hand. Half in French, half in German, he said to me, 'I am a Gestapo officer. I know you are Jewish. *Das ist mir ganz egal* (That doesn't interest me in the least). I am confident your passes are genuine. I know Captain Hannemann' – our *Ausweise* bore this signature but we did not, I repeat, know whether any Captain Hannemann existed – 'and I know his signature. If he issued you with passes he had his reasons. I don't want any trouble with him. You won't be going to prison.'

What followed this announcement I no longer remember. As I write all this down it is as if I am watching a screen: from time to time the film must break, for the screen goes blank.

The Glacier

H. RIDER HAGGARD

**Leo Vincey and Horace Holly have been travel-
ling for sixteen years in the wilds of Asia, in
quest of the mysterious 'She'. They are very
near the end of their resources and surrounded
by impassable mountains on every side: the
only way on, though suicidal, is over a glazier.**

There was the end of the road, and there were our own
footprints and the impress of the yak's hoofs in the snow. The
sight of them affected me, for it seemed strange that we should
have lived to look upon them again. We stared over the edge of
the precipice. Yes, it was sheer and absolutely unclimbable.

'Come to the glacier,' said Leo.

So we went on to it, and scrambling a little way down its root,
made an examination. Here, so far as we could judge, the cliff
was about four hundred feet deep. But whether or no the tongue
of ice reached to the foot of it we were unable to tell, since about
two thirds of the way down it arched inwards, like the end of a
bent bow, and the conformation of the overhanging rocks on
either side was such that we could not see where it terminated.
We climbed back again and sat down, and despair took hold of
us, bitter, black despair.

'What are we to do?' I asked. 'In front of us death. Behind us death, for how can we recross those mountains without food or guns to shoot it with? Here death, for we must sit and starve. We have striven and failed. Leo, our end is at hand. Only a miracle can save us.'

'A miracle,' he answered. 'Well, what was it that led us to the top of the mount so that we were able to escape the avalanche? And what was it which put that rock in your way as you sank into the bed of dust, and gave me wit and strength to dig you out of your grave of snow? And what is it that has preserved us through seventeen years of dangers such as few men have known and lived? Some directing Power. Some Destiny that will accomplish itself in us. Why should the Power cease to guide? Why should the Destiny be baulked at last?'

He paused, then added fiercely, 'I tell you, Horace, that even if we had guns, food, and yaks, I would not turn back upon our spoor, since to do so would prove me a coward and unworthy of her. I will go on.'

'How?' I asked.

'By that road,' and he pointed to the glacier.

'It is a road to death!'

'Well, if so, Horace, it would seem that in this land men find life in death, or so they believe. If we die now, we shall die travelling our path, and in the country where we perish we may be born again. At least I am determined, so you must choose.'

'I have chosen long ago. Leo, we began this journey together and we will end it together. Perhaps Ayesha knows and will help us,' and I laughed drearily. 'If not – come, we are wasting time.'

Then we took counsel, and the end of it was that we cut a skin rug and the yak's tough hide into strips and knotted these together into two serviceable ropes, which we fastened about our middles, leaving one end loose, for we thought that they might help us in our descent.

Next we bound fragments of another skin rug about our legs and knees to protect them from the chaffing of the ice and rocks, and for the same reason put on our thick leather gloves. This done, we took the remainder of our gear and heavy robes and, having placed stones in them, threw them over the brink of the precipice, trusting to find them again, should we ever reach its foot. Now our preparations were complete, and it was time for us to start upon perhaps one of the most desperate journeys ever undertaken by men of their own will.

Yet we stayed a little, looking at each other in a piteous fashion, for we could not speak. Only we embraced, and I confess, I think I wept a little. It all seemed so sad and hopeless, these longings endured through many years, these perpetual, weary travellings, and now – the end. I could not bear to think of that splendid man, my ward, my most dear friend, the companion of my life, who stood before me so full of beauty and of vigour, but who must within a few short minutes be turned into a heap of quivering, mangled flesh. For myself it did not matter. I was old, it was time that I should die. I had lived innocently, if it were innocent to follow this lovely image, this Siren of the caves, who lured us on to doom.

No, I don't think that I thought of myself then, but I thought a great deal of Leo, and when I saw his determined face and flashing eyes as he nerved himself to the last endeavour, I was proud of him. So in broken accents I blessed him and wished him well through all the aeons, praying that I might be his companion to the end of time. In few words and short he thanked me and gave me back my blessing. Then he muttered—
'Come.'

So side by side we began the terrible descent. At first it was easy enough, although a slip would have hurled us to eternity. But we were strong and skilful, accustomed to such places moreover, and made none. About a quarter of the way down we paused, standing upon a great boulder that was embedded in the ice, and, turning round cautiously, leaned our backs against the glacier and looked about us. Truly it was a horrible place, almost sheer, nor did we learn much, for beneath us, a hundred and twenty feet or more, the projecting bend cut off our view of what lay below.

The Glacier

So, feeling that our nerves would not bear a prolonged contemplation of that dizzy gulf, once more we set our faces to the ice and proceeded on the downward climb. Now matters were more difficult, for the stones were fewer, and once or twice we must slide to reach them, not knowing if we should ever stop again. But the ropes which we threw over the angles of the rocks, or salient points of ice, letting ourselves down by their help and drawing them after us when we reached the next foothold, saved us from disaster.

Thus at length we came to the bend, which was more than halfway down the precipice, being, so far as I could judge, about two hundred and fifty feet from its lip, and say one hundred and fifty from the darksome bottom of the narrow gulf. Here were no stones, but only some rough ice, on which we sat to rest.

'We must look,' said Leo presently.

But the question was, how to do this. Indeed, there was only one way to hang over the bend and discover what lay below. We read each other's thought without the need of words, and I made a motion as though I would start.

'No,' said Leo, 'I am younger and stronger than you. Come, help me,' and he began to fasten the end of his rope to a strong, projecting point of ice. 'Now,' he said, 'hold my ankles.'

It seemed an insanity, but there was nothing else to be done, so, fixing my heels in a niche, I grasped his ankles and slowly he slid forward till his body vanished to the middle. What he saw does not matter, for I saw it all afterwards, but what happened was that suddenly all his great weight came upon my arms with such a jerk that his ankles were torn from my grip.

Or, who knows? perhaps in my terror I loosed them, obeying the natural impulse which prompts a man to save his own life. If so, may I be forgiven, but had I held on, I must have been jerked into the abyss. Then the rope ran out and remained taut.

'Leo!' I screamed, 'Leo!' and I heard a muffled voice saying, as I thought, 'Come.' What it really said was – 'Don't come.' But indeed – and may it go to my credit – I did not pause to think, but face outwards, just as I was sitting, I began to slide and scramble down the ice.

In two seconds I had reached the curve, in three I was over it. Beneath was what I can only describe as a great icicle broken off short, and separated from the cliff by about four yards of space. This icicle was not more than fifteen feet in length and sloped outwards, so that my descent was not sheer. Moreover, at the end of it the trickling of water, or some such accident, had worn away the ice, leaving a little ledge as broad, perhaps, as a man's hand. There were roughnesses on the surface below the curve, upon which my clothing caught, also I gripped them desperately with my fingers. Thus it came about that I slid down quite gently and, my heels landing upon the little ledge, remained almost upright, with outstretched arms – like a person crucified to a cross of ice.

Then I saw everything, and the sight curdled the blood within my veins. Hanging to the rope, four or five feet below the broken point, was Leo, out of reach of it, and out of reach of the cliff; as he hung turning slowly round and round, much as – for in a dreadful, inconsequent fashion the absurd similarity struck me even then – a joint turns before the fire. Below yawned the black gulf, and at the bottom of it, far, far beneath, appeared a faint white sheet of snow. That is what I saw.

Think of it! Think of it! I crucified upon the ice, my heels resting upon a little ledge; my fingers grasping excrescences on which a bird would scarcely have found a foothold; round and below me dizzy space. To climb back whence I came was impossible, to stir even was impossible, since one slip and I must be gone.

And below me, hung like a spider to its cord, Leo turning slowly round and round!

I could see that rope of green hide stretch beneath his weight and the double knots in it slip and tighten, and I remember wondering which would give first, the hide or the knots, or whether it would hold till he dropped from the noose limb by limb.

Oh! I have been in many a perilous place, I who sprang from the

I grasped his ankles and slowly he slid forwards

Swaying Stone to the point of the Trembling Spur, and missed my aim, but never, never in such a one as this. Agony took hold of me; a cold sweat burst from every pore. I could feel it running down my face like tears; my hair bristled upon my head. And below, in utter silence, Leo turned round and round, and each time he turned his up-cast eyes met mine with a look that was horrible to see.

The silence was the worst of it, the silence and the helplessness. If he had cried out, if he had struggled, it would have been better. But to know that he was alive there, with every nerve and perception at its utmost stretch. Oh! my God! Oh! my god!

My limbs began to ache, and yet I dared not stir a muscle. They ached horribly, or so I thought, and beneath this torture, mental and physical, my mind gave. I remembered things: remembered how, as a child, I had climbed a tree and reached a place whence I could move neither up nor down, and what I suffered then. Remembered how once in Egypt a foolhardy friend of mine had ascended the Second Pyramid alone, and become thus crucified upon its shining cap, where he remained for a whole half hour with four hundred feet of space beneath him. I could see him now stretching his stockinged foot downwards in a vain attempt to reach the next crack, and drawing it back again; could see his tortured face, a white blot upon the red granite.

Then that face vanished and blackness gathered round me, and in the blackness visions: of the living, resistless avalanche, of the snow-grave into which I had sunk – oh! years and years ago; of Ayesha demanding Leo's life at my hands. Blackness and silence, through which I could only hear the cracking of my muscles.

Suddenly in the blackness a flash, and in the silence a sound. The flash was the flash of a knife which Leo had drawn. He was hacking at the cord with it fiercely, fiercely, to make an end. And the sound was that of the noise he made, a ghastly noise, half shout of defiance and half yell of terror, as at the third stroke it suddenly parted.

I saw it part. The tough hide was half cut through, and its severed portion curled upwards and downwards like the upper and lower lips of an angry dog, whilst that which was unsevered stretched out slowly, slowly, till it grew quite thin. Then it snapped, so that the rope flew upwards and struck me across the face like the lash of a whip.

Another instant and I heard a cracking, thudding sound. Leo had struck the ground below. Leo was dead, a mangled mass of flesh and bone as I had pictured him. I could not bear it. My nerve and human dignity came back. I would not wait until my strength exhausted, I slid from my perch as a wounded bird falls from a tree. No, I would follow him at once, of my own act.

I let my arms fall against my sides, and rejoiced in the relief from pain that the movement gave me. Then balanced upon my heels, I stood upright, took my last look at the sky, muttered my last prayer. For an instant I remained thus poised.

Shouting, 'I come,' I raised my hands above my head and dived as a bather dives, dived into the black gulf beneath.

Oh! that rush through space! Folk falling thus are supposed to lose consciousness, but I can assert that this is not true. Never were my wits and perceptions more lively than while I travelled from that broken glacier to the ground, and never did a short journey seem to take a longer time. I saw the white floor, like some living thing, leaping up through empty air to meet me, then – *finis*!

Crash! Why, what was this? I still lived. I was in water, for I could feel its chill, and going down, down, till I thought I should never rise again. But rise I did, though my lungs were nigh to bursting first. As I floated up towards the top I remembered the crash, which told me that I had passed through ice. Therefore I should meet ice at the surface again. Oh! to think that after surviving so much I must be drowned like a kitten and beneath a sheet of ice. My hands touched it. There it was above me shining white like glass. Heaven be praised! My head broke through; in this low and sheltered gorge it was but a film no thicker than a penny formed by the light frost of the previous night. So I rose from the deep and stared about me, treading water with my feet.

Then I saw the gladdest sight that ever my eyes beheld, for on the right, not ten yards away, the water running from his hair and beard, was Leo. Leo alive, for he broke the thin ice with his arms as he struggled towards the shore from the deep river.[1] He saw me also, and his grey eyes seemed to start out of his head.

'Still living, both of us, and the precipice passed!' he shouted in a ringing, exultant voice. 'I told you we were led.'

[1] Usually, as we learned afterwards, the river at this spot was quite shallow; only a foot or two in depth. It was the avalanche that by damming it with fallen heaps of snow had raised its level very many feet. Therefore, to this avalanche, which had threatened to destroy us, we in reality owed our lives, for had the stream stood only at its normal height we must have been dashed to pieces upon the stones. – L.H.H.

Flying Colours

C. S. FORESTER

**Captain Horatio Hornblower's ship the *Sut-
herland* is captured by the French after a fierce
sea battle which left many of the sailors on both
sides either dead or dying. Hornblower, Bush,
his injured first lieutenant and Brown the coxswain are taken to Paris to be tried and ex-
ecuted but on the way they manage to escape.
They steal a boat and row down the river Loire
until they reach the port of Nantes. There,
dressed in the uniform of members of the
French customs service, they search for a way
to get back to England.**

And then against the quay below the American ships they saw
something else, something which caused them to stiffen in their
seats. The tricolour here was hoisted above a tattered blue
ensign, flaunting a petty triumph.

'*Witch of Endor*, ten-gun cutter,' said Bush hoarsely. 'A
French frigate caught her on a lee shore off Noirmoutier last
year. By God, isn't it what you'd expect of the French? It's
eleven months ago and they're still wearing French colours over
British.'

She was a lovely little ship; even from where they were they could see the perfection of her lines – speed and seaworthiness were written all over her.

'The Frogs don't seem to have over-sparred her the way you'd expect 'em to,' commented Bush.

She was ready for sea, and their expert eyes could estimate the area of the furled mainsail and jib. The high graceful mast nodded to them, almost imperceptibly, as the cutter rocked minutely beside the quay. It was as if a prisoner were appealing to them for aid, and the flapping colours, tricolour over blue ensign, told a tragic story. In a sudden rush of impulse Hornblower put the helm over.

'Lay us alongside the quay,' he said to Brown.

A few strokes took them there; the tide had turned some time ago, and they headed against the flood. Brown caught a ring and made the painter fast, and first Hornblower, nimbly, and then Bush, with difficulty, mounted the stone steps to the top of the quay.

'Suivez-nous,' said Hornblower to Brown, remembering at the last moment to speak French.

Hornblower forced himself to hold up his head and walk with a swagger; the pistols in his side pockets bumped reassuringly against his hips, and his sword tapped against his thigh. Bush walked beside him, his wooden leg thumping with measured stride on the stone quay. A passing group of soldiers saluted the smart uniform, and Hornblower returned the salute nonchalantly, amazed at his new coolness. His heart was beating fast, but ecstatically he knew he was not afraid. It was worth running this risk to experience this feeling of mad bravery.

They stopped and looked at the *Witch of Endor* against the quay. Her decks were not of the dazzling whiteness upon which an English first lieutenant would have insisted, and there was a slovenliness about her standing rigging which was heartbreaking to contemplate. A couple of men were moving lackadaisically about the deck under the supervision of a third.

'Anchor watch,' muttered Bush. 'Two hands and a master's mate.'

He spoke without moving his lips, like a naughty boy in school, lest some onlooker should read his words and realize that he was not speaking French.

'Everyone else on shore, the lubbers,' went on Bush.

Hornblower stood on the quay, the tiny breeze blowing round his ears, soldiers and sailors and civilians walking by, the bustle of the unloading of the American ships noisy in the distance. Bush's thoughts were following on the heels of his own. Bush was aware of the temptation Hornblower was feeling, to steal the *Witch of Endor* and to sail her to England – Bush would never have thought of it himself, but years of service under his captain made him receptive of ideas, however fantastic.

Fantastic was the right word. Those big cutters carried a crew of sixty men, and the gear and tackle were planned accordingly. Three men – one a cripple – could not even hope to be able to hoist the big mainsail, although it was just possible that the three of them might handle her under sail in the open sea in fair weather. It was that possibility which had given rise to the train of thought, but on the other hand there was all the tricky estuary of the Loire between them and the sea; and the French, Hornblower knew, had removed the buoys and navigation marks for fear of an English raid. Unpiloted they could never hope to find their way through thirty-five miles of shoals without going aground, and besides, there were batteries at Paimboeuf and Saint Nazaire to prohibit unauthorized entrance and exit. The thing was impossible – it was sheer sentimentality to think of it, he told himself, suddenly self-critical again for a moment.

He turned away and strolled up towards the American ships, and watched with interest the wretched chain gangs staggering along the gang planks with their loads of grain. The sight of their misery sickened him; so did the bullying sergeants who strutted about in charge of them. Here, if anywhere, he told himself, was to be found the nucleus of that rising against Bonaparte which everyone was expecting. All that was needed was a desperate leader – that would be something worth reporting to the

Government when he reached home. Farther down river yet another ship was coming up to the port, her topsails black against the setting sun, as, with the flood behind her, she held her course close hauled to the faint southerly breeze. She was flying the Stars and Stripes – American again. Hornblower experienced the same feeling of exasperated impotence which he had known in the old days of his service under Pellew. What was the use of blockading a coast, and enduring all the hardships and perils of that service, if neutral vessels could sail in and out with impunity? Their cargoes of wheat were officially noncontraband, but wheat was of as vital importance to Bonaparte as ever was hemp, or pitch, or any other item on the contraband list – the more wheat he could import, the more men he could draft into his armies. Hornblower found himself drifting into the eternal debate as to whether America, when eventually she became weary of the indignities of neutrality, would turn her arms against England or France – she had actually been at war with France for a short time already, and it was much to her interest to help pull down the imperial despotism, but it was doubtful whether she would be able to resist the temptation to twist the British lion's tail.

The new arrival, smartly enough handled, was edging in now to the quay. A backed topsail took the way off her, and the warps creaked round the bollards. Hornblower watched idly, Bush and Brown beside him. As the ship was made fast, a gang plank was thrown to the quay, and a little stout man made ready to walk down it from the ship. He was in civilian clothes, and he had a rosy round face with a ridiculous little black moustache with upturned ends. From his manner of shaking hands with the captain, and from the very broken English which he was speaking, Hornblower guessed him to be the pilot.

The pilot! In that moment a surge of ideas boiled up in Hornblower's mind. It would be dark in less than an hour, with the moon in its first quarter – already he could see it, just visible in the sky high over the setting sun. A clear night, the tide about to ebb, a gentle breeze, southerly with a touch of east. A pilot available on the one hand, a crew on the other. Then he hesitated. The whole scheme was rash to the point of madness – beyond that point. It must be ill-digested, unsound. His mind raced madly through the scheme again, but even as it did so he was carried away by the wave of recklessness. There was an intoxication about throwing caution to the winds which he had forgotten since his boyhood. In the tense seconds which were all he had, while the pilot was descending the gang plank and approaching them along the quay, he had formed his resolution. He nudged his two companions, and then stepped forward and intercepted the fat little pilot as he walked briskly past them.

'Monsieur,' he said. 'I have some questions to ask you. Will you kindly accompany me to my ship for a moment?'

The pilot noted the uniform, the star of the Legion of Honour, the assured manner.

'Why, certainly,' he said. His conscience was clear; he was guilty of no more than venal infringements of the Continental system. He turned and trotted alongside Hornblower. 'You are a newcomer to this port, Colonel, I fancy?'

'I was transferred here yesterday from Amsterdam,' answered Hornblower shortly.

Brown was striding along at the pilot's other elbow; Bush was bringing up the rear, gallantly trying to keep pace with them, his wooden leg thumping the pavement. They came up to the *Witch of Endor*, and made their way up her gang plank to her deck; the officer there looked at them with a little surprise. But he knew the pilot, and he knew the customs uniform.

'I want to examine one of your charts, if you please,' said Hornblower. 'Will you show us the way to the cabin?'

The mate had not a suspicion in the world. He signed to his men to go on with their work and led the way down the brief companion to the after cabin. The mate entered, and politely Hornblower thrust the pilot in next, before him. It was a tiny cabin, but there was sufficient room to be safe when they were at the farther end. He stood by the door and brought out his two pistols.

'If you make a sound,' he said, and excitement rippled his lips into a snarl, 'I will kill you.'

They simply stood and stared at him, but at last the pilot opened his mouth to speak – speech was irrepressible with him.

'Silence!' snapped Hornblower.

He moved far enough into the room to allow Brown and Bush to enter after him.

'Tie 'em up,' he ordered.

Belts and handkerchiefs and scarves did the work efficiently enough; soon the two men were gagged and helpless, their hands tied behind them.

'Under the table with 'em,' said Hornblower. 'Now, be ready for the two hands when I bring 'em down.'

He ran up on deck.

'Here, you two,' he snapped. 'I've some questions to ask you. Come down with me.'

They put down their work and followed him meekly, to the cabin where Hornblower's pistols frightened them into silence. Brown ran on deck for generous supply of line with which to bind them and to make the lashings of the other two more secure yet. Then he and Bush – neither of them had spoken as yet since the adventure began – looked to him for further orders.

'Watch 'em,' said Hornblower. 'I'll be back in five minutes with a crew. There'll be one more man at least to make fast.'

He went up to the quay again, and along to where the gangs of galley slaves were assembling, weary after their day's work of unloading. The ten chained men under the sergeant whom he addressed looked at him with lack-lustre eyes, only wondering faintly what fresh misery this spruce colonel was bringing them.

'Sergeant,' he said. 'Bring your party down to my ship. There is work for them there.'

'Yes, Colonel,' said the sergeant.

He rasped an order at the weary men, and they followed Hornblower down the quay. Their bare feet made no sound, but the chain which ran from waist to waist clashed rhythmically with their stride.

'Bring them down on to the deck,' said Hornblower. 'Now come down into the cabin for your orders.'

It was all so easy, thanks to that uniform and star. Hornblower had to try hard not to laugh at the sergeant's bewilderment as they disarmed him and tied him up. It took no more than a significant gesture with Hornblower's pistol to make the sergeant indicate in which pocket was the key of the prisoners' chain.

'I'll have these men laid out under the table, if you please, Mr Bush,' said Hornblower. 'All except the pilot. I want him on deck.'

The sergeant and the mate and the two hands were laid out, none too gently, and Hornblower went out on deck while the others dragged the pilot after him; it was nearly quite dark now, with only the moon shining. The galley slaves were squatting listlessly on the hatchcoaming. Hornblower addressed them quietly. Despite his difficulty with the language, his boiling excitement conveyed itself to them.

'I can set you free,' he said. 'There will be an end of beatings and slavery if you will do what I order. I am an English officer, and I am going to sail this ship to England. Does anyone not want to come?'

There was a little sigh from the group; it was as if they could not believe they were hearing aright – probably they could not.

'In England,' went on Hornblower, 'you will be rewarded. There will be a new life awaiting you.'

Now at last they were beginning to understand that they had not been brought on board the cutter for further toil, that there really was a chance of freedom.

'Yes, sir,' said a voice.

'I am going to unfasten your chain,' said Hornblower. 'Remember this. There is to be no noise. Sit still until you are told what to do.'

He fumbled for the padlock in the dim light, unlocked it and snapped it open – it was pathetic, the automatic gesture with which the first man lifted his arms. He was accustomed to being locked and unlocked daily, like an animal. Hornblower set free each man in turn, and the chain clanked on the deck; he stood back with his hands on the butts of his pistols ready in case of trouble, but there was no sign of any. The men stood dazed – the transition from slavery to freedom had taken no more than three minutes.

Hornblower felt the movement of the cutter under his feet as the wind swung her; she was bumping gently against the fends-off hung between her and the quay. A glance over the side confirmed his conclusions – the tide had not yet begun to ebb. There were still some minutes to wait, and he turned to Brown, standing restless aft of the mainmast with the pilot sitting miserably at his feet.

'Brown,' he said quietly, 'run down to our boat and bring me my parcel of clothes. Run along now – what are you waiting for?'

Brown went unhappily. It seemed dreadful to him that his captain should waste precious minutes over recovering his clothes, and should even trouble to think of them. But Hornblower was not as mad as he might appear. They could not start until the tide turned, and Brown might as well be employed fetching clothes as standing fidgeting. For once in his life Hornblower had no intention of posing before his subordinates. His head was clear despite his excitement.

'Thank you,' he said, as Brown returned, panting with the canvas bag. 'Get me my uniform coat out.'

He stripped off his colonel's tunic and put on the coat which Brown held for him, experiencing a pleasant thrill as his fingers fastened the buttons with their crown and anchor. The coat was sadly crumpled, and the gold lace bent and broken, but still it was a uniform, even though the last time he had worn it was months ago when they had been capsized in the Loire. With this coat on his back he could no longer be accused of being a spy, and should their attempt result in failure and recapture it would shelter both himself and his subordinates. Failure and recapture were likely possibilities, as his logical brain told him, but secret murder now was not. The stealing of the cutter would attract sufficient public attention to make that impossible. Already he had bettered his position – he could not be shot as a spy nor be quietly strangled in prison. If he were recaptured now he could only be tried on the old charge of violation of the laws of war, and Hornblower felt that his recent exploits might win him sufficient public sympathy to make it impolitic for Bonaparte to press even that charge.

It was time for action now. He took a belaying pin from the rail, and walked up slowly to the seated pilot, weighing the instrument meditatively in his hand.

'Monsieur,' he said, 'I want you to pilot this ship out to sea.'

The pilot goggled up at him in the faint moonlight.

'I cannot,' he gabbled. 'My professional honour – my duty –'

Hornblower cut him short with a menacing gesture of the belaying pin.

'We are going to start now,' he said. 'You can give instructions or not, as you choose. But I tell you this, monsieur. The moment this ship touches ground, I will beat your head into a paste with this.'

Hornblower eyed the white face of the pilot – his moustache was lop-sided and ridiculous now after his rough treatment. The man's eyes were on the belaying pin with which Hornblower was tapping the palm of his hand, and Hornblower felt a little thrill of triumph. The threat of a pistol bullet through the head would not have been sufficient for this imaginative southerner. But the man could picture so clearly the crash of the belaying pin upon his skull, and the savage blows which would beat him to death, that the argument Hornblower had selected was the most effective one.

'Yes, monsieur,' said the pilot, weakly.

'Right,' said Hornblower. 'Brown, lash him to the rail, there. Then we can start. Mr Bush, will you take the tiller, if you please?'

The necessary preparations were brief; the convicts were led to the halliards and the ropes put in their hands, ready to haul on the word of command. Hornblower and Brown had so often before had experience in pushing raw crews into their places, thanks to the all-embracing activities of the British press-gangs, and it was good to see that Brown's French, eked out by the force of his example, was sufficient for the occasion.

'Cut the warps, sir?' volunteered Brown.

'No. Cast them off,' snapped Hornblower.

Cut warps left hanging to the bollards would be a sure proof of a hurried and probably illegal departure; to cast them off meant possibly delaying inquiry and pursuit by a few more minutes, and every minute of delay might be precious in the uncertain future. The first of the ebb was tightening the ropes now, simplifying the business of getting away from the quay. To handle the tiny fore-and-aft rigged ship was an operation calling for little either of the judgement or of the brute strength which a big square rigger would demand, and the present circumstances – the wind off the quay and the ebbing tide – made the only precaution necessary that of casting off the stern warp before the bow, as Brown understood as clearly as Hornblower. It happened in the natural course of events, for Hornblower had to fumble in the dim light to disentangle the clove hitches with which some French sailor had made fast, and Brown had completed his share long before him. The push of the tide was swinging the cutter away from the quay. Hornblower, in the uncertain light, had to time his moment for setting sail, making allowance for the unreliability of his crew, the eddy along the quayside, the tide and the wind.

'Hoist away,' said Hornblower, and then, to the men, 'Tirez'.

Mainsail and jib rose, to the accompaniment of the creaking of the blocks. The sails flapped, bellied, flapped again. Then they filled, and Bush at the tiller – the cutter steered with a tiller, not a wheel – felt a steady pressure. The cutter was gathering way; she was changing from a dead thing to a live. She heeled the tiniest fraction to the breeze with a subdued creaking of her cordage, and simultaneously Hornblower heard a little musical chuckle from the bows as her forefoot bubbled through the water. He picked up the belaying pin again, and in three strides was at the

'*Monsieur, I want you to pilot this ship out to sea*'

pilot's side, balancing the instrument in his hand.

'To the right, monsieur,' gabbled the individual. 'Keep well to the right.'

'Port your helm, Mr Bush. We're taking the starboard channel,' said Hornblower, and then, translating the further hurried instructions of the pilot. 'Meet her! Keep her at that!'

The cutter glided on down the river in the faint moonlight. From the bank of the river she must make a pretty picture – no one would guess that she was not setting forth on some quite legitimate expedition.

The pilot was saying something else now; Hornblower bent his ear to listen. It had regard to the advisability of having a man at work with the lead taking soundings, and Hornblower would not consider it for a moment. There were only Brown and himself who could do that, and they both might be wanted at any moment in case it should be necessary for the cutter to go about – moreover, there would be bound to be a muddle about fathoms and meters.

'No,' said Hornblower. 'You will have to do your work without that. And my promise still holds good.'

He tapped his palm with the belaying pin, and laughed. That laugh surprised him, it was so blood-curdling in its implications. Anyone hearing it would be quite sure that Hornblower was determined upon clubbing the pilot to death if they went aground. Hornblower asked himself if he were acting and was puzzled to discover that he could not answer the question. He could not picture himself killing a helpless man – and yet he could not be sure. This fierce, relentless determination that consumed him was something new to him, just as it always was. He was aware of the fact that once he had set his hand to a scheme he never allowed any consideration to stop his carrying it through, but he always looked upon himself as fatalistic or resigned. It was always startling to detect in himself qualities which he admired in other men. But it was sufficient, and satisfactory, for the moment, to know that the pilot was quite sure that he would be killed in an unpleasant fashion if the cutter should touch ground.

Within half a mile it was necessary to cross to the other side – it was amusing to note how this vast estuary repeated on a grand scale the characteristics of the upper river, where the clear channel serpentined from shore to shore between the sandbanks. At the pilot's warning Hornblower got his motley crew together in case it might be necessary to go about, but the precaution was needless. Closehauled, and with the tide running fast behind her, the cutter glided across, Hornblower and Brown at the sheets, and Bush at the tiller demonstrating once more what an accomplished seaman he was. They steadied her with the wind again over her quarter, Hornblower anxiously testing the direction of the wind and looking up at the ghostly sails.

'Monsieur,' pleaded the pilot. 'Monsieur, these cords are tight.'

Hornblower laughed again, horribly.

'They will serve to keep you awake, then,' he said.

His instinct had dictated the reply; his reason confirmed it. It would be best to show no hint of weakness towards this man who had it in his power to wreck everything – the more firmly the pilot was convinced of his captor's utter pitilessness the less chance there was of his playing them false. Better that he should endure the pain of tight ligatures than that three men should risk imprisonment and death. And suddenly Hornblower remembered the four other men – the sergeant and the mate and the two hands – who lay gagged and bound in the cabin. They must be highly uncomfortable, and probably fairly near to suffocation. It could not be helped. No one could be spared for a moment from the deck to go below and attend them. There they must lie until there was no hope of rescue for them.

He found himself feeling sorry for them, and put the feeling aside. Naval history teemed with stories of recaptured prizes, in which the prisoners had succeeded in overpowering weak prize crews. He was going to run no risk of that. It was interesting to note how his mouth set itself hard at the thought without his own volition; and it was equally interesting to observe how his reluctance to go home and face the music reacted contrariwise upon his resolution to see this affair through. He did not want to fail, and the thought that he might be glad of failure because of the postponement of the settlement of his affairs only made him more set in his determination not to fail.

'I will loosen the cords,' he said to the pilot, 'when we are off Noirmoutier. Not before.'

'You'll die in Singapore'

C. McCORMAC

Seventeen men escaped from the Japanese prison camp in Singapore in 1941, but the bid for freedom left two of their number dead. For the survivors, there was a hazardous journey ahead.

We decided to make our way to the Causeway in groups of twos and threes, with about twenty yards between each group. Don and I were to lead the way, for I was in familiar territory and knew the roads and the best points at which to cross them. We were to regroup on the far side of the Naval Base Road, which led to the Causeway. The latter was the danger spot and was certain to be well patrolled and guarded.

We set off, Don and I in front, the next group some twenty-five yards behind, from which distance they could just see our shadowy figures moving cautiously from tree to tree. At first we kept to the welcome gloom of the rubber trees on the south side of the Yio Chu Kang Road. We passed the W.T. station, then a small burned-out village. There was no sign of life among the charred ruins. Then we came to a woodland area again, close to where I had joined the road-blocking party before Singapore had fallen: how many weeks ago....

At last we reached the Naval Base Road, and saw at the

bottom of it the twinkling lights of the Causeway over the Johore Straits. On the other side were the mainland, the hills, the jungle, the guerrillas. Our chance of freedom. Near the Causeway Don and I stopped among the twisted trunks and roots of the mangroves, waiting for the rest of the party to catch up. It was agreed that if we got across the Straits we would again split into pairs and make our way independently towards the Kuala Lipis hills.

Once assembled we made a compact group and, bent low from the hips, we edged slowly forward across the mud-flats towards the water, which we could hear lapping against the shore. The mud-flats were slippery and quite devoid of cover. But there, thank God, drawn a little above the water's edge, were the two boats.

'Good old Rodriguez!' muttered a Welshman close behind me. 'So he played ball after all!'

'Shut up, you fool!' snapped Don.

Instantly all of us stiffened and froze motionless. Only ten yards away, dead in front of us, a number of dark figures were walking purposefully towards the boats. A Japanese patrol. Had we stood still and remained quiet, we might perhaps have got away with it. But from the rear of our party came a frightened yell.

'Japs!'

There were startled orders from the shadowy figures ahead, then the biting orange flashes of point-blank rifle-fire. We had only one chance. Springing forward as one man, we rushed the patrol. Clubs and bayonets wielded by desperate men are terrible weapons. In a second we were among them, and a slithering mass of bodies fought savagely beside the quietly lapping water. I saw the white gleam of a Jap's teeth and, like a maniac, slashed my bayonet at his face. Together we dropped onto the mud and I felt him squirming beneath me, his nails tearing into my thighs. I changed my grip on the bayonet and using it like a dagger, stabbed it again and again into the writhing body clawing round my legs.

'You'll die in Singapore'

As suddenly as it had started, the fight was over.

Together with seven others I scrambled over the fallen bodies and rushed towards the nearest boat. A couple of Japanese fled in silent terror into the fringe of the mangroves. And seven of our party lay dead or dying on the wet, shining mud.

'Come on,' someone muttered. 'In a minute the swines will be swarming out.'

There was just room for the eight of us in one boat, and this we together pushed and shoved down towards the water. It slid smoothly over the slime and mud and, once it was afloat, we tumbled in. The Welshman found a paddle lying in the bottom and with it he pushed off from the shore. He heaved hard, and the rest of us dragged our hands deeply through the water. Slowly – painfully slowly – we moved into the Strait.

'How many dead?' muttered Don.

'Seven, I think.'

'Only half of us left.' The speaker was another Welshman: a small, dark-haired man half-hanging over the gunwale. He was beating frantically at the water, using his hand as a paddle.

I looked round for oars or sail, but apart from the solitary paddle and a short stump of mast the bottom of the boat was almost empty. We tried paddling with our hands, using the paddle as a rudder, but seemed to make very little progress. In spite of our efforts we drifted eastward, parallel to the shore and towards the Causeway. Obviously we were caught in the five-knot current that comes sweeping in from the open sea towards the Causeway, only to turn northward at the last moment and again flow out to sea. As hard as we paddled to the northward we were carried towards the east, towards the Causeway, and the lights and the Japanese.

'Thank heaven it's dark,' growled Don.

But it was not dark for long. Suddenly from the Causeway a searchlight flashed out brilliantly. For a few seconds it flicked on and off, then it steadied into a full broad beam, moving slowly in a golden pathway across the water. There was no escaping it. It was swinging in our direction.

'Down!' I hissed sharply.

Huddled on the floorboards below the level of the gunwale, we lay perfectly still. Suddenly the boat floated into light; light was all round us; and then it was dark again as the beam passed on.

'Don't move,' muttered Don. 'It'll be back.'

It was. Again the pale golden light flooded over the boat; this time the beam steadied and remained trained on us. Every minute we expected to hear the rattle of machine-gun fire or the engine of an approaching launch. But after what seemed like hours, the light moved on and the boat was dark again.

Don peered over the gunwale. 'Keep down, chaps,' he ordered sharply.

There we lay, motionless and terrified, each of us feeling the adjacent bodies panting in and out, in and out.

'It's coming back again,' he grunted. 'Keep right down.'

The searchlight played around us, like a cat uncertain whether the mouse is dead; then suddenly it cut off. As, with grunts and groans, we pulled ourselves up from our cramped positions, I saw that the scattered lights on the Causeway were much further away. We must have moved round with the current, have drifted up to and parallel to the Causeway, and were now drifting away from it, westwards, out to sea.

'Not much point in trying to paddle,' I said. 'There's a five-knot tide here and it's taking us just about in the right direction.'

'Thank God for that!' Don began to button up his shirt, for the night wind, striking off the water, was keen and chill.

It was reassuring to see the lights of the Causeway fading further and further into the distance, away into the milky haze of the horizon. All the same we were heading out to sea, out into the broad Strait of Malacca. I hoped that the tide would sweep us up the Malay Peninsula, and that, once we had drifted a fair way from Singapore, we would be able to paddle ourselves ashore into the mangrove swamps along the west coast of Malaya.

It was cold in the boat and none of us were wearing more than a tattered shirt, shorts and shoes. Our limbs were aching after the twelve-mile rush across the island from Pasir Panjang to the Causeway. Our bodies weren't used to that sort of exertion. My own legs were still smarting from the clawing scratches of the Japanese soldier, and congealed blood had thickened where the barbed wire had cut into my head and shoulders. We were a motley-looking crew, huddled closely together for warmth on the floorboards of the dilapidated twelve-foot boat. The Welshman was singing softly.

I crawled on hands and knees round the boat, taking stock of our few provisions. Up in the bows I came across a small drum of water, nearly full, also a few strips of dried fish and some rotten fruit. We shared the food round and half the water. There wasn't much for each man, but the water was nectar to us. Over the stern of the boat was a half-disintegrated covering of old and wispy straw, and under it a short mast. It was all sadly derelict, but the boat stayed afloat. I was dog-tired and, remembering that sleep had escaped me the night before, I nodded off with the others to the slight rhythmic pitching of the boat. Only the night before! Surely too much had happened, too quickly, for it to have been only yesterday morning that we were paraded between the atap huts of Pasir Panjang. It seemed impossible to believe that we were no longer prisoners, that this morning there would be no Jap guards to prod us into wakefulness, that there would be no barbed-wire cage around us – nothing but the open sea. The dawn, I thought, would find us free men.

The sun rose cold, fresh, and pink, its rays shafting flatly across the sea, whose grey surface caught and reflected in a myriad flashes the new light of day. Over to the east, several miles distant, was a thin pencil of land. We had drifted far. In the drum there were only a few inches of water. Though our tongues were beginning to feel thick and furry and our lips dry, we decided to leave the water and hold out as long as we could; for we knew the heat of day could bring terrors as great as, if not greater than the cold of night. But at first we found the sun's warmth on our stiffened bodies comforting as a hot bath in frosty weather. We took turns on the paddle, using our strength economically in an attempt to head the boat north-east towards the land. We made little progress. Then we tried paddling in unison with our hands; we moved with the élan of a water-flea crossing the Pacific. After an hour we gave it up.

'There's a slight breeze, Don,' I said. 'Let's tie our shirts together and try to rig up a sail.'

We were just starting to peel them off when Don drew his breath in sharply.

'Hold it!' he snapped.

He pointed to the east and I followed the line of his finger towards the distant strip of land. There, low on the horizon, were two dots in the clear morning sky, becoming rapidly larger. Presently we heard the low hum of engines. Aircraft.

'Recognize 'em, Mac?'

'Not yet. They're fighters, I think.'

The planes were low over the water and flying directly towards us. A quarter of a mile away they seemed to be heading to the north of us; then one banked sharply towards us, followed immediately by the other.

'Look out!' I yelled. 'They're Zeros.'

'Overboard!' shouted Don. And he dived over the gunwale. In no time I was in beside him, and I remember my surprise at finding the water so warm. Three more of us jumped into the sea, but the others stayed crouched low in the bottom of the boat, their eyes following the aircraft as if hypnotized. The Zeros roared in only a few feet above us, then they climbed sharply until they were again mere specks in the sky. Then they turned in for the kill, sweeping down on the boat in a long shallow dive, their throttles wide open, little darts of flame spouting from the cannon at either wingroot. Those still in the boat tumbled over the side, one of them screaming 'Watch out for sharks!'

I swam away fast and, as my ears filled with the roar of the fighters, took a deep lungful of air and dived under the water with all the power I could muster. I held my breath as long as I could and then, when the strain was at breaking-point, I surfaced like a fish thrown up by an under-water explosion. Behind me, the sea was churned up by cannon-shells and the boat was upside down. I could see only three heads bobbing about in the fringe of the churned-up water.

'Look out, here they come again!' It was – thank God – an Australian voice: Don's. I dived again. Twice more the Zeros, cannon and machine-guns blazing, swept down on the boat; then they circled low over the water. Finally they climbed high into the western sky and headed away up the Malacca Strait. I made sure they were out of sight before I swam back to the shell-holed keel of the boat, which was upside down but still floating. Don reached it just before me, and we clung on breathlessly, looking round at the foamflecked waves for the other six. Only two heads appeared; and only two men, gasping for air, splashed their way over to my side of the keel and there sought a grip on the smooth, slippery wood.

'Let's turn it over,' panted Don, and he swam over to our side.

The four of us trod water and heaved together until the boat rolled sluggishly over, bringing a mass of water inside it, so that the gunwale was only just above the surface. We were scared of sharks, and pulling ourselves into the boat, started to bale out furiously with our hands.

There was no sign of the others. Don and I watched anxiously for them, but the sea, apart from our riddled boat and the distant haze of land, was empty and devoid of any sign of life.

I caught Don's eye.

'Sharks or bullets,' I said.

So now we were four. Four out of seventeen. Two had died on the jungle fringe, breaking out from Pasir Panjang; seven more on the moon-lit mud close to Kranji Point; now another four had found their grave in the warm, untroubled waters of the Malacca Strait. We had covered perhaps twenty out of the two thousand miles to Australia; and, so pitiably soon, there were only four of us left.

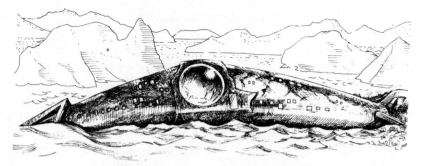

Want of Air

JULES VERNE

**Captain Nemo's amazing submarine, the
Nautilus, has got into trouble in Antarctic ice.**

Around the *Nautilus*, above and below, was an impenetrable
wall of ice. We were prisoners to the iceberg. I watched the
Captain. His countenance had resumed its habitual
imperturbability.

'Gentlemen,' he said calmly, 'there are two ways of dying in
the circumstances in which we are placed.' (This inexplicable
person had the air of a mathematical professor lecturing to his
pupils.) 'The first is to be crushed; the second is to die of
suffocation. I do not speak of the possibility of dying of hunger,
for the supply of provisions in the *Nautilus* will certainly last
longer than we shall. Let us then calculate our chances.'

'As to suffocation, Captain,' I replied, 'that is not to be feared,
because our reservoirs are full.'

'Just so; but they will only yield two days' supply of air. Now,
for thirty-six hours we have been hidden under the water, and
already the heavy atmosphere of the *Nautilus* requires renewal.
In forty-eight hours our reserve will be exhausted.'

'Well, Captain, can we be delivered before forty-eight hours?'

'We will attempt it, at least, by piercing the wall that
surrounds us.'

'On which side?'

'Sound will tell us. I am going to run the *Nautilus* aground on the lower bank, and my men will attack the iceberg on the side that is least thick.'

Captain Nemo went out. Soon I discovered by a hissing noise that the water was entering the reservoirs. The *Nautilus* sank slowly, and rested on the ice at a depth of 350 yards, the depth at which the lower bank was immersed.

'My friends,' I said, 'our situation is serious, but I rely on your courage and energy.'

Sir,' replied the Canadian, 'I am ready to do anything for the general safety.'

'Good, Ned!' and I held out my hand to the Canadian.

'I will add', he continued, 'that being as handy with the pick-axe as with the harpoon, if I can be useful to the Captain, he can command my services.'

'He will not refuse your help. Come, Ned!'

I led him to the room where the crew of the *Nautilus* were putting on their cork jackets. I told the Captain of Ned's proposal, which he accepted. The Canadian put on his sea-costume, and was ready as soon as his companions. When Ned was dressed, I re-entered the drawing-room, where the panes of glass were open, and, posted near Conseil, I examined the ambient beds that supported the *Nautilus*. Some instants after, we saw a dozen of the crew set foot on the bank of ice, and among them Ned Land, easily known by his stature. Captain Nemo was with them. Before proceeding to dig the walls, he took the soundings, to be sure of working in the right direction. Long sounding lines were sunk in the side walls, but after fifteen yards they were again stopped by the thick wall. It was useless to attack it on the ceiling-like surface, since the iceberg itself measured more than 400 yards in height. Captain Nemo then sounded the lower surface. There ten yards of wall separated us from the water, so great was the thickness of the ice-field. It was necessary, therefore, to cut from it a piece equal in extent to the waterline of the *Nautilus*. There were about 6,000 cubic yards to detach, so as to dig a hole by which we could descend to the icefield. The work was begun immediately, and carried on with indefatigable energy. Instead of digging round the *Nautilus*, which would have involved greater difficulty, Captain Nemo had an immense trench made at eight yards from the port quarter. Then the men set to work simultaneously with their screws, on several points of its circumference. Presently the pickaxe attacked this compact matter vigorously, and large blocks were detached from the mass. By a curious effect of specific gravity, these blocks, lighter than water, fled, so to speak, to the vault of the tunnel, that increased in thickness at the top in proportion as it diminished at the base. But that mattered little, so long as the lower part grew thinner. After two hours' hard work, Ned Land came in exhausted. He and his comrades were replaced by new workers, whom Conseil and I joined. The second lieutenant of the *Nautilus* superintended us. The water seemed singularly cold, but I soon got warm handling the pickaxe. My movements were free enough, although they were made under a pressure of thirty atmospheres. When I re-entered, after working two hours, to take some food and rest, I found a perceptible difference between the pure fluid with which the Rouquayrol engine supplied me, and the atmosphere of the *Nautilus*, already charged with carbonic acid. The air had not been renewed for forty-eight hours, and its vivifying qualities were considerably enfeebled. However after a lapse of twelve hours, we had only raised a block of ice one yard thick, on the marked surface, which was about 600 cubic yards! Reckoning that it took twelve hours to accomplish this much, it would take five nights and four days to bring this enterprise to a satisfactory conclusion. Five nights and four days! And we have only air enough for two days in the reservoirs! 'Without taking into account,' said Ned, 'that, even if we get out of this infernal prison, we shall also be imprisoned under the iceberg, shut out from all possible communication with the atmosphere.' True enough! Who could then foresee the minimum of time necessary for our deliverance? We might be suffocated before the *Nautilus* could regain the surface of the waves! Was it destined to perish in this ice tomb, with all those it enclosed? The situation was terrible. But everyone had looked the danger in the face, and each was determined to do his duty to the last.

As I expected, during the night a new block a yard square was carried away, and still farther sank the immense hollow. But in the morning when, dressed in my cork jacket, I traversed the slushy mass at a temperature of six or seven degrees below zero, I remarked that the side walls were gradually closing in. The beds of water farthest from the trench, that were not warmed by the men's mere work, showed a tendency to solidification. In presence of this new and imminent danger, what would become of our chances of safety, and how hinder the solidification of this liquid medium, that would burst the partitions of the *Nautilus* like glass?

I did not tell my companions of this new danger. What was the good of damping the energy they displayed in the painful work of escape? But when I went on board again, I told Captain Nemo of this grave complication.

'I know it,' he said, in that calm tone which could counteract the most terrible apprehensions. 'It is one danger more; but I see no way of escaping it; the only chance of safety is to go quicker than solidification. We must be beforehand with it, that is all.'

On this day for several hours I used my pickaxe vigorously. The work kept me up. Besides, to work was to quit the *Nautilus*, and breathe directly the pure air drawn from the reservoirs, and supplied by our apparatus, and to quit the impoverished and vitiated atmosphere. Towards evening the trench was dug one yard deeper. When I returned on board, I was nearly suffocated by the carbonic acid with which the air was filled. Ah! if we had only the chemical means to drive away this deleterious gas. We had plenty of oxygen; all this water contained a considerable quantity, and by dissolving it with our powerful piles, it would restore the vivifying fluid. I had thought well over it; but of what good was that, since the carbonic acid produced by our respiration had invaded every part of the vessel? To absorb it, it was necessary to fill some jars with caustic potash, and to shake them incessantly. Now this substance was wanting on board, and nothing could replace it. On that evening, Captain Nemo ought to open the taps of his reservoirs, and let some pure air into the interior of the *Nautilus*; without this precaution, we could not get rid of the sense of suffocation. The next day, 26th March, I resumed my miner's work in beginning the fifth yard. The side walls and the lower surface of the iceberg thickened visibly. It was evident that they would meet before the *Nautilus* was able to disengage itself. Despair seized me for an instant, my pickaxe nearly fell from my hands. What was the good of digging if I must be suffocated, crushed by the water that was turning into stone? A punishment that the ferocity of the savages even would not have invented! Just then Captain Nemo passed near me. I touched his hand and showed him the walls of our prison. The wall to port had advanced to at least four yards from the hull of the *Nautilus.* The Captain understood me, and signed to me to follow him. We went on board. I took off my cork jacket, and accompanied him into the drawing-room.

'M. Aronnax, we must attempt some desperate means, or we shall be sealed up in this solidified water as in cement.'

'Yes; but what is to be done?'

'Ah, if my *Nautilus* were strong enough to bear this pressure without being crushed!'

'Well?' I asked, not catching the Captain's idea.

'Do you not understand', he replied, 'that this congelation of water will help us? Do you not see that, by its solidification, it would burst through this field of ice that imprisons us, as, when it freezes, it bursts the hardest stones? Do you not perceive that it would be an agent of safety instead of destruction?'

'Yes, Captain, perhaps. But whatever resistance to crushing the *Nautilus* possesses, it could not support this terrible pressure, and would be flattened like an iron plate.'

'I know it, sir. Therefore we must not reckon on the aid of nature, but on our own exertions. We must stop this solidification. Not only will the side walls be pressed together; but there is not ten feet of water before or behind the *Nautilus*. The

On this day for several hours I used my pickaxe vigorously

congelation gains on us on all sides.'

'How long will the air in the reservoirs last for us to breathe on board?'

The Captain looked in my face. 'After tomorrow they will be empty!'

A cold sweat came over me. However, ought I to have been astonished at the answer? On 22nd March, the *Nautilus* was in the open polar seas. We were at 26°. For five days we had lived on the reserve on board. And what was left of the respirable air must be kept for the workers. Even now, as I write, my recollection is still so vivid that an involuntary terror seizes me, and my lungs seem to be without air. Meanwhile, Captain Nemo reflected silently, and evidently an idea had struck him; but he seemed to reject it. At last, these words escaped his lips:

'Boiling water!' he muttered.

'Boiling water?' I cried.

'Yes, sir. We are enclosed in a space that is relatively confined. Would not jets of boiling water, constantly injected by the pumps, raise the temperature in this part, and stay the congelation?'

The thermometer then stood at seven degrees outside. Captain Nemo took me to the galleys, where the vast distillatory machines stood that furnished the drinkable water by evaporation. They filled these with water, and all the electric heat from the piles was thrown through the worms bathed in the liquid. In a few minutes this water reached a hundred degrees. It was directed towards the pumps, while fresh water replaced it in proportion. The heat developed by the troughs was such that cold water, drawn up from the sea, after only having gone through the machines, came boiling into the body of the pump. The injection was begun, and three hours after the thermometer marked six degrees below zero outside. One degree was gained. Two hours later, the thermometer only marked four degrees.

'We shall succeed,' I said to the Captain, after having anxiously watched the result of the operation.

'I think', he answered, 'that we shall not be crushed. We have no more suffocation to fear.'

During the night the temperature of the water rose to one degree below zero. The injections could not carry it to a higher point. But as the congelation of the sea-water produces at least two degrees, I was at last reassured against the dangers of solidification.

The next day, 27th March, six yards of ice had been cleared, four yards only remaining to be cleared away. There was yet forty-eight hours' work. The air could not be renewed in the interior of the *Nautilus*. And this day would make it worse. An intolerable weight oppressed me. Towards three o'clock in the evening, this feeling rose to a violent degree. Yawns dislocated my jaws. My lungs panted as they inhaled this burning fluid, which became rarefied more and more. A moral torpor took hold of me. I was powerless, almost unconscious. My brave Conseil, though exhibiting the same symptoms and suffering in the same manner, never left me. He took my hand and encouraged me, and I heard him murmur: 'Oh, if I could only not breathe, so as to leave more air for my master!'

Tears came into my eyes on hearing him speak thus. If our situation to all was intolerable in the interior, with what haste and gladness would we put on our cork jackets to work in our turn! Pickaxes sounded on the frozen ice-beds. Our arms ached, the skin was torn off our hands. But what were these fatigues, what did the wounds matter? Vital air came to the lungs! We breathed! We breathed!

All this time, no one prolonged his voluntary task beyond the prescribed time. His task accomplished, each one handed in turn to his panting companions the apparatus that supplied him with life. Captain Nemo set the example, and submitted first to this severe discipline. When the time came, he gave up his apparatus to another, and returned to the vitiated air on board, calm, unflinching, unmurmuring.

On that day the ordinary work was accomplished with unusual vigour. Only two yards remained to be raised from the surface. Two yards only separated us from the open sea. But the reservoirs were nearly emptied of air. The little that remained ought to be kept for the workers; not a particle for the *Nautilus*. When I went back on board, I was half suffocated. What a night! I know not how to describe it. The next day my breathing was oppressed. Dizziness accompanied the pain in my head, and made me like a drunken man. My companions showed the same symptoms. Some of the crew had rattling in the throat.

On that day, the sixth of our imprisonment, Captain Nemo, finding the pickaxes work too slowly, resolved to crush the ice-bed that still separated us from the liquid sheet. This man's coolness and energy never forsook him. He subdued his physical pains by moral force.

By his orders the vessel was lightened, that is to say, raised from the ice-bed by a change of specific gravity. When it floated they towed it so as to bring it above the immense trench made on the level of the water-line. Then filling his reservoirs of water, he descended and shut himself up in the hole.

Just then all the crew came on board, and the double door of communication was shut. The *Nautilus* then rested on the bed of ice, which was not one yard thick, and which the sounding leads had perforated in a thousand places. The taps of the reservoirs were then opened, and a hundred cubic yards of water was let in, increasing the weight of the *Nautilus* to 1,800 tons. We waited, we listened, forgetting our sufferings in hope. Our safety depended on this last chance. Notwithstanding the buzzing in my head, I soon heard the humming sound under the hull of the *Nautilus*. The ice cracked with a singular noise, like tearing paper, and the *Nautilus* sank.

'We are off!' murmured Conseil in my ear.

I could not answer him. I seized his hand, and pressed it convulsively. All at once, carried away by its frightful over-charge, the *Nautilus* sank like a bullet under the waters, that is to say, it fell as if it was in a vacuum. Then all the electric force was put on the pumps, that soon began to let the water out of the reservoirs. After some minutes, our fall was stopped. Soon, too, the manometer indicated an ascending movement. The screw, going at full speed, made the iron hull tremble to its very bolts, and drew us towards the north. But if this floating under the iceberg is to last another day before we reach the open sea, I shall be dead first.

Half stretched upon a divan in the library, I was suffocating. My face was purple, my lips blue, my faculties suspended. I neither saw nor heard. All notion of time had gone from my mind. My muscles could not contract. I do not know how many hours passed thus, but I was conscious of the agony that was coming over me. I felt as if I was going to die. Suddenly I came to. Some breaths of air penetrated my lungs. Had we risen to the surface of the waves? Were we free of the iceberg? No; Ned and Conseil, my two brave friends, were sacrificing themselves to save me. Some particles of air still remained at the bottom of one apparatus. Instead of using it, they had kept it for me, and while they were being suffocated, they gave me life drop by drop. I wanted to push back the thing; they held my hands, and for some moments I breathed freely. I looked at the clock; it was eleven in the morning. It ought to be the 28th of March. The *Nautilus* went at a frightful pace, forty miles an hour. It literally tore through the water. Where was Captain Nemo? Had he succumbed? Were his companions dead with him? At the moment, the manometer indicated that we were not more than twenty feet from the surface. A mere plate of ice separated us from the atmosphere: could we not break it? Perhaps. In any case the *Nautilus* was going to attempt it. I felt that it was in an oblique position, lowering the stern, and raising the bows. The introduction of water had been the means of disturbing its equilibrium. Then, impelled by its powerful screw, it attacked the icefield from beneath like a formidable battering-ram. It broke it by backing and then rushing forward against the field, which gradually gave way; and at last, dashing suddenly against it, shot forwards on the icy field, that crushed beneath its weight. The panel was opened – one might say torn off – and the pure air came in in abundance to all parts of the *Nautilus*.

Free as a Running Fox

T. D. CALNAN

In 1942 Tommy Calnan's group of R.A.F. prisoners of war is being moved from Spangenberg Castle to a new prison. They have just been put on a train and he has decided it is a good chance to escape.

The train eventually pulled out of the station. I was sitting on a hard wooden bench with eight other prisoners and one German guard, armed with a rifle and a pistol, sharing the compartment. The guard sat in the outside corner seat, his back to the engine. My place was diagonally opposite to him, on the inside of the train, facing the engine. The windows of the compartment were closed and firmly wired in that position from the outside.

In front of me was a lavatory which had two doors, one from my compartment and the other giving access to the adjoining compartment. This next compartment was a mirror image of ours and had the same complement of one guard and eight prisoners.

In a third compartment, which did not in any way connect with ours as the carriage had no corridors, was another small party of prisoners, including the SBO, adjutant and other staff, together with the German officers and NCOs in charge of us.

After we had been journeying for a while and everybody had settled down, I asked the guard if I could use the lavatory. He said not to shut the door, to remember that his rifle was loaded and that he had orders to shoot any prisoner attempting to escape. But he remained relaxed and made no effort to accompany me.

The lavatory had its own window, this time of frosted glass, and it was solidly fixed in the shut position by some arrangement outside the window. It was obvious that if I could get this window open, escaping from the train was going to be no problem.

I heaved down with all my weight on the handle at the top of the window and was delighted to find that it yielded for a tiny fraction of an inch, which gave me a gap just sufficient to slide a knife blade through and explore the system the Germans had used to close it. It seemed to be primitive enough – a tough piece of wire anchored above the window by a large nail hammered into the carriage side and bent over and, at the other end, by another nail hammered into the wooden frame of the window. The way out was so simple, it seemed unbelievable.

My inspection of the lavatory had not taken two minutes and I came back into the compartment buttoning up my trousers for the sake of the German guard. From now on it was essential to keep him happy and unsuspicious. It was also necessary to prevent anyone else from making any bungling attempts which would interfere with my plans. I still had a lot of difficult work to do on the window before I could get it to open easily when the time came and still look firmly secure both from the inside and the outside.

There was only one way of ensuring that I got no interference and that was to announce my intentions, which I did immediately.

Marcus Marsh was sitting next to me and I whispered to him that I was going out through the lavatory window as soon as it was dark and asked him to pass the word around. I added that I would welcome any one person who wanted to come with me, but that I thought two was the limit, if we were to have a hope of getting away undetected. I also asked for food, especially concentrated foods, like chocolate, raisins and sugar.

The word got round the compartment fairly fast. We did not, in fact, have to be particularly cautious because it was obvious that, unless he was a very cunning fellow and a remarkably good actor, our guard spoke not a word of any language but his own. Nevertheless we whispered, probably because the atmosphere had become conspiratorial.

Everybody in turn looked at me as they got the message but I saw no response in anybody's eyes. I had rather expected somebody to signify that they would like to come along, but at that early stage I was not particularly concerned as my mind was working out methods to get the window fixed. And there were still five or six hours of daylight.

Marcus reminded me of the stolen maps, which I had completely forgotten. I got them out of my pocket and put them inside the cardboard box which I held on my knees. I sorted out Marcus's Deutschmarks and slipped them into his hand. Surreptitiously he counted them.

'Here, Tommy,' he said, nudging my elbow, 'take these. There are fifty marks. If you don't get away, let me have them back.'

'Thanks a lot, Marcus. They'll be very useful. If you don't mind I'll go through these maps later. First I want to get started on the lavatory window. There'll be lots of time to waste before it gets dark.'

I had glanced very briefly at the crumpled maps and realized that they represented a real treasure. I wanted to go through them calmly and in detail.

I spent the next half an hour retrieving my tools from their hiding places and secreting them in various pockets. I also took my German knife, which looked as if it might be the most useful tool of all of them.

It was time to get to work.

I asked the guard if I could go and visit the next compartment, passing through the lavatory, to talk to my friends there and borrow some cigarettes. The guard agreed but said I was to leave both lavatory doors open. This was no handicap as the guard could not see what was happening in the lavatory from where he sat.

I did not go through to the next compartment, but spent five minutes in the lavatory working on the window. I discovered that I could reach the nail above the window with my German knife and, after much struggling to obtain the right leverage, I managed to move it. If the extruding part of the nail, which was bent upwards, could be rotated through ninety degrees, the retaining wire could be slipped off and there would be, as far as I could judge, no obstacle to letting the window down. Even if the wire could not be dislodged, I could cut through it with my hacksaw blade in a matter of seconds.

As soon as I was satisfied that I could move the nail, I returned it to its vertical position with the wire in place and intact. I then went back to the compartment and gave the guard one of my few precious cigarettes.

From where he sat, Marcus could see what I was doing in the lavatory and give me warning if our guard got restive or suspicious. He was a natural conspirator and I knew that I could rely on him completely to cover all my moves.

When I sat down again beside him, I asked him to go through to the next compartment and tell them what was going on.

'Tell them there is still room for one more on this job,' I reminded Marcus, 'and get them to start a regular exchange of visits with us.'

I wanted both guards to get used to a casual exchange of prisoners between the two compartments because, in this way, if I did manage to get out of the window, my absence would not be immediately noticed.

During the long afternoon of that tedious train journey, a regular interchange of visits between the compartments gradually became an accepted move by the two guards. But nobody offered to come with me through the window.

Escape Stories

On my third visit to the lavatory I worked on the nail until it would move freely through ninety degrees and back again, without the retaining wire becoming detached. I calculated that that was as much preparation as was needed. I was quite confident that, when the moment came, I could rotate the nail through 180 degrees and slip the wire off. Then all I had to do was to pull down the window and get out.

I was concentrating all my attention on the delicate task of getting the nail back into its original position, when there was a great crash from the compartment.

I whipped round and saw Marcus bending down to retrieve a Red Cross box which had apparently fallen off the rack. The look he gave me was a warning of immediate danger and I hurriedly jammed the window fully shut and stowed my tools in my pockets.

I whipped down my trousers and squatted on the lavatory seat. A few seconds later, the guard appeared in the doorway. He was embarrassed to find me so occupied and retreated.

'Später, später,' he muttered as he turned his back.

'Ich bin fertig,' I called after him, as I pulled the plug. I redressed quickly and left the lavatory free for the guard. I should have thought of it, the poor bastard had not relieved himself in four hours.

After that scene, it was obvious that I would have to stay out of the lavatory for some time. I settled down to examine the stolen maps and to complete all my preparations for a getaway.

I studied the maps one by one, well covered by the open top of my Red Cross box, which lay on my knee. There were eleven maps in all. For my own use I selected a large-scale plan of the docks of Stettin and another of the docks at Danzig. The Schaffhausen crossing was also covered in minute detail, and I put it aside. At that point in time, I had no idea which way I would be heading after getting off the train.

There were smaller-scale maps of Poland and Czechoslovakia, and of Austria, showing its borders with Italy, Switzerland and Germany, and of the south-west corner of Germany showing the whole Swiss border. There was a map of northern Germany, including the Dutch and Danish frontiers.

I did not want to be greedy so I added two more maps to my stock. One of central Germany, which would cover the area we were travelling through, and the one showing the Swiss–German border.

The rest I gave to Marcus, not doubting that he could get them through the search which was to be expected on arrival at the new camp.

There was still a long wait until dark and my other preparations were soon made. I had no civilian clothes, but was wearing an airman's uniform and quite a smart airman's greatcoat which, with the brass buttons replaced, would pass muster. At least it was better than my Polish greatcoat, which was packed in my kitbag. I decided that as soon as I was off the train I would cut off the brass buttons and replace them with buttons made of wood, which I would whittle from whatever suitable bit of wood I found. I had a needle and cotton.

I stowed my maps and my compass in my pockets and decided to take only the lockpick of my collection of tools as well as the strong penknife. The rest I handed over to Marcus to get through if he could.

My major preoccupation now was food. I had none at all. I discussed the situation with Marcus. He confirmed that there were Red Cross parcels travelling with us on the train, but he had no idea who had charge of them, or where they were. He offered a slight ray of hope.

'I've got the feeling,' he said, 'that we are bound to make a stop soon. We've been going steadily for four hours now and the engine is bound to run out of water or coal or whatever they burn. You can find out where the parcels are at the next stop.'

'Let's hope so,' I replied, 'because there isn't much time. It will be dark in two hours.'

Marcus was right. Less than an hour later, the train stopped at a wayside station and we were allowed off. We were served with hot soup which was most acceptable if not very nourishing. I went looking for the escape committee and eventually ran one of them to earth. I came straight to the point.

'The food,' I demanded, 'the parcels, where are they? I'm getting out as soon as it is dark and I've got to have my escape rations now, at this stop.'

'Don't kid yourself,' he answered, 'you won't get off the train. We're too well guarded.'

I was getting angry.

'Where are those parcels?' I insisted with slow emphasis and subdued fury.

He suddenly became apologetic.

'Well, you see, what happened was this. The Germans transported them to the station for us and there they were put in a separate truck with all the other stores. We can't get at them unless the Germans decide to give them out.'

'Really far-sighted organization on your part,' I said sarcastically. 'What do I do now? Go and ask the Germans for some food because I want to escape?'

'Now listen, Tommy, there is no need to lose your temper.' But I had turned my back and gone to look for Tony.

Tony's news was half good. They had started cutting the floorboards but these were thicker and harder than he had expected and the saw kept breaking. Nevertheless, he hoped to have made a hole big enough to get out of before morning.

'Why don't you join us and bring your saw?' Tony invited.

'I'm sorry, Tony, but I've got my way out all ready. I'm getting off as soon as it's dark. See if you can get the Leutnant to let you swap with somebody in our carriage. So far, nobody has offered to come with me.'

But Tony felt that he could not abandon his hole in the cattle-truck floor and the others who were working with him. I preferred my lavatory window, so we continued our journey in different sections of the train.

Before leaving Tony I gave him my walking-stick, the one with the file in it.

'You can cut a new saw with the file,' I said. 'If you don't get out, try and get it through the search at the new camp. It's the most useful tool we have.'

He took the walking-stick.

'Good luck,' he said. 'Where are you going to aim for?'

'I've just no idea, it depends where I get off the train.'

When the train got moving again it was late in the evening and the light was fading fast. I was getting more and more tense as darkness approached and I was still very angry about the food fiasco. I sensed that my nervousness and rebellious mood were embarrassing to my companions and disturbing their peace.

I asked every fit man in the compartment, directly, whether he wanted to come with me. I got no takers.

This depressed me. In the first place, I wanted company. Secondly, I began to think that they were right and I was wrong. Even if I got safely away from the train, I needed a whole series of miracles to have any hope of reaching and crossing a frontier, with no food and no civilian clothes. Looked at calmly and logically, it was probably wiser to sit back on one's wooden bench in a third-class carriage and hope that a more suitable opportunity would occur some day in the future.

But I could not see it that way. For me, the fact of escaping, even if to nowhere, was a notable victory over my captors. Getting one up on them gave me enough personal satisfaction to make my imprisonment bearable for a long time to come, even if I was recaptured.

I did not even bother to canvass the second compartment. If anybody wanted to escape, he would at least have the energy and initiative to come and tell me.

It was obvious that I was going to have no companion, but I still needed food. I started asking direct questions of each prisoner in turn. Had he any chocolate, raisins, sugar, glucose – anything? I was asking for precious things, rarely seen and jealously hoarded. Heads were shaken and nothing was produced. And my provisions for the great journey into the unknown consisted of a complete loaf of black bread about a foot long and three inches square – the ration for the compartment –

and a one-pound tin of Lyle's Golden Syrup. Two more cumbersome articles could not have been imagined. I considered them in despair as I wondered how I was going to carry them when I wriggled my way through the small window of the lavatory. Again I cursed the obstinacy and inefficiency of the escape committee.

It was now beginning to get really dark and I had the old familiar feeling in my stomach that comes with excitement and fear. Marcus was going to help me out of the window and then close it after me, attempting to push the nail and wire back to their original positions. Marcus had studied the mechanics of the operation and felt sure that, with his knife, he could close the window again so that it looked normal at a casual glance.

When it was fully dark, I turned to Marcus.

'I'm going out at the next stop, whenever that is. As soon as the train starts slowing down, I'll go into the lavatory and get the window ready. You follow me casually just when the train stops.'

'Roger,' he answered. 'Get somebody to come through here from the other compartment, we want a little to-ing and fro-ing.'

The train clattered on through the night. The countryside was completely black and there was no moon. The curtains of the compartment were closely drawn to prevent the faint light of a single bulb in the ceiling being visible outside. There was a noticeable tendency for most of my companions to settle down to sleep and, indeed, I was feeling very sleepy myself. I hoped I would not have to wait too long for the next stop because it was getting more and more difficult to dragoon anybody into making an occasional visit to the other compartment. And it was essential to keep the guard used to this movement and unsuspicious of it.

It must have been about two hours after dark when I felt the brakes go on. Quite definitely the train was slowing down. I waited tensely for a long minute. The deceleration became more pronounced. We were going to stop. I touched Marcus' knee and, as casually as I could, strolled into the lavatory. I had the tin of treacle and the loaf tucked into the top of my tunic, so that my hands were free.

The train was now going very slowly and I started to work feverishly on the window, afraid that I had left it too late. I found I was sweating slightly, although the night was cold. I jerked the window down as hard as I could and got a half-inch gap through which I could work on the nail. The nail rotated easily through the first ninety degrees and I then changed my leverage to work it round to the vertical. I got it down another thirty degrees and found that I could push the wire loop away from the nail – and the window was free.

Marcus was standing right behind me now. The train was barely moving. The brakes went on again and it juddered to a complete halt. Looking through the slit at the top of the window I judged that we had stopped at a signal way out in the country. There was no station, no buildings, no lights, no danger. I nodded to Marcus, pulled the window down cautiously and poked my head out to have a look around.

There was a man standing on the track, less than three yards away, clearly visible in the light from the firebox of the engine. I shut the window fast but quietly. He had his back to me and had not seen anything. Obviously it was the engine driver or his mate and I could not get out of the window while he was standing there.

I explained the situation to Marcus.

'I'll have to wait until we get started again, then when the fireman climbs back into the cab, I'll get out as fast as I can.'

At that moment the train started again, in a series of jerks. I waited while I counted ten to let the fireman get back on board, then pulled down the window. All clear, but we were gathering speed. Hurrying desperately, I leant backwards through the window, reaching upwards on the outside to find a grip for my hands. I got a good hold and then started easing my bottom and legs out through the window. Marcus was shoving and it was a considerable struggle, which, although it may only have lasted seconds, seemed much too long to me, with the train accelerating every second. My loaf of bread jammed and Marcus grabbed it saying he would throw it out after me. Suddenly my feet were out and I was dangling by my hands on the side of the train. I found a purchase for my feet and lowered my handhold to the window sill. I then found a lower platform for my feet and turned to face forwards, hanging on with one hand. The train was now moving frighteningly fast and there was no time to be lost. I pushed off outwards into space with all the force of my legs and one arm, hit the ground with stupefying violence and rolled, falling forward. My elbows and forearms took the brunt of the fall, but as they were well protected by my greatcoat, I did not get hurt. I got a last glimpse of Marcus framed in the window.

I lay absolutely still on the ground, with my head between my arms until the whole length of the train had passed and then, looking up very cautiously, watched its red tail light receding into the darkness.

I stared at the tail light for long minutes, until it had disappeared. Then I listened to the receding noise of the engine. As long as it made the regular chugging, it meant that my escape had not been discovered. And the noise did not stop. It just faded into the distance. I had made a clean getaway.

I was unwilling to move, although I knew I should get as far away from the railway as I could, as soon as possible. The effect of adrenalin which had been pumping into my bloodstream while I was getting through the window had completely worn off. I felt a lassitude, a sense of depression and a sudden complete loss of confidence in myself. I wanted to smoke a cigarette, but dared not.

My eyes had now become adjusted to the dark and I tried to take stock of my immediate surroundings. The first thing I saw was a black object not more than six inches from my nose. I felt it and discovered it was an iron staunchion, made from a piece of rail, stuck vertically into the ground. I thanked my guardian angel for my perfect timing. A tenth of a second later and I

I was dangling by my hands on the side of the train

would have smashed my head on that unfriendly piece of iron.

I pulled myself together and started searching for the loaf that Marcus had thrown after me, crawling on my hands and knees in the pitch dark. The loaf should have been a little way ahead of me and, perhaps, a little farther away from the lines. I felt around for ten minutes, but could not find it and was forced to decide that I would have to abandon my loaf and get away from the area. This depressed me even more. Now I had only a tin of treacle and I would have to eat it with a knife.

The Boiling Water
HAMMOND INNES

Whilst helping to mine manganese ore on a remote Indian Ocean island Commander Bailey gets caught in a freak storm. As he drives his runabout out to *The Strode Trader*, the parent ship which is towing a barge full of the ore, he realises that he is in great danger.

My whole mind, my every nerve became instantly concentrated on driving the boat forward, intent on reaching the ship before she got under way. I had the throttle wide open, leaning forward over the engine casing as though I could by sheer will-power drive her faster. The stern sank in a trough and I heard the break of the wave almost at the moment it thumped me in the back, spilling across the stern, flooding over the gunn'ls as it carried the boat forward like a surfboard. And at the same moment lightning forked across the ship, showing it very near now, so that I could see the prop beginning to thresh the water. The thunder crashed. The barge was swinging away from the ship's side and it was the barge I hit. And as the bows splintered and the boat began to sink under me I jumped, caught the steel edge of the barge's side and hauled myself aboard. Lying there, panting on the grit-grimed plating, I could feel the strong pulsing beat of the *Strode Trader's* engines transmitted through the barge's hull every time it rammed its blunt nose against the ship's side.

I tried to attract their attention, of course, but no human voice could be heard above the turmoil of the storm. A wave broke and then another. The barge's flank was like a breakwater, the waves pouring over the side and cascading down into the half-empty hold. I struggled to my feet, balancing myself to the pitch and roll of the ungainly hulk and in the next flash of lightning waved my hands. But there was nobody on deck. There was a shuddering jar, the clank of steel on steel, and beyond the open cavern of the barge's hold I could see the dark side of the ship towering above me. Food and warmth, the cosy familiarity of my cabin all so near, but nobody to tell Reece to stop his bloody engines and get me off the barge.

The ship was gathering way fast now. She had turned her fat stern to the island and was running down wind. The barge yawed, grinding its bows. I stood and waved and shouted, and still nobody answered.

I began working my way for'ard then. I had almost reached the broader platform of the bows when the stern of the barge was lifted and flung sideways. She lay wallowing for an instant, rolling her topsides into the waves, water pouring over me. Then the bow line tautened with a jerk. It steadied her and I started forward again. It was a mistake, for the bows swung in, both vessels rolling towards each other. The crash as they met caught me off balance. I can remember falling, but that's all.

I came to, gasping and sobbing for breath, a great roaring in my ears. I knew I was drowning and I fought with all my strength, clawing and kicking, with the water gurgling in my lungs and throat and one little horrified corner of my brain aware that my hands and feet were motionless as in a nightmare where the struggle is in the mind and not transmitted into physical action. My brain, groping towards full consciousness, recorded sluggishly – the feel of grit under the palms of my hands, the hardness of solid steel beneath my body, the slosh of

No human voice could be heard above the turmoil of the storm

water resounding loud as in a tank.

I lay still a moment. Then I was gulping air, my mouth filled with grit and the sickening salinity of sea water. Somewhere my head was hurting, a raw burn of pain, and I retched, vomiting nothing but grit and slime. A blinding jar, the crash of steel, a great swooping movement. I was riding a roller-coaster and the water was back. I was afloat in a great sea and being battered to death against a shingle beach. It changed to a sea wall; I could feel its vertical sides as I clawed at it, calling for help, conscious that however hard I called nobody would come to save me since no sound was coming out of my mouth. Another jar and the tide receding – or was I trapped in the engine-room of a sinking ship? Steel under my hands – cold steel, pitted with rust and filmed with grit. A great searing flash and my smarting eyes saw the rusty pit with its vertical steel walls, the pile of ore awash, and the water flooding back at me as the stern lifted, a wall of black filthy water that spilled over me.

This time my muscles responded to the call of my brain. I struggled to my feet and the water broke, knocking me backwards and forcing me to my knees, and as it receded I was sick again. I felt better then and when the water trapped in the bottom of the barge came back at me I was ready for it, my body braced against the steel side. It broke harmlessly against me, surging round my knees, reaching finally to my waist before it receded, sucking at the heap of unloaded ore. The barge was close against the ship's side then, grinding at the steel, and the faint throb that was transmitted to my body told me that the *Strode Trader* was still under way.

The clouds overhead were low, and in the stabs of lightning I could see dark bellying masses constantly on the move, a pattern of suspended vapour that was never still. I could also see that there was no way out of the hold in which I was trapped. It was like a tank, sheer-sided, and roofed at the edges by the overhang of the side deck, and the water inside it rolled back and forth with the movement of the waves; each time I braced myself to withstand the surge and suck of it and each time the effort sapped a little more of my strength. The ship was steaming broadside to the storm now. Her side was a steel wall, rolling and toppling above me, the seas breaking against it. How long before Reece stopped his engines, or would he steam all night? He couldn't anchor now. It was too deep. I looked at my wrist-watch, but my eyes were tired and all I could see in the flickering lightning was the pale disc of it spattered red with the blood dripping from my head. There was a gash somewhere in my scalp below the hair. In fact, the glass was broken and the watch had stopped. Dawn was a long way off.

Ten hours! I wondered whether I could last that long. I felt light-headed and I was shivering, but not with cold for sea and air were both warm; it was exhaustion. The water came and went, rolling nodules of ore. The noise of it sloshing back and forth along the empty barge walls was constant, unending, and behind it were other sounds, the surge of the ship's bow wave, the growl of thunder, the crackle of lightning. It was a wild night and we seemed to be travelling with the storm for it stayed with us, the clouds hanging in great masses so low they seemed pressing down against the high glimmer of the mast-head lights. And then the rain came as it had before in a solid downpour of water, the roar of it drowning out all other sounds.

Time passed and the rain stopped. As before it had flattened the sea so that I no longer had to fight the surge of the water. The wind had gone, too, and the barge lay snugged against the ship's side, not bumping now nor even grinding at the plates, but steady, and the water lapped around my knees. My eyelids drooped and closed, the eyeballs strained by the violent contrasts of million-voltage light and pitch darkness, seared with salt. I dozed standing, never quite losing consciousness, but relaxed now that I didn't have to fight the water. I could survive till dawn. Drowsily I wondered how Peter was faring, what it was like shut up in that small hut with fourteen frightened Pakistanis, and then I was thinking of Reece, wondering what the hell he was playing at. To up anchor and put to sea, that was reasonable enough. He was responsible for the safety of his ship and any captain might reasonably have thought his position insecure. But to go on steaming away from the island . . .

I became conscious then of a change in the beat of the engines. The drowsiness vanished and I was suddenly wide awake. The ship's engines had slowed. The surge of the bow wave died to a murmur. In a brief pause in the thunder I thought I heard the slow threshing of the screw. Then that ceased and I sensed the ship was losing way. I moved out from the side of the barge, climbing the heap of ore so that I could see the ship in the lightning. But of course nothing had changed, it was only that sounds which had become familiar had now ceased. The storm alone remained, thunderous and crackling. It was all forked lightning now. It stabbed and banged around us, the ship's superstructure lit by flashes so that the effect was of a vessel going in with the first wave of a seaborne landing.

Somebody shouted then. I remember it very clearly because it was the first human voice I had heard for what seemed a very long time. He must have been out on the starboard bridge wing for the sound of his voice was clear and distinct. 'Full astern; Full . . .'' The thunder cracked and lightning stabbed, obliterating the rest of it. I think it was Reece and in the momentary silence that followed the thunder I heard the beat of the engines, the thresh of the screw. There was a visual change, too. The ship slid away from me. For one ghastly moment I thought the bow line had been let go and the barge set adrift, but it wasn't that; it was just that the barge was swinging as the ship went astern.

I waited, my head bent back, watching as the side of the ship moved away from me, its position changing. The barge checked at the end of its securing wire. Soon it would swing in again, port side on as the ship gathered stern way. But it didn't. It stayed like that, bows-on to the *Strode Trader*. A figure came out on to the bridge wing. A torch glimmered palely in the flash brilliance of a fork of lightning. The man was peering down. His hand waved. Still nothing happened, the barge bows-on and steady at the end of the bow line, which was taut – a single, slender strand of wire. It was a strange sight, the ship standing there, the lights bright in the darkness, dim as glow-worms when the lightning banged, and not moving though I could hear the engines and the frenzied turning of the screw. A flash, brighter still and close behind me, and in the succeeding blackness the mast, the bridge, the whole superstructure limned with a blue-green light, the ship's whole outline traced in a sort of St. Elmo's fire. And then it happened.

There was a flash, a great sizzling firework fork of electricity – a thousand million volts stabbing down, striking straight at the foremast. I heard it hit. There was a crack as the full blast of power touched the mast top, a crackling and a sizzling, and then the ear-splitting unbelievable sound of the cloud-clash that had sparked it. And with the sound the mast crumpled, falling slowly to lean in drunken nonchalance against the bridge before the heat of that great charge of electricity burned the metal to a molten white. Flames burst like bright orange flowers as the woodwork caught, and then the whole bridge went up, a shower of sparks, a soft whoof of heat rising. It was spectacular, fantastic, beautiful but deadly. *Tiger, tiger, burning bright . . .* My God! I thought. This is it – the ship on fire a thousand miles from any help. And something else – something even more appalling. It had been nagging at my brain, and now suddenly the position of the barge, the man peering down at the water, the call for full astern – it all came together in my mind. The ship was aground.

Aground and on fire, and myself imprisoned in that barge, a helpless spectator as the flames licked higher and higher and figures lit by the glare and the forked flashes ran shouting about the decks. Lightning stabbed again, struck with a blue flash. A lascar seaman caught on the bridge deck was withered instantly, a blackened rag doll dying with a piercing shriek. Hoses were being run out and a jet of water sprang from the nozzle, insignificant against the flames licking up from the bridge superstructure. And where the jet struck the heat of the fire it sent up a little puff of steam that was instantly burned out in the heat. Two more jets and then another bolt of lightning. The ship, with her steel bottom firmly stranded on the sea bed, was earthed; she was acting as a huge lightning conductor.

The flames, the lightning, the ship aground where no land should be – my mind reeled before the extent of the disaster, dazed and unable in that moment to comprehend it. The flames licked the humidity out of the night air and a red glow lit the storm clouds overhead. The heat was intense. My clothes dried on me, became stiff with salt and sweat and the darker streaks of my own blood. I watched for a time, held stupefied by the roaring holocaust of fire, by the sheer fascination of it as a spectacle, not conscious then of any fear, only of the childlike need to gape. But the bow line was not more than fifty or sixty feet long and soon the heat forced me to crouch, seeking the protection of the barge's steel plates. By then my eyeballs were burned dry, my skin parched, my hair like grass. I was glad then of the water in the bottom. I bathed my face and finally lay full-length in it, floating and watching the storm flickering and banging in the red inferno of the clouds.

It was no longer immediately overhead. In fact, that third lightning stab proved to be the last. But lying there in the bottom of the barge with the water buoying me up I wondered whether perhaps the poor wretch who had been fried by that second bolt of lightning wasn't the lucky one. I could hear the roar of the flames, could see the leap and glow of them reflected in the sky, but no longer distracted by the visual excitement of them, my mind groped towards an appreciation of my situation, and the result was frightening. I was like a rat trapped in a giant bath, the heat increasing all the time, the water getting warmer, and if I survived till the fire burned itself out – what then? A lingering death, for I'd no fresh water, no food, no prospect of being rescued. I was tied to a ship that would never move again in seas that were unvisited and in an area that was in the process of volcanic change.

Sparks flew in the night, some burning embers fell with a hiss

into the water close by my feet. My left shoulder was beginning
to stiffen. My whole body ached from my fall and I wished to
God I had never recovered consciousness. I closed my eyes,
wearied to death with the glare and the flicker. I pretended then
that I was back in London, in the little flat I'd rented, lying in a
hot bath. God! I was tired. Would Ida still be in London, or was
she back in Dartmouth now, in the room above the antique shop
where I had first met her? With my eyes closed, the red glare
through my eyelids was like the light of the maroon lampshade
in the bedroom. I saw her then as I had seen her that last night
we had spent together, her slim, warm, golden body emerging
and then the closeness and the warmth, the soft yielding, the
sense of being one. Would she have a child, or had she taken
precautions? I didn't know. Strangely, I found myself hoping it
was the former, hoping that between us we had found new life to
replace the old that would die here in this filthy steel tank. The
thought of that, of life reproducing itself, switched my mind to
John and Mary. All their hopes, and now this. How would they
view my death? Would they feel I had let them down? I felt my
mind recoil from their contempt, seeking to obliterate the
thought of how they'd feel. For their sake, if not for my own, I
must struggle for survival. I knew that. But I was drifting now,
drifting away from the thought of the effort, the terrible ghastly
effort that is involved in dying slowly.

I slept, pretending to myself as I dozed off that I was lying in
my bath, having a little nap, and that soon I'd get up and dry
myself and put on my pyjamas and go to a soft, cool bed. And
Ida was there her dark eyes looking straight into mine, her cheek
pressed against me, her hair falling about her and her hand was
holding me tight, not letting me go, refusing to let me slip away,
but keeping me just on the edge of consciousness. Was this the
knife-edge between life and death? Somewhere there was a
rending crash, the splash and hiss of flaming débris quenched in
water. The thunder died, the lightning, too. The world became
deathly still, only the roar of the fire in the grate, and then that
died down and there were shouts from the pavement below and a

fire engine playing water on a gutted ship across the street.

My mind recorded things, blurring them with the desire for an ordinary setting, an ordinary explanation, whilst I drifted half unconscious. And suddenly the glow was gone and a grey light filtered through my closed eyelids. Dawn was breaking.

I had floated against the remains of the barge's load of ore and was reclining against the piled-up heap. My body ached and my skin was crinkled white with long immersion. It was an effort even to shift my position and I lay there with my eyes open, staring at the rusty interior of the barge, at the water, black and filthy and quite inert. Nothing stirred. There was no sound of the sea. I might have been lying in a tank on dry land for all the movement. The sun came up, a rosy glow for a moment, but then a bright, hard light casting dark shadows. When I stirred – when I made the awful effort of struggling to my feet . . . what should I find? A gutted ship, the crew all gone? Would I be the only living thing? I called out. But my voice was weak. I did not want to call too loudly for then I could continue to lie there, fooling myself that they had not heard. The sun climbed quickly till it touched my body with its warmth, and then the full heat of it was shining directly on me and I knew I had to move, for the sun's heat meant thirst.

I forced myself to my feet and standing on the shingle heap of ore turned and faced the ship. The barge still lay bows-on to it at the full extent of its securing line, held apparently in the grip of some current. The *Strode Trader* was an appalling sight. All the bridge was gone, the whole superstructure a twisted heap of blackened, tortured metal, with here and there charred fragments of wood still clinging like rags of flesh to a burned carcass. The timbers of the hatch covers were scorched but not consumed. The cargo booms, too, though scorched, were still identifiable in the contorted wreckage of the masts. The only structure to escape the fire was the deck housing on the poop aft and as I stood there the sound of Eastern music came faint on the still morning air.

At first I refused to believe it. I was afraid it was in my head,

The Boiling Water

for it was a singing sound – a siren song in the midst of
desolation. The minutes passed and I stood rooted. But still that
music floated in the stillness, something live and real and
unbelievable. It was pipes and drums and a girl's voice singing
sweetly, and all so soft, so insubstantial, so impossible in the
midst of chaos and ruin.

It was a radio, of course. Some poor devil had been listening in
as the lightning struck, one of the lascar crew in the quarters aft,
and he had run, leaving his little portable radio still switched on.
I turned, dejected, but still glad of the sound, and as I turned to
find a means of reaching the barge's deck, I caught a glimpse of
something moving, and then a voice called, giving an order. He
was on the poop, looking over the stern, a man in a rag of a shirt
and clean white trousers neatly creased, all the hair scorched
from his head. It was the second officer – Lennie – and before I
knew it I was standing on the deck of the barge, scrambling to
the bows and shouting to him. 'Lennie! Lennie!'

He turned and I can still see him, standing shocked and
unbelieving as though he thought I were a ghost. And then he
called back, dived limping to the deck house, and a moment later
half a dozen lascars like demon beggars dressed in rags and black
as sweeps came slowly, wearily along the deck to pull on the bow
line and bring the barge alongside.

'I didn't know,' Lennie said as they hauled me up at the end of
a rope to what had once been a white scrubbed deck of laid pine
and was now black charcoal with the plates all showing, buckled
by the heat. 'Nobody knew you were there.' And then Reece
arrived and Blake, their eyes red-rimmed and sunk deep in their
sockets, all moving and speaking slow with the dazed look of
men who have gazed into the mouth of hell and do not yet
believe that they are still alive.

'What happened?' I asked. 'Why is the ship aground?' But it
was no good asking questions of men so tired they could hardly
stand. In any case, they didn't know, they barely cared. They'd
fought a fire all night and somehow they had won. That was
enough – for the moment.

White Coolies

BETTY JEFFREY

**Betty Jeffrey was an Australian army nurse in
the Second World War. When Singapore was
attacked, all the nurses were evacuated by boat.**

But the planes had not finished with us. Over they came again
and machine-gunned the deck and all the lifeboats – rather
effectively. The ropes holding the three lifeboats on our side
were severed. Two dropped into the sea. One filled and sank, the
other turned upside down and floated away. The third was
already manned by two Malay sailors and I'm sure they never
anticipated such a quick trip down. I couldn't help laughing at
the expressions on their faces as they hit the water and found
that their boat had filled almost immediately and left them.

Beth Cuthbertson searched the ship when it was at a very odd
angle to make sure all wounded people had been taken off and
that nobody remained, while other nurses were busy getting
people into the sea.

At this stage there were quite a few people in the water –
including the ack-ack crew, who had been blown there with the
first bombs – and the ship was listing heavily to starboard. The
oldest people, the wounded, Matron Drummond and some of
our girls with all the first-aid equipment, were put into the
remaining lifeboats on the starboard side and lowered into the

sea. Two boats got away safely. Greatcoats and rugs were thrown down into them and with bright calls of, 'See you later!' they rowed away. The last I saw of them, some sisters were frantically bailing out water with their steel helmets.

The third boat was caught by the ship when she started to roll on her side and so had to be evacuated very smartly.

Matron Paschke set a superb example to us all by the calm way in which she organized the evacuation of the ship. As the Australian sisters went over the side, she said, 'We'll all meet on the shore girls and get teed up again.'

It was our turn. 'Take off your shoes and get over the side as quickly as you can!' came the order. Off came our shoes – I'll never do that again; I am still shoeless – and we all got busy getting over.

One sister thought the order silly. 'I'll drown anyway, as I can't swim,' was her comment as she went over in her shoes. Sixteen hours later she landed – in her shoes, and she still has them.

It was wonderful to see the way those girls jumped over or crawled down rope ladders into the sea. They made no more fuss than if they had been jumping into the swimming pool at Malacca.

Land was just visible, a big hill jutting up out of the sea about ten miles away.

I had been so busy helping people over the side that I had to go in a very big hurry myself. Couldn't find a rope ladder so tried to be Tarzan and slip down a rope. Result, terribly burnt fingers, all skin missing from six fingers and both palms of my hands; they seemed quite raw. I landed with an awful thud and my tin hat landed on top of me.

What a glorious sensation! The coolness of the water was marvellous after the heat of the ship. We all swam well away from her and grabbed anything that floated and hung on to it in small groups. We hopelessly watched the *Vyner Brooke* take her last roll and disappear under the waves. I looked at my watch – twenty to three. (Most of our watches are still twenty to three.)

Then up came oil – that awful, horrible oil, ugh!

I was swimming from group to group looking for Matron Paschke, who that very morning had jokingly asked me to help her swim for it if we had to go over the side. Nobody had seen her leave the ship, so I went on searching wherever I saw groups of girls in grey uniform. I met Win Davis and Pat Gunther clinging to an upturned canvas stretcher and stayed with them for a while, then went on again through that revolting oil when I saw a raft packed with people and more grey uniforms. There was Matron, clinging to this crowded thing. She was terribly pleased with herself for having kept afloat for three hours, and as she was no swimmer I quite agreed with her. Never have I met such an amazing spirit in any person.

On this raft were two Malay sailors, one a bit burnt, who were ineffectively trying to paddle the thing, but had no idea how. Sister Ennis was holding two small children, a Chinese boy aged four and a little English girl about three years of age. There were four or five civilian women and Sisters Harper, Trennery, and McDonald from the 13th A.G.H., Sister Dorsch from the 2/4th C.C.S., and Matron Paschke and Sisters Ennis, Clarke, and myself from 2/10th A.G.H. There seemed no hope of being picked up, so we tried to organize things a little better. Our oars were two small pieces of wood from a packing case and nobody seemed to be able to use them to effect, so more re-arranging was done. Those who were able hung on to the sides of the raft, those who were hurt or ill sat on it, while Matron, Iole Harper, and I rowed all night long in turn. Iole was wonderful, when not rowing she would get off, swim all round, count everybody, and collect those who got tired of hanging on, making them use their feet properly to assist in pushing the thing along.

We seemed to pass, or be passed by, many of the sisters in small groups on wreckage or rafts. Everybody appeared to be gradually making slow progress towards the shore, and every one of us felt quite sure she would eventually get in.

The last thing we saw before night fell was the smoke from at least five ships on the horizon and we thought we were saved.

Surely this was the British Navy? Later on we saw motor-boats searching for people in the darkness; we shouted to them, but they missed us. We eventually came in close to a long pier, but were carried out to sea again. We saw a fire on the shore and knew the lifeboats had made it, so we paddled furiously to get there. We gradually got nearer and nearer and saw the girls, even heard them talking, but they could neither hear nor see us because of a storm, which took us out to sea again. We tried again; it was a lighthouse this time, but once more we missed it by a narrow margin. We seemed helpless against those vile currents. A ship's officer floated past us sitting on a piece of wreckage; he told us where to go when we landed and wished us luck. We didn't see him again.

The two small children with us were very good and they slept most of the time in Sister Ennis's arms. It was very rough and dark and we rocked and tossed until everybody was sick. During this storm the little girl awakened and her tiny voice said, 'Auntie, I want to go upstairs.' Poor little soul, she was absolutely saturated with salt water, but Ennis had to take off her pants before she was convinced that it would be all right. Those two children behaved extremely well, cried very little, and were certainly no trouble.

We came in towards the lighthouse again and I suggested to Matron, 'Let's give her twenty and we'll make it.' We nearly did, but the currents wouldn't let us, and out to sea we went for the third time. We saw large rocks ahead and paddled over, but to our amazement found them moving slowly towards us – ships! As the first went slowly past us we had to push ourselves off from its sides with our feet and the oars. There was no light nor any sound of life at all as they stopped. From the third ship came many large motor-boats, each one packed with armed Japanese soldiers; they surrounded us, chatting away, then one boat came alongside – what an awful sinking feeling we had! They looked hard at us, spoke to us in Japanese, then away they went in a fan-shaped formation towards the town of Muntok. All this left a pretty awful taste in our mouths, for we then realized we didn't have a chance of getting away from them at this stage. We were told that the Japs didn't take prisoners . . . .

When daylight came we were all very tired and just as far out to sea as we were when bombed, but miles farther down the coast; beaches had disappeared and all we could see was a distant line of tree-tops and what looked like jungle. Behind us were about fifteen ships, some of them firing guns towards Muntok.

As we were not getting anywhere and the load was far too heavy, the two Malays, Iole Harper, and I left the raft to swim alongside and so lighten the load. My hands were badly cut about now and too swollen to even cling to the ropes, also we were too tired to row any longer. Two other sisters took over and at last we made progress. We were all coming in well, we four swimming alongside and keeping up a bright conversation about what we'd do and drink when we got in – then suddenly the raft was once more caught in a current which missed us and carried them swiftly out to sea. They called to us, but we didn't have a hope of getting back to it; they were travelling too fast for us to catch them. And so we were left there.

We didn't see Matron Paschke and those sisters again. They were wonderful.

We didn't see the two Malays after about an hour – they just disappeared.

I kept my eye on Iole as she got farther away from me. My stinging, swollen hands were nearly driving me crazy and my progress was very slow. Iole was visible only as a blob about four hundred yards away. Now and again there would be a white blob and I realized then that she was turning round looking for me. I waved; she waved back. Then the blob was black again, going on its way.

Iole was swimming thus away and ahead of me in a different current and so reached the trees first – no beach, just mangrove swamps. She was there a long time before I arrived, which was well after midday. We could tell that by the sun, and we both went to sleep immediately, hanging on to a dead and leafless tree, our bodies still floating in water that was well out of our depth.

Later we discussed our prospects of swimming to Australia!

We spent the remainder of that day swimming up creeks and down again – because they all ended in dense jungle. Our progress was slow, for we had to swim breast-stroke. Thank God we had lifebelts, though the canvas had already rubbed our chins raw. The peculiar animals, crabs, and fish we met along the way didn't exactly inspire good cheer. We would be swimming along through these swamps, when suddenly something would go flop into the water beside or behind us. And fish would go flipping along the surface of the water in an upright position on their tails. If only we could get along at that rate!

In the late afternoon the tide went out, leaving exposed sharp mangrove roots and long hard spikes, which cut our hands and legs still more and our tummies until we were just about at screaming point.

But there was one humorous interlude. Iole was about fifteen yards ahead of me when suddenly she turned round and called out, 'Oh, by the way, what's your name?' We had been swimming together for twenty-eight hours!

So we paused, while we formally introduced ourselves, looked each other over, and exchanged names and addresses. As we belonged to different units we had never met before. She was a little person, about five feet high, had very wet, short black curly hair and the smallest and prettiest hands I had ever seen.

The water was far too salty to drink; we were swimming up the creeks to see if we could get to fresher water, for we were beginning to get thirsty. There was no sign of land or civilization.

When it was dark the tide was right out, and we couldn't make any further headway, sinking in mud up to our thighs. Once when I was sinking in that slimy soft mud and my legs and arms had disappeared in it, I suddenly saw ahead of me very plainly the white sheepskin mat in front of the fireplace at home – I also saw my father sitting in his armchair with a *Herald* over his face, asleep. He has often done that. It certainly made me snap out of it and get free of that patch.

We crawled and scrambled through this to a dead tree-trunk and climbed to the top of it, where there was just enough room for us. We sat there changing places every few minutes because we were getting numb. Huge birds flew at us hitting our faces with their wings – they were horrible.

Soon the tide rose again and we kept on moving to stay out of the water, because it was still dark. During the night Iole kept pointing down at the oily black water and saying to me, 'There are the beds, why don't you get into one?' – and was furious when I refused. I could see Sister Win Davis giving an orderly a glass of water and asking him to bring it to us; I saw this every time I closed my eyes for the next two days, so perhaps I was just as crazy as Iole. I know we were both terribly hot.

When the water reached us we floated off and swam all that day, pausing only to watch planes dog-fighting overhead. We must have swum many miles that day towards the beach at Muntok. We saw a few crocodiles. Late that night we found a river – a big one this time – so we swam up until we were too tired to swim any farther. Then we found something that looked like grass, so we got out on to it. It was grass, but very squashy. We broke palm leaves with our elbows because our hands were too badly infected and made a bed there. Then we heard a dog bark; we were thrilled to know we were on the right track at last. Again we had to keep moving, for we kept sinking in the mud and we were bothered with mosquitoes and sandflies. There must have been thousands of them! While there we heard the splash of oars. We rushed to the water again and called to two natives in a small boat, but they didn't take the slightest notice of us.

During the night we heard some animal coming slowly towards us, snapping dead twigs as it came. We were scared stiff. Then two large eyes appeared above us; it sniffed us all over, and – thank Heaven – went away again.

Again we heard dogs barking and knew we must be near a native village and decided then and there to swim on up the river. We got back into the water and later heard the Malay fishermen coming back in their boat. They called to us and paddled alongside, all smiles, and helped us into their boat. What a relief after three days in the water! We produced our scanty Malay, asking for a drink of water and food; they smiled and nodded, and everything seemed to be pretty good.

We went quite a long way upstream with them, and eventually reached their village. First thing we noticed was a row of thirteen sharks lying on the ground to dry! We were taken to the fisherman's hut, where we sat in the kitchen – after he had put the fowls outside – and dried ourselves by a stove. His wife and a small boy gave us cold tea first, then made us a pot of hot tea and some small hot cakes, which we ate as they came out of the oven. I haven't tasted anything better since!

The Silver Sword

IAN SERRAILLIER

It is 1945; Ruth, Edek and Bronia Balicki, together with Jan an orphan boy, are travelling from Poland to Switzerland to find their parents who were taken prisoner early in the war. On their way through Bavaria, they are given a home for a while by a kindly farmer and his wife. However, the time has now come for them to move on: the Burgomaster, who represents the military authorities in the area, has discovered the children, and he has orders that all Poles must be shipped back to Poland.

The farmer did not normally milk the cows himself – that was left to others. But when he felt depressed or in need of a little reflection, he sometimes took his turn. To sit on a stool with his forehead pressed against a cow's flank and the milk splashing between his fingers into the pail – this, he found, was an attitude which inspired reflective thought.

All afternoon he had been wondering how to beat the Burgomaster and get the family safely away. Telegrams to the International Tracing Service, to Berne and to the Swiss consul in Munich, a hide-out in a cave in the hills – these and other unfruitful ideas had flashed across his mind. Having by milking-time found no solution, he took himself to the cowshed.

And there, at the fifteenth splash into the pail, the idea sprang into being.

As soon as the milking was done, he assembled the family and took them up into the attic. Under a dusty heap of brown paper, broken cases, the boys' skis and some old boots, he found two long canvas bags. Their leather handles were green with mildew. It must have been years since anyone had touched them.

'Ruth and Jan can take this one, Edek can help me with the other,' said the farmer. 'Mind – they're heavier than they look. Bronia, you come down last and close the trap-door behind us. Be careful not to fall down the ladder.'

Wholly mystified, the family did as they were told.

In a pother of dust by no means to Frau Wolff's liking (she was rolling pastry), the bags were dumped on the kitchen floor. She made them take them into the yard.

So out they staggered with their burdens. A few stray hens flew clucking away. And the children clapped their black hands against their clothes.

'Gently, gently,' said the farmer, as they fumbled clumsily with the fastenings.

Ruth's bag was the first open. On top of musty lengths of stuff – was it canvas, was it rubber? – lay a bundle of sticks with metal clasps at the end. Whatever could it be?

Now the other bag was open, and the contents looked similar.

'Don't mix the two up,' said the farmer. 'I'll assemble the one while you all watch. You can do the other yourselves.' And when asked for the umpteenth time what it was all about, all he would say was, 'Ah!'

Out came the sticks first, and with the metal clasps the farmer joined them together – six sets of much the same length, which he fastened at the ends. The sticks grew into a skeleton. And before the farmer had started to give it flesh, Jan cried out, 'A canoe!'

'It's a bit of a gamble,' said the farmer, 'but your only chance.

Has any of you ever canoed before?'

'Yes,' said Ruth and Edek both together.

'Father took us one summer in the Pieniny mountains,' said Ruth. 'We hired two-seaters to take us downstream, then sent them back by train.'

'One of these is a two-seater,' said the farmer. 'They belonged to my sons. Have you tried wild water?'

'The Dunajec wasn't particularly wild, except in one place where there were some rocks sticking out,' said Edek.

'There are only two difficult patches on the Falken River,' said the farmer, 'the rapids ten kilometres below the village, and the part where the river joins the Danube. Keep to mid-stream and clear of the broken water and you'll be all right.' He did not tell them just how tricky the rapids were, and that it was a long time before he had allowed his boys to tackle them unaccompanied. Nor did he drop a hint of his other fear. The canoes were years old. Would they still hold the water out?

Working together, Edek and Jan assembled the second canoe according to the farmer's directions. After a time, soiled and battered but recognizable, two canoes lay stretched out on the ground.

'Of course we'll have to try them out,' said the farmer, 'and it's advisable to leave that till after dark.'

'What about the paddles?' said Edek.

A second visit to the attic produced three double paddles, one of them snapped in two, another with a broken blade. The farmer saw to the carpentry, having packed the family off to a meal and bed. They must get a few hours' rest, for the plan would not work unless they were away in the small hours of the morning while it was still dark. There were many other things that could go wrong. Parts of the river were highly dangerous. Was any watch kept upon it where it ran past the village? Much luck and not a little skill would be needed for the venture to succeed. But it was their only chance.

It took him till dark to repair the paddles and the cracked floor-boards. Of the four buoyancy balloons (one for each end) three were punctured and the fourth had perished. There was no time to get hold of new ones, so the three had to be patched.

The moon had not yet risen when, with tractor and trailer, he carried the canoes down to the river to try them out. The larger one was all right, but the single-seater leaked in several places. The top skin of waterproof linen seemed sound enough. It was the under skin of rubberized cloth which needed attention. All he had to help him was some talc, and, working by torchlight, he made the best job of it he could.

Soon after 3 a.m. four sleepy-eyed youngsters were bundled into the trailer and driven over the bumpy track down to the river. Frau Wolff sat with them.

'I found the waterproofs which go with the canoes and I've mended them for you,' she told them. 'Mind you fit them tightly round the splashboards, or you'll get swamped. And I've packed you up some food as well.'

'Go easy with the food, dear,' shouted the farmer, above the noisy splutter of the tractor. 'We don't want to sink them.'

Reaching the river, he shut off the engine. Under the dark trees they could see the river only dimly, but the gentle rushing sound of the water was music in their ears. On, on to the Danube. On to Switzerland, it sang.

'Say goodbye to Ludwig for me,' said Jan. 'I shall miss him dreadfully.'

'Ludwig's in the wood somewhere. I heard him bark,' said Bronia.

'Ludwig's asleep in his basket at home,' said Frau Wolff.

'Listen, all of you,' said the farmer. 'Your safety depends on your not making any stupid mistakes. Edek and Jan – you'd better have the two-seater. We'll stow the luggage with you. Put on these waterproofs – the elastic grips round your faces and wrists and round the splashboard. They'll keep the water out of the canoe. Ruth and Bronia – you'll both have to fit into one waterproof as best you can. Keep the waistband tight round the splashboard.'

When they were all aboard and the little luggage they had was safely stowed, he gave them final instructions. 'It's only fifty kilometres to the Danube, so you've not far to go. Keep to mid-stream where you can – the river's fastest there. There's no need to paddle much, except in the broken water where there are rocks. For the rest, just keep the canoes headed straight and the current will do all the work. If you get into difficulties, draw in to the side. The water's sluggish there and quite shallow. Remember – not a sound as you pass the village. There's no moon now and you shouldn't be seen. But if there's any firing, lie as flat as you can. Goodbye, and good luck to you.'

'God bless you, my dears,' said Frau Wolff.

'We can never thank you enough for all you've done for us,' said Ruth.

'I'll paint a picture of the farm, with both of you in it – and I'll remember you for ever,' said Bronia.

The two boys waved their paddles.

The farmer gave each bow a gentle push. Ruth, tightly squeezed with Bronia inside the ash-wood rim of the single-seater, drove hard in with her paddle and headed for midstream, with Edek and Jan close behind. Glancing back over her shoulder, she saw the two pale figures under the trees waving silently – silently and, she thought, rather sadly. The darkness quickly swallowed them.

'It's lovely and warm in here – like being in a nest,' said Bronia. 'I'm so glad I'm in your boat, Ruth. I bet the others are envious.'

They were in the grip of the current now, floating gently and steadily downstream. Edek and Jan were a length behind. She could hear the splash of their paddles in the water and Jan's voice calling. Had something gone wrong?

She backed water till they drew alongside.

'Don't shout, Jan,' she said.

'We're down at the bows. There's something very heavy inside, Ruth,' said Jan.

'Pass the stuff back to me. There's room astern,' said Edek.

Jan lifted the waist of his waterproof clear of the rim and

reached underneath.

'Ow! It's wriggling – it's alive – and wet!' said Jan.

'Perhaps a fish has come up through the bottom,' said Bronia, much alarmed.

But Jan had guessed already what was hiding there. The wet thing was a nose. The stowaway was Ludwig. He thrust up eagerly for air, licking Jan's fingers and wriggling with delight at the success of his plans. As for Jan, even if this unexpected passenger meant shipwreck, he could not have been better pleased.

The current was swift. In the darkness the great wooded hills swept by. For a moment the moon peeped from a cloud and turned the rippling surface of the stream to silver.

'Stay away, moon,' Ruth muttered. 'Don't come out again till we've passed the village.'

Side by side, the two canoes sped on.

On the left bank the line of the hills curved downwards. Were those dim shapes houses? Had they reached the village?

Again the moon appeared. It had chosen quite the wrong moment, for this was indeed the village, with houses crowded about both banks, and on the left bank suddenly an open space with lorries in it. They were so close together that they were almost touching, and there were several rows of them. These must be the lorries that were to take the Polish refugees back to Poland. With a tightening of fear in her throat, Ruth realized that if they were spotted now, they would be taken back too.

'Look out for the bridge,' said Edek.

He and Jan shot ahead, aiming for the centre of the three arches. Edging away from the square, Ruth paddled towards the right-hand arch.

Edek's canoe shot under the arch and disappeared into the shadows. Too far to the right, Ruth got caught in sluggish water. She drifted broadside on to the base of the arch.

The water was noisy and Ruth did not hear the footsteps on the bridge. But she saw a man's shadow on the water and it was moving. she paddled frantically to get free. 'The water's coming in. I can feel it damp under me,' said Bronia.

A man shouted, and his shadow leaned far out over the water.

The canoe was still across the base of the arch, with the water thrusting against each end, threatening to break its back. She jabbed hard with the paddle and managed to ease it a little.

The man was right overhead, shouting and waving, but she could not understand what he was saying. In the distance a dog was barking.

A pair of legs dangled over the parapet and scraped against the stone. An American soldier. ·

With a last effort she thrust at the stonework, and the canoe broke free. But the soldier had clambered down and jumped into the water where it was shallow at the side. He caught at the paddle and clung on.

Ruth tugged, twisted, then let go of it, and the canoe swung sideways into the shadows under the arch. The soldier, not expecting her to let go, toppled over backwards and fell with a splash into the river.

As the canoe shot out beyond the bridge, Ruth realized that she was at the mercy of the current. Bronia had no paddle and could not help.

Two or three shots from the bridge whizzed past her cheek, and she pushed Bronia's head down against the canvas. She peered ahead to see if she could see anything of the other canoe.

Then the moon went behind a cloud, and the darkness hid her.

There were no more shots now, but she felt helpless as the current drove them wherever it chose. On and on they sped, the water foaming against the bows, spitting and bubbling against the canvas.

'I'm sitting in the river,' said Bronia.

But Ruth took no notice. 'Edek! Jan!' she shouted.

As they rounded a bend, they were thrust towards the right bank. The river was quieter here, and soon they felt the bottom of the canoe scrape over pebbles and slow them to a halt.

He caught at the paddle and hung on

Ruth put her hand over the side and down into the water and tried to shove them off. But they were stuck. There was a pale light in the sky now, and the rim of the hills stood out dark against it. It was still too dark to see much, but she could make out rocks in the water, rounded like hippos' backs.

'We'll have to get out and push,' she said.

They stepped into the water, which was little more than ankle-deep, and at once the canoe floated. With the painter in her hand and Bronia beside her, she drew it gently along till they came to a large V-shaped rock that seemed to project from the bank. She pulled the canoe high and dry on to a shoal of pebbles, then lifted Bronia on to the rock.

'We must wait here till daylight,' she said.

And they sat there shivering and clinging to each other till the shadows brightened and they could see the whole sweep of the river, white and broken in the middle, rock-strewn and shallow at either side, with the wood-muffled hills hemming it in, and not a soul in sight. No sign of Edek and Jan. They could not have felt lonelier.

Then Bronia saw something which gave them hope. Down in the water, near the point of the V-shaped rock, was a stick that looked as if it might serve as a paddle. She climbed down to get it and found it was the very paddle they had lost. This was luck indeed.

They turned the canoe over and poured the water out. Then, with new confidence, they launched it again. Stepping aboard, they headed for midstream. And the current caught them and carried them on towards the rapids.

The river grew faster, and the bank flashed past. Soon they were in a kind of gorge, where the river squeezed past great boulders, some of them as high as houses. Some of the swells were over a foot high, and the spray dashed over the bow and stung their faces. The water roared here so that even the loudest shout could not be heard. Out to the left there were huge oily surges that looked as if they would pound you down into the depths if you got caught in them.

Bronia closed her eyes and clung to her sister's waist. Ruth was not as scared as she had expected to be. With a triumphant sense of exhilaration she flashed in with her paddle, heading always for the open stream, away from the white broken water where the rocks lay hidden. Now and then a boulder loomed up, and she knew that if they struck it they would be dashed to pieces. But a quick dip of the paddle at the right moment was enough to shoot them safely past.

In no time the river broadened, the boulders eased, and the banks were wooded again. The terrors of the rapids were over. Ruth hoped that Edek and Jan, whose two-seater was much less easy to manoeuvre, had been as successful as they had.

There seemed no need for the paddle now, for the water was clear of rocks and the current smooth and swift. They could lie back and let the canoe take care of itself.

Bronia closed her eyes and fell asleep. Ruth lay back and watched the blue sky overhead and the climbing sun. It was to be another scorching day, and she too became sleepy and dozed.

A grating, tearing sound brought her to her senses, and she woke to find herself thigh-deep in water. The canoe had grounded on a shoal and a sharp stone had ripped the canvas underneath. She looked about her. The river was very broad here, and they were near the right bank, where it was shallow and easy to wade ashore. So they stepped out and scraped the waterlogged craft over the pebbles to the bank and hauled it ashore.

'The tear's too long to mend,' said Ruth. 'We shall have to leave the canoe and walk. It can't be far to the Danube now.'

They found a path which threaded its way through the trees on the bank, and they followed it to the last big bend before the river joined the Danube at Falkenburg. There were no woods here, only green fields, a dusty country road, and a gently sloping bank that reached far out into the river.

Ruth made for the bank, for she thought it would give her a good view of the river in both directions and some chance of seeing Edek and Jan. Except for a couple of unfinished haystacks, the bank was deserted. She did not know that two sentries had posted themselves here for most of the morning, on the look-out for their canoe. Weary with waiting, they had climbed to the top of one of the haystacks and taken it in turns to go to sleep.

The first she knew of their presence was when a half-eaten apple struck her on the shoulder. Then there was a bark, and Ludwig was licking her ankles.

'Where have you been all this time? We thought you must have come to grief in the rapids,' said Jan, who was standing on top of the stack. He gave the sleeping Edek a shove, and the boy landed – with hay sticking out of his hair and his shirt, right at Bronia's feet.

It was a merry meeting.

'We came to grief too,' said Edek, 'same way as you did, but we travelled further before we went aground.'

Not a hundred yards away a convoy of American lorries swept up the road in a pother of dust. They were crammed with refugees, most of them Poles and all grimly silent. But the children were so busy talking and laughing over their experiences that they did not even notice.

Captain of Foot

RONALD WELCH

Christopher Carey, a lieutenant in Sir John Moore's army fighting in Spain during the Peninsular War, was captured by the French during the British retreat to Corunna.

When Chris recovered consciousness again he was lying with his back against a rock. His head was throbbing heavily with a dull and sickening pain, and the whole of one side of his face was wet. Afraid of what he would find he explored gingerly with his fingers, but all that he touched was a large and very painful lump above his ear. The wetness on his face was rain, and not blood.

As the pain shot through his head again he groaned, and then he heard the clink of feet on stones. He looked up slowly, for any sudden movement made his head spin, and saw above him a French officer.

'You are unhurt, m'sieur?'

Chris nodded cautiously. His knowledge of French was reasonable, though he could understand considerably more than he could speak.

'That is your regiment on the bridge?'

Chris tried to control his whirling brain. He must be careful of what he said, for all ranks in the 43rd had been warned that if they were taken prisoner, they must give their names and rank

261

only, though the identity of the regiment might not cause much harm if that was known.

'Your name and rank, m'sieur?'

'Lieutenant Carey.'

'Your regiment?'

The Frenchman shrugged his shoulders when Chris made no reply. He was holding Chris's battered shako, his fingers touching the bugle-horn badge and the short green tuft.

'Light Infantry,' he said, and then, as one of his men handed him a British cross-belt, taken from the man who had been shot through the head, Chris thought, he pointed to the number on the brass plate.

'43rd Foot,' he added. 'I congratulate you, Lieutenant, on your regiment. Never before have I seen the Chasseurs of the Guard driven off by infantry in line,' and he laughed, glancing down the valley, as if he was not altogether sorry to see the famous Chasseurs worsted for once. Chris grinned feebly, too, for he shared the infantryman's feelings of rivalry with the cavalry.

He was not asked any more questions, much to his relief. Instead, he was helped to his feet and taken farther from the bridge, and then allowed to sit down, huddled up in his greatcoat, with the remains of his shako perched on his head, back to the driving rain, feeling very cold and sick and miserable.

But he watched the French with interest as they made ready for another assault on the bridge. Infantry were pushed out on either flank towards the steep banks of the Esla, while a larger column marched up the road towards the bridge itself.

On the farther bank Chris saw Napier's company, and Colonel Stewart had sent forward another company as well to their flank. The bridge was not going to be abandoned yet, then, though the main body of the army must have gained a clear lead of twenty-four hours by this time. To add to that, the French would spend the best part of a day throwing pontoons across the river, assuming that they would waste no time bringing up the heavy and cumbersome equipment.

A crackle of musketry broke out on either flank. The French were hoping, perhaps, to force back the two flanking companies of the 43rd, and Chris shook his head. It would take more than that to shift them, and there was still the formidable Thomas Lloyd on the bridge. He would soon give the French a lesson in how the 43rd dealt with an infantry column.

As the column neared the bridge, the French officers waved their swords in the air; bugles blew insistently, the drums rolled out across the valley, and with shrill cheers the infantry quickened their pace. Chris forgot his aches and his misery, and jumped to his feet.

There was an ominous silence from the bridge, though it was possible to see a line of black shakos and the long barrels of the muskets above the piled carts and tree trunks. Then the muzzles spurted flame, and the scene was blotted out by the smoke. Chris heard the familiar crash of a disciplined British volley, and the leading files of the French column were swept away as if a giant finger had flicked them to the gound.

But the French had not smashed the armies of Europe by lack of courage or determination. Again the bugles blew and the drums rolled, and once more the column rushed forward. But again there came the sudden pin-points of flame from the barricade, the same crash of muskets, the white, drifting smoke, and another heap of French soldiers littered the ground.

That was the last attempt to storm the bridge, for the light was failing, and the French fell back down the valley, leaving behind them nearly fifty men in the mud and slush of the road, Chris reckoned.

He was brought some food, and a cup of very raw Spanish wine. He was to be well treated, then, though he had expected nothing else. If he had been a Spaniard he would almost certainly have been shot an hour ago, for the atrocities of the Spanish guerrilla forces encouraged the French to retaliate whenever they had the chance. But for the British the French soldier had the professional sympathy of one soldier for another.

Chris ate his poor supper, and listened to the Frenchmen as they settled down for the night around him. They were dapper little fellows in broad-shouldered and swallow-tailed coats, baggy trousers, and shakos very similar to the British ones. They were a merry crowd, despite their failure to rush the bridge, and the lack of fires, for there was no timber in the valley, did not seem to affect their spirits. Chris could imagine the grumbles of his men under similar conditions.

He turned his head quickly. From the other side of the Esla came a familiar bugle call. 'Retreat and close! Retreat and close!' The 43rd were falling back at last.

A vivid sheet of flame shot up from the bridge, lighting up the whole valley like a gigantic flash of lightning. Then a long, rumbling roar of the explosion, and stones, tree trunks and broken carts went up in the air as the thick arches of the bridge tumbled into the torrent below. The bridge of Castrogonzalo had been blown, and the Light Brigade had finished its rearguard action.

Chris sighed. Suddenly he realized his position. He was lonely and homesick. His horse, his servant, his pack and all his spare clothes and the few luxuries that made life endurable in these mountains were on the other side of the river. And here he was in the chill, wet darkness, a prisoner of the French, whilst his regiment marched away to the coast and to England.

Chris began to curse furiously. He cursed the day he had ever taken a commission; he cursed the retreat from Spain, these dreadful mountains, the biting cold, the wind with its everlasting moan, the drenching rain that never stopped, the French around him, the aching lump on his head, his sodden coat and trousers, and the intolerable stupidity of a war that had uprooted him from a comfortable home and thrown him down in this uncivilized corner of a filthy country in the depths of winter.

Two days later Chris was sitting in a Spanish bullock cart, jolting slowly over the roads that led down from the mountain passes. Then for several days more the cart rolled across the interminable plain of Léon, though Chris, with memories of the dust on the same roads in the summer, was glad to see that the sandy soil had been washed down by the rain into thick mud. He was bound, so he had been told, for Valladolid and the Headquarters of the French army of Castile.

Sleeping under a roof, warm fires and reasonably good food had helped Chris to recover from his depression, and already he was wondering about the chances of an escape. No one had asked him for his parole, an oversight perhaps, but he had decided that he would not give it if he were asked to do so. He assumed that he would be sent on to France from Valladolid, so that he must escape before he crossed the French frontier.

The Spaniards loathed the French with a savage and bitter hatred. If it came to that, they disliked all foreigners, but they would probably be disposed to give some help to a British officer, or so Chris hoped.

Valladolid was quite the dirtiest town that Chris had yet seen in Spain. The houses were old and decrepit; open sewers ran down the centre of the streets, and foul-smelling heaps of filth and refuse littered the squares.

The column of carts containing the French wounded creaked through the town and into a large barracks that had once been used by the Spanish troops. Chris was taken across the great square to a corner block, up a flight of stairs and into a tiny, white-washed room with one chair, a low bed, and the wonderful sight of a fire. So luxurious did it all seem that he barely noticed the ominous locking of the door behind him.

He had been given a razor and some soap by a friendly French officer, and he began to pull off his clothes. A shave, a wash, he decided, and then he must try to clean his uniform, for at the moment he looked more like a tramp than an officer of the 43rd.

He was sitting on his bed contemplating the mud on his trousers when the door was unlocked, and a tall French officer in the uniform of a regiment of Cuirassiers stalked into the room. He bowed to Chris, his spurs clinking loudly.

'Lieutenant Carey?'

Chris had jumped to his feet, still holding his trousers, and very conscious of his shirt tails and underwear. But he managed a bow in return, and said that he was indeed Lieutenant Carey. The Cuirassier handed him a folded paper, and as Chris read the few lines written there his eyebrows shot up in surprise.

Au Quartier General á Valladolid.
Le 15 Decembre, 1809.
Le Maréchal de l'Empire, le Duc d'Elchingen, prie Monsieur Carey de lui faire l'honneur de venir diner chez lui aujourd'hui, à 5 heures.
Répondez s'il vous plaît.

Chris looked up. The Cuirassier was about his own age, a dark-faced and pleasant-looking young fellow in his extremely smart uniform.

'Étienne Laborde, at your service, m'sieur.' The long black riding boots clicked together with a snap and a jingle of spurs. 'Of the 2nd Cuirassiers, and A.D.C. to the Marshal Duke.'

'Er . . . thank you,' Chris said, waving the confounded trousers. 'I shall be delighted, and honoured, to accept the invitation of the Marshal to dinner. But . . .' and he waved the offending trousers once more, 'my uniform, you see, it is very dirty, and . . .'

Laborde grinned, and Chris liked him from that moment. 'If I may send my servant, m'sieur Carey—' he said. 'He is an excellent valet.'

'By all means,' Chris said thankfully.

'Good! Then I shall call for you in an hour. Au revoir, m'sieur.' Another click of boots, an even louder jingle and the Cuirassier had gone.

Chris sat down on the hard bed again, and let out a long, low whistle. The Marshal Duke of Elchingen. Now, which one was that? Soult? No. Then Augerau? No, of course, it was Ney, red-haired Ney, the Fighting Marshal of the Empire, one of those men who had risen from the ranks during the Revolution. Well, he was a Duke now, and one of the great soldiers of Europe, with his name in the history books of the future. Chris whistled again, and grinned. It would be a fascinating experience to sit down at the same table with one of the legendary Marshals of France.

Laborde's servant arrived a few minutes later, a dark-jowled and wiry little man who beamed at Chris, and set to work with a swift and deft precision that betrayed the well-trained valet. He chattered with a freedom that Chris knew was common in France now, but would have been treated as insolence in an English servant. Chris took no offence, though many of his fellow officers might well have done so. But then they all told him he was too easy going.

The creased and muddy clothes were made presentable in a short time, though the Frenchman clicked his teeth over the shako. Rain and the sabre of the Chasseur had reduced that unfortunate piece of uniform to a state that no tailor could have remedied.

Chris tipped the man, for fortunately he still had his small supply of Spanish money. That would come in useful when he escaped, he thought, as he thanked the man for his help.

'A pleasure, m'sieur, a pleasure,' and Chris was alone once more.

He dressed himself carefully, revelling in the feeling of dry, clean clothes, his blue-grey trousers that once more had a crease in them, in the red coat, cut short in front and with small tails behind, the leather sword belt over his right shoulder, though he had no sword now as a prisoner of war, and finally the long red sash worn by all officers, which he rolled twice around his waist, with the heavy silken tassels hanging down from one side.

Reasonably presentable, he thought, as he combed his fair hair, and inspected the result in a small mirror on the wall. The sun, the wind, and the exposure of the last few months had given him a tanned and weather-beaten appearance. Almost as leathery as the skin of his elder brother, Peter, after a voyage to the West Indies, and as dark as a gipsy, Chris thought.

Lieutenant Laborde arrived for him punctually. They walked across the barrack square, and out into the narrow and crowded streets of Valladolid, for the Spaniards had finished their midday siesta, and were strolling about, swarthy men in wide-brimmed sombreros and long cloaks flung over their shoulders, and black-haired and dark-eyed women with short skirts and bright petticoats and flashing white teeth.

They all stepped politely out of the way as Chris and Laborde picked their way through the piles of filth. Laborde clanked along with a clink of spurs, talking cheerfully, and ignoring the Spaniards. Did he notice the quick glances, Chris wondered, the scowls and the expressions of sheer hatred? I would not like to be a French officer in Spain, he decided.

They turned off the street through a pair of high gates, past two French sentries, and up the steps of an imposing house.

'The Marshal's Headquarters,' Laborde said over his shoulder as he led Chris across the cool hall into a long room with windows looking out on to a walled garden.

There were half a dozen French officers standing there, all of whom stared curiously at Chris's red coat. But they bowed politely as Laborde introduced him, and expressed their regrets at his position as a prisoner.

Chris mumbled suitable replies in his halting French until the double doors were flung open, and a tall man with dark reddish hair and long side whiskers strode into the room. He was in the undress uniform of a Marshal of the Empire, a dark blue coat with much gold lace at the shoulders and around the high collar, white breeches with long top boots that came up to the knee.

Chris bowed. He did not need Laborde's introduction to realize that this was Marshal Ney.

The Marshal's quick, darting eyes ran up and down Chris's figure, and then he held out his hand, and smiled pleasantly.

'It is a pleasure to meet you, m'sieur,' he said. 'I have read a report on the behaviour of your regiment. You are to be congratulated, Lieutenant Carey.'

Chris flushed, and once more summoned up his best French. But the Marshal interrupted him quickly.

'But you have no sword, m'sieur. Laborde! Hilaire! There is a sword in my office. Fetch it for the Lieutenant.'

An embarrassed Chris stood there while a Marshal of France handed him a long French cavalry sword, and helped him to slip it into the empty belt at his side.

The dinner was superb. The food and wine would have been worth comment in any house, Chris thought, but after the hardships of the past weeks he found it difficult to disguise his delight as he worked his way steadily through the various courses. Attentive mess servants refilled his glass whenever he showed signs of trying to empty it, and for a moment he wondered if this was deliberate, and part of a plan to make him talk too much, and perhaps give away some military information. But he was asked no questions, and the conversation was quite normal. He was being treated, he decided, with just sheer courtesy.

He learnt that he would be leaving Valladolid the next morning. The Marshal condoled with him on his fate as a prisoner, and assured him that he would take a personal interest in the possibility of an exchange. Chris thanked him again for his kindness, and was escorted back to his little room in the barracks.

'I shall be riding with you,' Laborde said. 'I am taking dispatches to Paris.' He beamed with delight. 'Paris! And I hope I never see this infernal country again! Good night, m'sieur. Could you be ready to move at seven?'

Chris undressed slowly. Tomorrow! He had hoped for a few days in Valladolid. There might have been a chance of breaking out from the barracks, a poor chance, perhaps, but a better one than trying to escape from the middle of a strong cavalry escort such as Laborde would take with him as bearer of dispatches to Paris.

Chris rode out of Valladolid by the side of Laborde. In front and behind clattered a troop of Hussars, and Chris shrugged his shoulders as he saw them. He could do nothing but watch the scenery slip past, and listen to Laborde's cheerful chatter about the delights of Paris, and the hope of being posted to Italy. His father, so Chris gathered, was a General, and now at the French

War Office, so Laborde was confident that the necessary strings could be pulled, and he would not have to return to Spain.

They rode along the straight roads of Spain for the next three days, through Burgos with its towers and spires, the beautiful cathedral and the fine houses along the banks of the river, and out on to the great Royal Road of Spain that ran as straight as a musket barrel towards the Pyrenees. The surface was poor, though, Chris thought, accustomed to the magnificent turnpike roads of England. But he had not seen a passably good road in either Portugal or Spain, and this was no exception.

They spent the nights at small fortified strong points which the French had built along the main roads at intervals of every thirty miles or so, and intended for couriers such as Laborde, and columns of soldiers or trains of wounded and supplies. There was not the slightest hope of an escape, Chris realized with a growing feeling of depression, and they would be over the frontier in a few days, Étienne told him.

For they were 'Étienne' and 'Chris' to each other now, and there was little about Laborde's life and history that Chris did not know by this time.

'I have some French relations,' Chris said one afternoon. 'Very distant ones, and my uncle helped them to escape from France during the Revolution.' He told Étienne what he knew of the story. 'My uncle married one of the family, but her brother insisted on staying in France. I believe he is in the army now.'

'Indeed,' Étienne said with great interest. 'What is his name, Chris?'

'Armand d'Assailly.'

'But of course! He is of the old nobility. Some of them came back, you know, after the Terror. The Vicomte is a Colonel now, in the Guides. I have met him once. He is on the Staff in Italy,' and Étienne was off again on his hopes for the future.

They crossed the Ebro at Logroño, a pretty little town of snow-white houses, and then on through lovely, undulating country, the most delightful that Chris had yet seen in Spain, with old castles perched on the hills, clean villages, and a prosperous-looking countryside.

Some ten miles beyond Logroño two of the horses in the escort went lame. Chris tried to follow the argument that broke out, conducted in rapid French and with much gesticulation and shrugging of shoulders. But if he could not understand what was being said, he could appreciate the difficulty. It was the everlasting one of Spanish guerrillas, haunting all the main roads. They might not often attack so strong a detachment as this, but two riders alone, and on lame horses, would never reach their destination.

The Hussar Captain in charge of the escort agreed eventually with Laborde, deferring, Chris guessed shrewdly, to Étienne's position as A.D.C. to the Marshal. Half the escort would return to Logroño with the lame horses, and the rest would push on. Travanca, the next fort along the road, was barely twelve miles ahead.

'I'm not wasting another day in this country,' Étienne said as he shook his reins. 'Paris in ten days if we're lucky, Chris.'

They halted for the usual midday meal under the shelter of some trees by the side of the road. The ground fell away into a tangle of little valleys and gentle hills beyond the trees, and a stream tinkled cheerfully away to the right, a pleasant spot without a house in sight, as Chris noticed when he was dismounting.

He had finished his meal, and was sitting on the grass beside Étienne who was chattering away as usual. This time it was about his home in Provence, but Chris was wondering why the Hussars had not posted any sentries. Perhaps he was too critical, he decided, brought up in the strict rules of the Light Brigade. Probably he would have done the same as the French if he had been in their place, five miles from a French fort, in a peaceful part of Spain, and not very far from the French frontier.

'You must come and stay with me after the war,' Étienne said. 'I'll show you Paris first, and then we'll . . .'

Muskets crashed behind them. A tremendous blow struck Chris in the back, high up by his left shoulder. He was thrown forward violently, sprawling awkwardly on his face. Another scattered volley, and he heard the bullets whistle over him. From Étienne there came a grunt as he clapped his hands to his leg and watched in stunned amazement the blood pouring through his fingers.

A horde of screeching men rushed across the grass, Spanish guerrillas in large round hats and brown cloaks, waving muskets and swords and long knives. The surviving Hussars disappeared in a ring of hacking, stabbing figures, amidst a wild chorus of shouts and screams and thudding blows.

And then it was all over, in a bare two minutes perhaps, Chris thought dully, as he tried to stand up, and listened to the quick Spanish voices, exultant and excited at their easy victory. Two men turned and came across to where Chris was swaying on his feet.

'*Inglés! Inglés!*' he shouted, and tried to hold out his arms to display the distinctive scarlet coat. But his left arm sent a sudden stab of pain through his back and across his shoulder and all he could do was mutter, '*Inglés* officer! *Inglés* officer!'

One of the guerrillas, the leader to judge by his shouted orders, came up to Chris, peered at his uniform, and said something to him in Spanish. Chris shook his head. He had picked up a few phrases in Spanish, like all the officers of the 43rd, but certainly not enough to understand this.

The guerrilla was unusually dark-skinned even for a Spaniard and his dress was richer and more colourful than the others, with yellow ribbons in his sombrero, and silver buttons on his brown coat and velveteen waistcoat. He was holding a pistol in one hand, and wicked-looking knife in the other. Stuck in the belt at his waist was another pistol, and with his dark, almost black face, his slightly bent knees and air of competent ruthlessness, he was anything but a comforting figure to Chris at that particular moment.

But at any rate the muzzle of the pistol moved away from Chris, and was pointing now at Étienne, still sitting on the grass and unable to stand.

Captain of Foot

'No, no!' Chris shouted. 'Friend! Friend! Don't shoot!'

The guerrilla shrugged his shoulders. Flame spurted from the pistol, and it kicked sharply in his hand. Étienne was knocked back, arms outflung, his face turned up to the hard blue of the Spanish sky that he had disliked so much. Chris bent over him. But there was nothing he could do for poor Étienne Laborde now; there would be no holiday in Paris for him, no posting to the Army of Italy, and Marshal the Duke of Elchingen would have to find another A.D.C.

'Do not distress yourself, *señor*,' the guerrilla said in slow and halting French. 'He was only a Frenchman.'

The guerrilla's white teeth showed for a second in a grimace of hatred as he glowered down at Étienne's body. He stuffed the pistol, with a faint whiff of smoke still curling from the muzzle, into the wide belt at his waist, and turned away to shout orders at his men.

They were ransacking the packs and pouches of the Hussars, collecting weapons and ammunition, and rounding up the frightened horses. Two men had pulled off the boots of dead Frenchmen, and were trying them on their own feet.

But the whole scene seemed to waver in front of Chris; he felt curiously light headed, and his knees were shaking. Blood was still trickling down inside his shirt, warm and sticky, and his shoulder was beginning to throb and burn as if a red-hot bayonet was being poked into his back.

One of the guerrillas started to pull off his tunic for him. Chris clenched his teeth as his arm came out of the sleeve, and he stood there, blinking and swaying in the bright sunshine as they tied a thick pad against the wound to stop the bleeding, and then pushed him towards a horse, and helped him up into the saddle. He grabbed the reins with one hand, and shut his eyes, for the trees and the horse's head seemed to spin round in a sickening circle as if he was drunk.

'*Vamos!*' the guerrilla leader shouted. '*Vamos!* We're off!'

Chris tried to keep his balance as his horse moved away, following the others through the trees and down a narrow track

273

towards the hills in the distance.

Well, he had escaped, Chris was thinking, though not quite as he had planned it. He had earned a bullet in his shoulder, and poor Étienne had lost his life, together with a dozen unfortunate French Hussars.

They rode steadily through an undulating and empty countryside for an hour or so, penetrating more deeply each mile into the mountains, though Chris was barely aware of what was happening, or of how long he clung painfully to his reins, and stayed erect in that high saddle. He was in a dreamy, semiconscious condition when he was helped down, and with a guerrilla on either side, holding him up on his feet, he stumbled into what seemed a long, dark tunnel, and was then allowed to lie on his back, and close his eyes. With a sigh he put his head back, and gave way to the tide of oblivion that he had fought against for so long.

When he opened his eyes again, he peered into darkness, broken by a flickering light on a low roof just above his head. He could smell wood smoke, and hear Spanish voices talking close by. But he was too weak to move his head, and drifted off into sleep again in a few minutes, too exhausted to wonder where he was or what had happened.

The sun was streaming across his face when he awoke for the second time. He could see where he was now, in a cave, with the smooth stone roof just above his staring eyes. A hand touched his, and a swarthy, bearded face bent over him. A metal cup was put against his lips, and he drank gratefully and greedily; some rough Spanish wine, he thought, but he gulped it down his parched throat, wincing as he felt the hot, searing pain in his shoulder.

'*Mas, señor?*' the man asked. 'More, *señor?*'

Chris nodded his head, and another cup was brought.

'*Estese usted quieto, señor,*' the guerrilla said, 'remain quiet.'

Chris had no inclination to do anything else. The slightest movement sent sharp stabs of pain through his shoulder and side, and he knew that the bullet was still in his back. Unless it was taken away, he would die. Even if some amateur surgeon tried to cut the bullet out, he would probably still die of gangrene; he had seen it happen with his own wounded men.

A little later that day a circle of guerrillas gathered around him. He listened dully to the quick chatter of Spanish, but he understood nothing of what was said. Then surprisingly gentle hands turned him over on to his face, and the bandages on his back were slowly unrolled. He groaned as the pad, which had stuck to the wound, was pulled away, but far worse was to come, the dreadful agony of the probes and the knife, until mercifully he fainted, and the rest of the crude operation was finished whilst he was unconscious.

He was still lying in the same place when he awoke again. But the pain had gone, leaving behind a dull ache, unpleasant, but bearable. He tried to move and lift his head, but he was too weak to do even that, and closed his eyes wearily, to lie there for several days while the guerrillas nursed him as best they knew.

He should have died, of course, either from shock after the operation, or from gangrene and dirty instruments; the odds were heavily against a recovery. But luck, perhaps, and his own good health and youth pulled him through. After a week he was on his feet again, very tottery and weak, and he was able to eat the spiced meat and sausages, all tainted, from his point of view, with too much pepper and garlic that was the staple diet of the Spaniards.

From sheer necessity he was forced to learn Spanish, words and phrases at first, and then he could put sentences together, and his quick brain and retentive memory made him remarkably fluent in a very short time.

He had learnt a good deal about this particular band of guerrillas by the end of a few weeks. Their leader was called El Empecinado, 'the Inky Face', for he was unusually dark of skin, even for a Spaniard. Probably a double dose of Moorish blood, Chris thought, remembering his Spanish history. He had been a regular trooper in the Spanish cavalry, had been captured by the

French, treated with atrocious cruelty, and had managed to escape. For the French he still retained a bitter and savage hatred that appalled Chris, when he recalled the courtesy and genuine kindness with which he had been greeted at Valladolid.

Chris did not move far from the cave at first. The guerrillas made four raids in that time. Local villagers kept them well informed of French troop movements, and if El Empecinado thought the chances were good enough, he made an attack. Normally he waited for convoys of supplies, or stragglers, but there was nothing heroic about his methods, as he openly admitted to Chris. If there was the slightest doubt he refused to move, and that was the invariable rule amongst all the guerrilla bands. Why should they take chances, Chris thought, hiding in their impregnable lairs up in the mountains, with ample warning of any French search party?

After four weeks, Chris rode out with them. He disliked the idea of a cold-blooded ambush of French soldiers, but after all, he was supposed to be fighting against the French, too, and he could hardly refuse to help the men who had saved his life.

The band were all mounted, mostly on captured French horses. They were a picturesque looking crowd in their brown jackets and gaiters, the breeches slit down the side below the knee; all wore large, round sombreros; a blanket was strapped to the saddle, and every man carried a French musket, and usually a pistol as well, in addition to the inevitable knife.

El Empecinado had been told of a large French convoy bound for the Army of Castile. It was almost certainly much too strong for him to tackle, but there were bound to be stragglers, he told Chris, and he drew his long brown fingers across his throat suggestively, his teeth bared, startlingly white against the blackness of his face. Chris frowned instinctively. This was not war as he knew it, but murder.

'You would think differently, *señor* Carey,' the guerrilla said quickly, 'if you were a Spaniard, and came to your home to find it in ashes, and your father and mother dead on the road.' He turned away, and Chris stared after him, still frowning. Yes, perhaps he would think differently, he decided.

They halted some two hundred yards above the main road from Burgos, and everyone dismounted. The horses were hidden carefully behind the crest of the hill, and the guerrillas lay down to wait as patiently as they could. The French convoy had left Travanca that morning an hour after dawn, so El Empecinado had discovered, and was bound for Logroño.

Chris made himself comfortable behind a tree, and puffed contentedly at a cigar, stretching out his legs in the warm sunshine. His back was stiff, and he would have a red, puckered scar below the shoulder for the rest of his life, but otherwise the wound had healed perfectly. He could be grateful to El Empecinado for that, he knew, for it was the guerrilla leader who had cut out the bullet.

Chris wished that he could feel grateful, but there was much about the guerrilla that repelled him. He was a sullen, brooding man, sometimes sitting by the fire in the cave for hours on end without speaking, and then changing without warning to a mood of violent passion, when the rest of the band avoided him, and the glance of his hot, furious eyes. They had no great love for him, that was clear, but he had led them to many victories over the French. That was the only test for a guerrilla chief.

The hours passed slowly. El Empecinado became restless, fidgeting with his knife, throwing pebbles against the tree, or examining the priming of his pistols. Chris could guess what was in his mind. The last two raids had been failures. Another disaster, and the guerrillas would wander away to find another leader, quickly forgetting the many times El Empecinado had been successful.

A low whistle came from the right. El Empecinado let out a hiss of relief, and scrambled to his feet. A cloud of brown dust was floating slowly over the hillsides in the distance.

Chris put his telescope on a boulder; it was a beautifully made instrument which he had bought from Dollond's in London, and through the thick dust he could see the twinkle of steel breastplates and helmets. 'Cavalry as the advance guard,' he muttered, and then behind were the long columns of the infantry, gaitered legs moving steadily up and down, and the files of black shakos stretching back out of sight.

As Chris put down his telescope, he saw El Empecinado looking at it curiously. Chris handed it to him. The guerrilla grunted, and spent five minutes inspecting the approaching column. He seemed reluctant to hand back the glass, and stroked the shining cover with his brown fingers.

'A fine glass, *Inglés*,' he said.

'Yes, it is.'

'It cost a great deal of money?'

Chris nodded and held out his hand for the telescope. El Empecinado grunted, and turned back to watch the column. There was nothing that either he or his band could do for the moment, though. The French advance guard was much too powerful for the guerrillas to attack, and they were forced to lie there and watch the columns of infantry plod past and down the road to Logroño. Mainly recruits, Chris thought, noticing the clean uniforms.

The infantry were past now, and behind them came the long baggage train, solid-wheeled carts, screeching and bumping over the road, long lines of mules, and spare horses. El Empecinado watched them greedily. The capture of a French commissariat train would be a resounding feat. But the risks were too great. There were two more troops of cavalry at least riding on either side of the road, Dragoons, Chris thought, to judge by their brass helmets and long black top boots.

Then the wagons, too had gone, and there were only the usual stragglers, small groups of tired men, trudging along slowly half a mile or so behind the rest.

El Empecinado jumped to his feet, and waved to his men. Reluctantly Chris mounted and followed the guerrillas as they rode down towards the road. But he could admire the way El Empecinado made use of cover, and brought his men to within fifty yards of the road before they were seen by the French. And by that time it was too late for the French.

El Empecinado pulled out a pistol, shouted loudly, and set his horse to a gallop. A wave of shrieking Spaniards flooded down the last slope, and as they came, the French tried to close up.

'Hold your fire,' Chris muttered under his breath, his professional instincts as an infantry officer getting the better of him. But the French were such obvious recruits, and badly frightened ones at that. They banged away a feeble and scattered volley at extreme range, and while they were still trying to reload, the guerrillas were in the middle of them.

Chris pulled up above the road, and well out of the massacre that was taking place below. It was as well for the Spaniards that he did so. To his left he saw the brass helmets of a troop of French Dragoons suddenly bursting into sight over a slight ridge. He yelled and waved his hands. The guerrillas turned their horses, and made for the shelter of the trees several hundreds of yards above the road. But one group was cut off, and the Dragoons rode them down with a relentless fury.

Chris saw no reason why he should wait. He was already half-way up the hill and within reach of safety when he slowed down to see what was happening behind him. Most of the guerrillas had escaped; two were just clear of the road, and Chris recognized El Empecinado and a fellow called Pablo, nominally the second in command of the band.

As Chris watched, another splutter of fire came from the survivors of the French infantry. El Empecinado's horse reared up, and then toppled sideways. The guerrilla was a fine horseman, though, due to his cavalry training; he flung himself nimbly from the saddle just before his horse would have rolled over on him.

Two of the Dragoons spurred towards him, swords in the air. Pablo glanced over his shoulder, and shot past Chris and into the trees, followed by the rest of the band. What happened to their leader was clearly no affair of theirs.

Chris hesitated. He had two pistols in his belt, and whatever might be his failings as a platoon commander, and Thomas Lloyd had often told him they were numerous, he was a fine shot with a pistol.

He shook his reins, and cantered down the slope, thumbing back the cocking piece of one pistol. It was a French one, and he had never fired it before, but he had checked the priming and the flint an hour ago.

He was barely in time. El Empecinado had no lack of courage. He was waiting for the Dragoons, though he must have known that the odds were hopelessly against him. One of his pistols was empty; he had only one shot left, and a man on foot faced with two mounted men who knew how to handle their swords was a dead man.

The Dragoons made the mistake of over-eagerness; one was well ahead of the other, and so intent upon El Empecinado that he never saw Chris coming down behind him. Chris swung up the heavy pistol and fired. The Dragoon threw up his arms, and crashed to the ground. As he did so, El Empecinado fired, too, and the second Dragoon, with a clatter of helmet and breastplate, rolled over on the hard turf.

'Catch his horse!' Chris shouted.

The guerrilla leapt for the riderless horse and swung himself into the saddle. Head down, and kicking the horse vigorously, he galloped after Chris and into the trees. They did not stop there, but crashed on through the copse and into the bewildering tangle of hills and valleys beyond where they knew the French would never bother to pursue them.

They found the rest of the band dismounting on a small plateau, some of them drinking and eating. El Empecinado watched them in smouldering silence, and they glanced up at him, and then down again, disgruntled, tired and somewhat guilty, Chris thought. The only man who faced El Empecinado was Pablo.

'So!' he said. 'You lead us into another trap, El Empecinado.'

El Empecinado jumped down, and cursed the man fluently, and Spanish, as Chris had learnt by now, was a language quite unequalled in Europe for its choice of abuse, and its vocabulary of searing, insulting terms.

Pablo scowled and shook his head. He was a big man, with broad shoulders and long arms, a dangerous, bull-necked and obstinate fellow.

El Empecinado finished at last. 'You would make a better leader than I, eh, Pablo?'

'*Con muchogusto!*' Pablo grunted. 'With much pleasure. We are tired of these army methods of yours, El Empecinado. You think that because you were in the regular cavalry no one else knows how to lead an attack on the French.'

'And you know, do you, Pablo?'

'We all know,' Pablo said fiercely. He turned to the others. '*Que dicen ustedes?* What do you all say?'

They shuffled their feet, but said nothing. Chris smiled. They would remain neutral, or until the question of the leadership was settled between these two.

'There is only one leader here,' El Empecinado said. He pulled out the long, heavy knife from his belt, and draped his cloak over his left arm.

A sigh came from the circle of men. Pablo stepped back hastily. Out came his knife, and his cloak fluttered, too. The guerrillas moved into a circle of dark, swarthy faces, eyes gleaming as they watched the two men in the centre.

Knees slightly bent, Pablo and El Empecinado were pacing round each other on tip-toe; now forward, then back or to the side with an odd and unnatural grace of movement, like two dancers in a stately minuet in some resplendent ballroom, Chris thought.

But if this was a dance, it was a dance of death. Each man was holding his knife with the thumb on top of the blade, the point inclined upwards, the wrist down. The first false step, the slightest hesitation or miscalculation of distance, and one of those long, heavy blades would end the fight with a single stab.

Chris had learnt to box, and he could admire the footwork of the two men, badly matched though they might have seemed at first sight; Pablo, broad and tall, long of reach, and heavily, even clumsily built, face to face with El Empecinado, much shorter, leaner and more nimble, turning on the balls of his feet like one of those ballet dancers Chris had seen at the theatre in Lisbon.

Then the brown cloaks fluttered as Pablo came in with a sudden rush, one long arm shooting out. He moved with a deceptive speed for a man of his build, but El Empecinado sidestepped and turned and struck. His blade ripped into Pablo's cloak, and left a jagged tear in the thick cloth.

A hiss of pent-up breath went round the intent circle, and Chris leant forward in his saddle, peering over the ring of brown sombreros, fascinated, horrified, by this murderous business.

Once again the two were circling around each other another quick rush by Pablo, the same sidestep by his opponent, but Pablo seemed to anticipate the move. Up went El Empecinado's arm and cloak as he pivoted on his feet, but he was too close to Pablo. He leapt back and grunted. Blood was staining the arm of his jacket, and there was a long rip in the cloth. He bared his teeth, his eyes half closed, feinted to the right, darted back to the left, and lunged with his knife. It came up, flickered past Pablo's face, and a gasp went up from the guerrillas as Pablo scuttled clear on his long legs.

Another feint from El Empecinado, a double feint this time, another lunge, and Chris heard the thump as the knife went home on Pablo's chest. Then Pablo was on his back, coughing out his life while the guerrillas watched him impassively.

El Empecinado was tying up the gash on his arm. 'My thanks, *señor* Carey,' he said. 'You saved my life a few minutes ago.' He climbed into his saddle. '*Vamos!*' he cried, and trotted away. The guerrillas mounted and followed him in silence like sheep.

Chris drew a deep breath, and wiped away the perspiration on his forehead, before he, too, cantered up the hill.

Chris surveyed the damp walls of the cave, the flickering fire light, and not for the first time during the last few weeks decided that he had lived long enough with Spanish guerrillas. The cave itself was a pigsty, full of wood smoke, the smell of garlic, of fleas and unwashed Spaniards. And the Spanish flea, the men of his platoon had often said, was the worst flea in Europe. Chris could

*Knees slightly bent, Pablo and El Empecinado were pacing
round each other*

well believe it.

Spain seemed a country of extremes, he thought. He had never experienced such contrasts of heat and cold; nor had he seen such wild and picturesque scenery, or such bare and savage plains that might well be called deserts. The people were the same, charming and civilized, or like these guerrillas, barbarous, cruel, with the unrestrained habits of animals.

Chris had asked El Empecinado to make inquiries about British warships off the coast, but so far the villagers had no information of value. The line of battle ships would be well out in the Bay of Biscay, Chris realized, but frigates must surely come close inshore. If so, a fishing boat could take him out.

But no frigates had been seen for several weeks, apparently. Probably the Navy was too busy convoying home Sir John Moore's army, Chris thought gloomily. He wondered if it might be wiser to make for the coast and lie hidden up in some fishing village until a frigate was sighted. Anything, he felt, would be preferable to living much longer with El Empecinado.

But on the third day after the unsuccessful raid on the French convoy, a man found his way up to the cave. He was from a village far to the north, and Chris questioned him.

He was a farmer, and answered to the name of Camillo, a tubby, round-faced little man, self-important and fussy, and not at all at his ease in the presence of El Empecinado.

'I can take you to Lequeitio, *señor*,' he said.

'Where's that?'

'About fifty kilometres along the coast from San Sebastián, *señor*.'

That would mean a journey due north of approximately sixty miles, Chris reckoned; three days at the most, on horseback.

'Are there any French troops near Lequeitio?' he asked.

'No, *señor*. None. The nearest are at Bilbao and San Sebastián.'

'And will the local people give me away? This red coat is conspicuous,' Chris said, pointing to his faded tunic.

Camillo shook his head emphatically. 'There are no *alfrance-*

sados in Lequeitio, *señor*,' he protested.

'There had better not be,' El Empecinado said, and Chris half smiled. Collaborators with the French received little mercy from their fellow Spaniards.

'You will be safe with Camillo,' the guerrilla leader added. 'Eh, Camillo?' and he eyed the little farmer.

Camillo nodded his head violently, his eyes on El Empecinado, his round face anxious, like a cheerful little puppy so ready to please, but wary of a swift kick at any moment.

Chris left the next morning. He and Camillo had decided to use mules rather than horses, for horses, especially French horses, would attract too much attention. Chris said good-bye to El Empecinado, and thanked him, no easy task, for he disliked the man. On his part, El Empecinado was all Spanish courtesy and charm, very different from his normal manner, and Chris received the impression, startling though it might be, that the guerrilla both liked and respected him.

Not until an hour after they had left the cave did Chris discover that his telescope was missing. He scowled angrily at the empty pouch. There was little doubt in his mind about the thief. Should he ride back? He started to laugh. El Empecinado was not the man to face with an accusation of theft, and Chris remembered the fight with Pablo. At this moment he was probably lying outside the cave inspecting the surrounding countryside through an expensive, London-made telescope. Well, it was worth it to be free of the guerrillas, and Chris nudged his mule to follow Camillo once again.

Camillo soon regained his normal cheerfulness once he was several miles from the guerrillas, and Chris asked him why he was so afraid of El Empecinado, and why he had travelled so far from his home to give information about British ships.

Camillo's plump brown face screwed up with distaste. 'El Empecinado is the most important chieftain in these parts, *señor*,' he said. 'If he suspects one of being an *alfrancesado*, then . . .' he drew his finger across his throat, and gulped realistically.

'Do the French ever send patrols to Lequeitio?'

'Oh, no, *señor, puedo asegurar a usted,* I can assure you,' Camillo said hastily. 'We have the guerrillas instead,' he added gloomily.

'And what do they do?'

'We have to supply them with food, *señor*. And they never pay.'

Chris grinned. 'I don't suppose the French would pay, either.'

'*No hay duda, señor,*' Camillo said. 'No doubt. War is very hard for us farmers, *señor,*' and he sighed deeply.

On the first night they stayed in a village where the name of El Empecinado was enough to furnish Chris and Camillo with accommodation, and in a clean house, in comfortable beds with fresh linen, a wonderful change for Chris after the filth and discomfort of the cave up in the hills.

After supper, a lamb stew, spiced as usual with garlic and pepper and excellent vegetables, Chris sat out in the evening sun, an object of much curiosity to the villagers, probably the first Englishman they had ever seen.

The older people settled down on the stone benches outside their houses, the men smoking cigars, and the women chatting, while the girls of the village danced their wild boleros and fandangos to the click of castanets and the clash of tambourines. Chris was delighted with it all, the colour, the whirling figures, the tremendous vitality, as the brown-skinned girls, black-eyed, black-haired, in blue jackets and slit sleeves, with red stockings and bright petticoats, whirled and stamped in front of him.

He would have to describe all this to his mother and his sisters, and they would want to know the details of the dresses. But perhaps his mother would not have approved of this dancing; or would she? She had lived in India with his father when Sir Henry served in the East India Company, and they must have seen native dances out there. He would like to visit India, too, Chris thought as he went upstairs to the small, white-washed bedroom. But he would have to get out of Spain first.

Captain of Foot

After a breakfast of hot chocolate and *salchichas*, the highly-seasoned Spanish sausages, Chris and Camillo set off again. They kept well away from the main roads, and up in the hills. The only people they met were the shepherds in their sheepskin clothing, carrying long guns, and followed by huge and extremely dangerous-looking wolf dogs.

On the next evening they arrived at Camillo's farm, a low, white building overlooking the sea, so Camillo said, for the sun was down, and Chris could see nothing. They ate supper, cooked with great skill by Camillo's wife, a bustling woman with a loud laugh and a sharp tongue. Two small children sat by the fire and stared open-eyed at Chris, never moving, fascinated and enthralled by this strange visitor.

'They have never seen an *Inglés* before, *señor*,' Camillo said. 'Now, as for me, I am a travelled man and . . .' A loud cackle from his wife interrupted him, and Chris grinned. It was quite clear that Camillo had never seen an Englishman before, either.

Camillo went down to Lequeitio immediately after breakfast to make inquiries. He advised Chris to stay on the farm. There was no danger for him in the village, but it was not worth taking any risks. So Chris spent most of the day walking, followed by the children, far too shy to do more than nod when he spoke to them. But he found a piece of high ground behind the farm, and from there he saw the sea, a deep blue, far below, with a rocky coastline, and steep cliffs, broken here and there by narrow inlets. Chris sat and looked at this lovely sight for an hour, cursing El Empecinado for the theft of his telescope.

But the only sails he saw were obviously those of fishing boats. There was no sign of a warship on the whole expanse of sea.

Camillo was full of news, though. 'There are British ships in the Bay, *señor*,' he said. 'Pedro Servillas saw one yesterday. He will take you out each day when he fishes.' The little farmer hesitated. 'He will want money, *señor*.'

Chris nodded. He had been afraid of this. In his pocket was a small roll of Spanish notes, but he knew from experience that the ordinary Spaniard of the countryside was not interested in anything but coins, and he had none.

'Gold, *señor*, if you have any,' Camillo added.

The only gold that Chris possessed was his watch, and that, he had decided, would be his farewell present to Camillo, for he liked the portly little farmer, and Camillo had never raised the question of payment, and Chris did not think he would.

'I have a silver flask, Camillo,' he said, and showed it to the farmer.

'A fine flask, *señor*,' Camillo said. 'Wasted on a mere fisherman like Pedro.'

Chris grinned. Clearly a farmer such as Camillo would be a far more suitable person. 'If this Pedro puts me on board a British warship, the Captain will pay him well, and in gold,' Chris added.

Camillo nodded his satisfaction. 'If you give Pedro this flask, *señor*, and promise him the gold, I think he will help you. I will take you down to Lequeitio in the morning. And I will mention the name of El Empecinado to Pedro Servillas. I have no fear of such a person as a mere guerrilla myself, you must understand, *señor* Carey,' and Chris nodded gravely, 'but an ignorant fisherman, ah, that will be different,' and Camillo nodded emphatically.

They went down on mules to the village, and Chris felt very conspicuous in his red coat with the white facings as they rode down the single street. But he had refused to wear Spanish clothes. If he was captured by the French in civilian dress, he could be shot as a spy.

Pedro Servillas was on the little quay. He was a large, swarthy fellow, sulky and morose, and he listened in brooding silence while Camillo spoke of silver flasks and gold from an English captain. He held out a grimy hand for the flask, and shook his head.

Camillo played his trump card then. 'The *señor* is a friend of El Empecinado, the guerrilla chieftain, Pedro,' he said importantly. 'And you know how El Empecinado deals with his enemies.'

Pedro spat loudly. 'That for El Empecinado,' he said.

Chris nearly laughed out aloud as he saw the horror on Camillo's face. 'If you put me aboard a British ship, Pedro,' he said, 'I will see that the Captain rewards you in addition to the flask.'

'In gold?'

'Yes, in gold. *Puedo asegurar a usted.* I can assure you.'

Pedro stared at the water in silence for a moment, while Camillo shifted impatiently from one foot to the other. Chris was quite confident. He possessed one supremely useful gift, though he was not fully aware of the fact, in that he could often tell with surprisingly accuracy how a person would react to a particular problem. And he was quite certain now that Pedro would agree. The man's hesitation was a mere pose; he did not want them to think that he was a man who rushed like a child into a decision.

'I will take the *Inglés* out to sea,' he said at last, and Camillo let out an enormous sigh of relief, though he tried, much too late, to conceal it from Pedro.

'When?' Chris asked.

'Tomorrow, *señor*. Be here an hour after sunrise.'

They were on the quay early the next morning; the sea was calm so Camillo said, though privately Chris thought there was quite a considerable breeze blowing out in the bay. He brought out his gold watch, and handed it to Camillo.

'I want you to have this, Camillo,' he said. 'It is all I have left of any value.'

Camillo gasped as he took the heavy watch. 'This is a gold watch, *señor*?'

'Yes.'

'An English watch?'

'Oh, yes. Made in London.'

Camillo took off his sombrero, and his brown eyes were moist. 'You are a great nobleman, *señor* Carey,' he said. 'There is no one in Lequeitio, not even the priest, who has such a watch as this.'

Chris smiled at the little man. 'Well, don't tell Pedro,' he said. 'Pedro Servillas!' Camillo said with scorn. 'That lump of offal,' and he went on to describe the fisherman with a wealth of Spanish abuse that made Chris choke with delight.

Pedro appeared at that moment. '*Buenos días, señor*,' he said gruffly. 'I am ready to sail.'

Chris shook hands with Camillo, still muttering courtly Spanish phrases, and went on board the little fishing smack. As they slipped away from the quay, the last Chris saw of Camillo was the fat little man inspecting his watch with an air of the most tremendous importance, and then holding it to his ear, his mouth wide open in delight.

Pedro was no conversationalist, Chris discovered. He left Chris to himself, and took the boat out to sea without a word. They fished a mile or so from the coast all that morning, and then moved farther out after midday, until the coast was low on the horizon.

But there was no sign of any sails out to sea, and when the sun went down Chris went below to the single cabin, and tried to sleep in the flea-ridden bunk.

The wind had freshened when he came on deck again, and the boat was rolling and pitching. Chris refused a sausage, and ate some dry bread for breakfast. His stomach, he was afraid, would not stand up to garlic on a choppy sea.

'Sail, sail!' It was one of the two boys who helped Pedro with his fishing.

Chris made his way towards the bows, and followed the pointing finger of the boy. For a moment he could see nothing, and then a white speck showed against the blue horizon.

'French or British?' Chris asked Pedro.

The Spaniard shrugged his shoulders, and spat over the side. 'Not many French ships at sea, *señor*,' he said. 'Too many *Inglés*.'

Chris yearned for his telescope, and once again he muttered curses on the head of the distant El Empecinado. He could distinguish the three masts of the approaching ship now, but she was still too far away to pick out her flag. '*Inglés!*' Pedro said suddenly, and nodded his head.

'Are you certain?' Chris asked.

'*Lo estoy seguro*,' Pedro said curtly. 'I am quite certain of it.'

He had swung the tiller over, and they headed out to sea to cut off the ship. Chris eyed him doubtfully, but there was little he could do. In his belt was one pistol, but that would not be of much use against a boatload of Frenchmen.

He strained his eyes, staring across the water. That was a warship, a frigate almost certainly, and there was her flag. A Tricolour or the White Ensign? One look through his telescope, and . . .

'You will not forget the gold, *señor*?' Pedro asked.

'If it's an English frigate, you'll have your gold,' Chris said. There would certainly be no difficulty about that. His elder brother, Peter, was a Captain in the Navy, in command of a frigate too, and somewhere on the French coast with the Channel fleet, Chris believed. His name would be a good enough introduction for a Naval Captain to advance Chris all that he needed.

The frigate was turning. Instead of three masts Chris could see only one now, and a single pyramid of white sails as the frigate came straight for the fishing boat. Well, he would soon know whether she was French or English.

Fifty yards away, and the frigate seemed as if she would swoop past Pedro's little boat, as she heeled over in the wind, her high, sharp bows throwing up a creamy bow wave, with an occasional shower of spray leaping up above her jib.

Then she spun round into the wind and came to a stop, rising and falling gently on the waves, her black and white hull broken by the gun ports, and from the mizzen mast Chris at last could see the Ensign, blowing stiff and clear to the eye in the breeze.

'Come alongside!' a voice roared, the first English voice that Chris had heard for three months.

Pedro brought his boat alongside the towering hull, and a rope ladder was flung down. One of the boys grabbed it, and

Chris scrambled into the bows.

'The gold, *señor*, the gold!' Pedro called out in anguish from the tiller.

'*Si, en verdad*, Pedro!' Chris shouted, as he put his foot on the first rung of the ladder.

Climbing a rope ladder up the side of a frigate in a slightly choppy sea was an unnerving business, Chris discovered, as he swayed back and then bumped into the hull with a jerk that nearly sent him tumbling into the water. Then a hand caught him by the shoulder, and heaved him up over the bulwark.

Chris took a deep breath of sheer happiness as he saw the white, freshly scrubbed deck, the immaculately coiled ropes and the gleaming brasswork. Even the sailors who stood around him seemed scrubbed and shaven and spotless after the succession of dark, swarthy, and dirty faces with which he had lived for so many weeks.

'I'm a British officer,' he said. 'Escaped from the French. Where's the Captain?'

'Captain Carey's on the quarterdeck,' a Lieutenant said.

'Who?' Chris said incredulously.

'Good Lord! The prodigal son returns!' a voice shouted. 'Bring out the fatted calf and make merry! Where the deuce did you spring from, Chris?'

Chris looked with delight at his brother's grinning face. 'Hullo, Peter,' he said. 'This is a piece of luck meeting you. I . . .'

A voice was roaring from the fishing boat down below, and Chris caught the familiar words. '*El oro! El oro, señor!*'

Chris laughed. 'He wants his reward, Peter. Have you any sovereigns on board? I promised this fisherman some gold if he put me on board a British ship.'

'I've got something better than that,' Peter Carey said. 'Spanish gold doubloons. We have a supply in case we want to buy fresh food from the Spanish. Will twenty satisfy this fellow?'

But Pedro was already clambering over the side, and he

dropped down on to the deck of the frigate, a huge and tattered-looking figure by the side of the British sailors.

'Does he speak any English?' Peter asked, looking at him with distaste. 'I don't think much of your Spanish friends, Chris. Hi! Stop that, you filthy swab!'

But he was too late. Pedro had spat out a long stream of liquid tobacco over the white deck, the greatest crime that could be committed on a British warship, and Chris turned his head to stifle his grin as he saw the expressions of horror on the faces of Peter and his officers. Even the sailors were staring aghast, and one had already snatched up a mop and a bucket of water.

But he spoke hurriedly to Pedro in his fluent Spanish. 'Yes, he'll take twenty doubloons, Peter.'

'He can have fifty if he gets off my deck,' Peter said. 'I'll have to have a receipt, though, Chris. The Admiralty Paymaster won't pass twenty guineas without some proof. Can this fellow write?'

'I shouldn't think so,' Chris said. 'Give me some paper, and I'll put it down in Spanish and English, and he can make a cross for his signature.'

Pedro's dark eyes gleamed as he watched the heavy gold coins being counted, and he quickly hid them away inside his brown coat. Chris read out the form of receipt.

'Received from Captain Peter Carey, of H.M.S. *Heron*, the sum of twenty doubloons for delivery of one British army officer, escaped from the French.'

Pedro took the pen in his huge fist and scrawled an untidy cross. Then he embraced Chris, breathing garlic over him with profusion, and went down over the side.

Chris leant over and waved to the boys below. He heard Peter shouting orders behind him as the frigate heaved and turned, and Chris took a last look at the faint coastline of Spain. Hot water, soap, razor, steaming coffee, clean sheets and blankets, were the thoughts that went through his mind as he saw the fishing boat slip away behind them.

The Cruel Sea

NICHOLAS MONSARRAT

When *Compass Rose*, one of the Atlantic convoy patrol ships is torpedoed, she sinks within minutes and her crew are left to fight the horrific, seeping cold of the North Atlantic. In these conditions few men can survive . . .

Some – a few – did not die: Lieutenant-Commander Ericson, Lieutenant Lockhart, Leading Radar Mechanic Sellars, Sick-Berth Attendant Crowther, Sub-Lieutenant Ferraby, Petty Officer Phillips, Leading-Stoker Gracey, Stoker Grey, Stoker Spurway, Telegraphist Widdowes, Ordinary-Seaman Tewson. Eleven men, on the two rafts; no others were left alive by morning.

It reminded Lockhart of the way a party ashore gradually thinned out and died away, as time and quarrelling and stupor and sleepiness took their toll. At one stage it had been almost a manageable affair: the two Carleys, with their load of a dozen men each and their cluster of hangers-on, had paddled towards each other across the oily heaving sea, and he had taken some kind of rough roll-call, and found that there were over thirty men still alive. But that had been a lot earlier on, when the party was a comparative success . . . As the long endless night progressed, men slipped out of life without warning, shivering and freezing to death almost between sentences: the strict account of dead and living got out of hand, lost its authority and became meaningless. Indeed, the score was hardly worth the keeping, when within a little while – unless the night ended and the sun came up to warm them – it might add up to total disaster.

On the rafts, in the whispering misery of the night that would not end, men were either voices or silences: if they were silences for too many minutes, it meant that they need no longer be counted in, and their places might be taken by others who still had a margin of life and warmth in their bodies.

'Christ, it's cold . . .'

'How far away was the convoy?'

'About thirty miles.'

'Shorty . . .'

'Did anyone see Jameson?'

'He was in the fo'c'sle.'

'None of *them* got out.'

'Lucky bastards . . . Better than this, any road.'

'We've got a chance still.'

'It's getting lighter.'

'That's the moon.'

'Shorty . . . Wake up . . .'

'She must've gone down inside of five minutes.'

'Like *Sorrel*.'

'Thirty miles off, they should have got us on the Radar.'

'If they were watching out properly.'

'Who was stern escort?'

'*Trefoil*.'

'Shorty . . .'

'How many on the other raft?'

'Same as us, I reckon.'

'Christ, it's cold.'

'Wind's getting up, too.'

'I'd like to meet the bastard that put us here.'

'Once is enough for me.'

'Shorty . . . What's the matter with you?'

'Must be pretty near Iceland.'
'We don't need telling that.'
'*Trefoil's* all right. They ought to have seen us on the Radar.'
'Not with some half-asleep sod of an operator on watch.'
'Shorty . . .'
'Stop saying that . . . ! Can't you see he's finished?'
'But he was talking to me.'
'That was an hour ago, you dope.'
'Wilson's dead, sir.'
'Sure?'
'Yes. Stone cold.'
'Tip him over, then . . . Who's coming up next?'
'Any more for the Skylark?'
'What's the use? It's no warmer up on the raft.'
'Christ, it's cold . . .'

At one point during the night, the thin crescent moon came through the ragged clouds, and illuminated for a few moments the desperate scene below. It shone on a waste of water, growing choppy with the biting wind: it shone on the silhouettes of men hunched together on the rafts, and the shadows of men clinging to them, and the blurred outlines of men in the outer ring, where the corpses wallowed and heaved, and the red lights burned and burned aimlessly on the breasts of those who, hours before, had switched them on in hope and confidence. For a few minutes the moon put this cold sheen upon the face of the water, and upon the foreheads of the men whose heads were still upright; and then it withdrew, veiling itself abruptly as if, in pity and amazement, it had seen enough, and knew that men in this extremity deserved only the decent mercy of darkness.

Ferraby did not die: but towards dawn it seemed to him that he *did* die, as he held Rose, the young signalman, in his arms, and Rose died for him. Throughout the night Rose had been sitting next to him on the raft, and sometimes they had talked and sometimes fallen silent: it had recalled that other night of long ago, their first night at sea, when he and Rose had chatted to each other and, urged on by the darkness and loneliness of their new surroundings, had drawn close together. Now the need for closeness was more compelling still, and they had turned to each other again, in an unspoken hunger for comfort, so young and unashamed that presently they found that they were holding hands . . . But in the end Rose had fallen silent, and had not answered his questions, and had sagged against him as if he had gone to sleep: Ferraby had put his arm round him and, when he slipped down farther still, had held him on his knees.

After waiting, afraid to put it to the test, he said: 'Are you all right, Rose?' There was no answer. He bent down and touched the face that was close under his own. By some instinct of compassion, it was with his lips that he touched it, and his lips came away icy and trembling. Now he was alone . . . The tears ran down Ferraby's cheeks, and fell on the open upturned eyes. In mourning and in mortal fear, he sat on, with the cold stiffening body of his friend like a dead child under his heart.

Lockhart did not die, though many times during that night there seemed to him little reason why this should be so. He had spent most of the dark hours in the water alongside Number Two Carley, of which he was in charge: only towards morning when there was room and to spare, did he climb onto it. From this slightly higher vantage point he looked round him, and felt the cold and smelt the oil, and saw the other raft nearby, and the troubled water in between; and he pondered the dark shadows which were dead men, and the clouds racing across the sky, and the single star overhead, and the sound of the bitter wind; and then, with all this to daunt him and drain him of hope, he took a last grip on himself, and on the handful of men on the raft, and set himself to stay alive till daylight, and to take them along with him.

He made them sing, he made them move their arms and legs, he made them talk, he made them keep awake. He slapped their faces, he kicked them, he rocked the raft till they were forced to rouse themselves and cling on: he dug deep into his repertoire of filthy stories and produced a selection so pointless and so disgusting that he would have blushed to tell them, if the extra blood had been available. He made them act 'Underneath the Spreading Chestnut Tree', and play guessing games: he roused Ferraby from his dejected silence, and made him repeat all the poetry he knew: he imitated all the characters of ITMA, and forced the others to join in. He set them to paddling the raft round in circles, and singing the 'Volga Boatmen': recalling a childhood game, he divided them into three parties, and detailed them to shout 'Russia', 'Prussia', and 'Austria', at the same moment – a manoeuvre designed to sound like a giant and appropriate sneeze . . . The men on his raft loathed him, and the sound of his voice, and his appalling optimism: they cursed him openly, and he answered them back in the same language, and promised them a liberal dose of detention as soon as they got back to harbour.

For all this, he drew on an unknown reserve of strength and energy which now came to his rescue. When he climbed out of the water, he had felt miserably stiff and cold: the wild and foolish activity, the clownish antics, soon restored him, and some of it communicated itself to some of the men with him, and some of them caught the point of it and became foolish and clownish and energetic in their turn, and so some of them saved their lives.

Sellars, Crowther, Gracey and Tewson did not die. They were on Number Two Carley with Lockhart and Ferraby, and they were all that were left alive by morning, despite these frenzied efforts to keep at bay the lure and the sweetness of sleep. It was Tewson's first ship, and his first voyage: he was a cheerful young cockney, and now and again during the night he had made them laugh by asking cheekily: 'Does this sort of thing happen *every* trip?' It was a pretty small joke, but (as Lockhart realized) it was the sort of contribution they had to have . . . There were other contributions: Sellars sang an interminable version of 'The Harlot of Jerusalem', Crowther (the Sick-Berth Attendant who had been a vet) imitated animal noises, Gracey gave an exhibition of shadow-boxing which nearly overturned the raft. They did, in fact, the best they could; and their best was just good enough to save their lives.

Phillips, Grey, Spurway, and Widdowes did not die. They were the survivors of Number One Carley, with the Captain; and they owed their lives to him. Ericson, like Lockhart, had realized that sleep had to be fought continuously and relentlessly if anyone were to be left alive in the morning: he had therefore spent the greater part of the night putting the men on his raft through an examination for their next higher rating. He made a round-game of it, half serious, half childish: he asked each man upwards of thirty questions: if the answer were correct all the others had to clap, if not, they had to boo at the tops of their voices, and the culprit had to perform some vigorous kind of forfeit . . . His authority carried many of the men along for several hours: it was only towards dawn, when he felt his own brain lagging with the effort of concentration, that the competitors began to thin out, and the clapping and shouting to fade to a ghostly mutter of sound: to a moaning like the wind, and a rustling like the cold waves curling and slopping against the raft, the waves that trustfully waited to swallow them all.

The Captain did not die: it was as if, after *Compass Rose* went down, he had nothing left to die with. The night's 'examination' effort had been necessary, and so he had made it, automatically – but only as the Captain, in charge of a raftful of men who had always been owed his utmost care and skill: the effort had had no part of his heart in it. That heart seemed to have shrivelled, in the few terrible minutes between the striking of his ship, and her sinking: he had loved *Compass Rose*, not sentimentally, but with the pride and the strong attachment which the past three years had inevitably brought, and to see her thus contemptuously destroyed before his eyes had been an appalling shock. There was no word and no reaction appropriate to this wicked night: it drained him of all feeling. But still he had not died, because he was forty-seven, and a sailor, and tough and strong, and he understood – though now he hated – the sea.

All his men had longed for daylight: Ericson merely noted that it was now at hand, and that the poor remnants of his crew might yet survive. When the first grey light from the eastward began to creep across the water, he roused himself, and his men, and set them to paddling towards the other raft, which had drifted a full mile away. The light, gaining in strength, seeped round them as if borne by the bitter wind itself, and fell without pity upon the terrible pale sea, and the great streaks of oil, and the floating bundles that had been living men. As the two rafts drew together, the figures on them waved to each other, jerkily, like people who could scarcely believe that they were not alone: when they were within earshot, there was a croaking hail from a man on Lockhart's raft, and Phillips, on the Captain's, made a vague noise in his throat in reply.

No one said anything more until the rafts met, and touched; and then they all looked at each other, in horror and in fear.

The two rafts were much alike. On each of them was the same handful of filthy oil-soaked men who still sat upright, while other men lay still in their arms or sprawled like dogs at their feet. Round them, in the water, were the same attendant figures – a horrifying fringe of bobbing corpses, with their meaningless faces blank to the sky and their hands frozen to the ratlines.

Between the dead and the living was no sharp dividing line. The men upright on the rafts seemed to blur with the dead men they nursed, and with the derelict men in the water, as part of the same vague and pitiful design.

Ericson counted the figures still alive on the other Carley. There were four of them, and Lockhart and Ferraby: they had the same fearful aspect as the men on his own raft: blackened, shivering, their cheeks and temples sunken with the cold, their limbs bloodless; men who, escaping death during the dark hours, still crouched stricken in its shadow when morning came. And the whole total was eleven . . . He rubbed his hand across his frozen lips, and cleared his throat, and said:

'Well, Number One . . .'

'Well, sir . . .'

Lockhart stared back at Ericson for a moment, and then looked away. There could be nothing more, nothing to ease the unbearable moment.

The wind blew chill in their faces, the water slopped and broke in small ice-cold waves against the rafts, the harnessed fringe of dead men swayed like dancers. The sun was coming up now, to add dreadful detail: it showed the rafts, horrible in themselves, to be only single items in a whole waste of cruel water, on which countless bodies rolled and laboured amid countless bits of wreckage, adrift under the bleak sky. All round them, on the oily, fouled surface, the wretched flotsam, all that was left of *Compass Rose*, hurt and shamed the eye.

The picture of the year, thought Lockhart: 'Morning, with Corpses.'

So *Viperous* found them.

The Professionals

JOHN HARRIS

**Martin Falconer and his friend 'Bill' Sykes
have crash landed behind the front line in
Belgium during the First World War. Together
they escape from the German prison camp and
with the help of Marie-Ange, a young Belgian
girl, they start the long walk to the coast.**

We set off from Noyelles soon after dark and, since the autumn
had now arrived, it wasn't late. Marie-Ange appeared at the
entrance to the barn wearing a cloak with a hood, and stout boots
and thick stockings. They gave her a lost-little-girl look, with
the drizzle on her hair and eyelashes. Her parting from her
mother seemed particularly emotional and the old lady's eyes
were streaming. Sykes was grave and silent and made kissing
Madame's hand seem twice as important, then we were tramp-
ing through the rain in the increasing darkness.

Marie-Ange knew her way all right. 'I have walk before to
Middelkerke,' she said. 'One time we walk to Ghent to see my
father.'

We didn't speak much and tramped through the puddles
silently, aware of the drizzle soaking our clothes. Marie-Ange
seemed to be made of fine springs and never seemed to be tired
and I decided that working on a farm was better practice for this

302

sort of thing than sitting in an aeroplane. I was tired long before
she was.

We halted to eat bread and meat from the haversack Sykes
carried, sitting in the shadows at the side of the road under a
clump of trees. As it was growing daylight, Marie-Ange pointed
to a timbered barn in a field. 'We will rest the day there,' she
said. 'I have write them a letter. They know we will be there, but
they are not interest to seeing us. They have much fear.'

The barn was dry and comfortable and there was plenty of
fresh straw. And placed prominently on an old crate was a bottle
of rough wine, a loaf and cheese.

Marie-Ange smiled delightedly. 'Someone has leave their
supper,' she said.

We were all hungry after the night's march in the cool air and
drizzle and we tore the loaf apart and shared the cheese and
wine. When we'd finished, we dug into the straw. It was warm
under there and I was half-asleep before I was even comfortable.

It must have been late in the afternoon when I awoke. Marie-
Ange's head was on my shoulder but she started to wakefulness
immediately I moved.

'Soon it is time to walk again,' she said.

The drizzle had stopped but there was a lot of cloud and it
seemed chilly with the damp of the low-lying fields. The farm
seemed deserted but somewhere not far away I could hear a
woman's voice and the sound of wood being sawn.

No one came near us, however, and we slipped away in the
dusk and began to head north again. Sykes was walking well but I
found the big boots Marie-Ange had found for me were heavy
and beginning to rub my heel.

'You are limping,' Marie-Ange said.

'It's having such big feet,' Sykes said mercilessly. 'More to
rub.'

That night was much colder than the previous one and the
wind was blowing from the west again bringing with it the thud
of guns and a hint of more rain. We still had about sixty kilometres
to go and I was already tired.

Through my mind a whole host of thoughts were running. I was making up a brave little farewell speech for when we had to leave Marie-Ange behind. I wasn't looking forward to it but I felt I had to put on some sort of show to make her realize how grateful we were and how pleased I was that I'd met her. It all seemed a little inadequate, however, and as I tried to improve on it the speech grew in my mind into an oration in which I made it clear how brave I thought her, how intelligent, how beautiful, and how delightful when she laughed, and I wondered if I ought to accompany it with a chaste kiss. Sykes, I thought, might even have the grace to turn his back for a while so that I could put my arms round her and make a proper job of it for a change.

She seemed to sense something was troubling me and after a while, she touched my hand as though to encourage me and we walked hand-in-hand in the darkness. But walking hand-in-hand belongs to warm evenings and strolling across fields, not slogging heavily in the damp night air, and we soon reverted to the steady trudge, one foot after the other, left, right, left, right, left, right.

I was walking head down, indifferent to the flickering western horizon and not really thinking about anything, when Sykes, who was just in front, stopped so suddenly I crashed into his back. I scraped my nose on the buckle of the haversack he was carrying and cursed him.

'Shut up,' he said sharply.

'What is it?' Marie-Ange demanded.

'Look,' Sykes said, jerking a hand.

It was only just possible to make him out and when I looked through the darkness to where he was pointing all I could see was what looked like the end of a large building among the trees.

'It's only a barn,' I said.

'Is it?' Sykes said. 'Look to the left a bit.'

We were in a small depression at the time, where the road ran between higher ground on either side. My eye moved to the left and I saw a pair of parallel lines against the sky – and V-shaped struts between them. And then a shark-like nose and a propeller.

'Aeroplanes,' I breathed.

'German aeroplanes,' Sykes agreed.

Marie-Ange looked agitated. 'We must not to stay here,' she said. 'There will be guards.'

Sykes took her arm and pulled her into the shadow of some low shrubs. 'Where are we?' he demanded.

'This is Phalempon. The village is over there.'

Sykes drew a deep breath. 'Marie-Ange,' he said. 'This is as far as we go.'

She looked puzzled. '*Je ne comprends pas.*'

'I have a better idea than going by boat. Let's *fly* back.'

'In an aeroplane?' I said.

'I hadn't thought of feathers.' Sykes jerked a hand and we moved forward to the rising ground, and crept slowly up it. Lying flat in the damp grass at the top, we could see a wide space and more aeroplanes which had been invisible from the lower ground. What I had thought was a barn was a canvas hangar.

'Albatros DIIIs or DVs,' Sykes said. 'Couldn't *we* fly 'em?'

'No!' Marie-Ange's reaction was vehement. 'This is not good!'

For once I didn't agree with her. What Sykes was suggesting made sense. 'Marie-Ange,' I said. 'Instead of taking all night to sneak past the German patrol boats, it'll take only half an hour.'

'See any guards?' Sykes asked.

In the distance across the field I could see lights but no movement. 'I'll bet they're there all right,' I said. 'They told me when they caught me it'd be no good trying to grab an aeroplane.'

'*One* of us might,' Sykes said. 'If we start something at opposite ends of the line.'

We spent the next few minutes arguing fiercely over the merits and demerits of Sykes' idea. Marie-Ange obviously didn't like it. She knew nothing about aeroplanes and she gripped my hand fiercely as we talked in low voices.

'You will be shot!'

Neither of us was listening to her now, though. Our minds

were racing with the possibility of what lay in front of us.

'We couldn't fly an aeroplane off on a pitch-black night,' I said.

Sykes gestured. 'We've flown in the dark, he said. 'Both of us.'

'We'd be better leaving at first light.'

Suddenly the plan seemed foolhardy, but Sykes prevailed and we agreed to scout round the field. Marie-Ange was unhappy about the whole thing. Her mind seemed full of foreboding and she was anxious to get away before we were found. But Sykes had got the idea firmly fixed in his head now and we decided to move round the perimeter away from where the lights lay.

'It's hopeless,' I said after a while. 'The machines are all too close to the huts. We'd be safer in a boat.'

Marie-Ange looked hopeful but Sykes pulled a face. 'Always seasick,' he said. 'Rotten sailor.'

I didn't believe him because I knew he had his mind set on doing the job by air. But it seemed impossible to steal an aeroplane from in front of the hangars and after a lot of arguing we decided to spend the rest of the night among the bushes at the end of the field farthest from the huts and hangars and watch what happened the following day. Marie-Ange fought fiercely against it. 'No,' she said. 'It is bad. It is much dangerous.'

I thought so, too, but we found a spot in the bushes to hole up in and crouched together in a huddle. Against the growing morning light, Sykes' face had a bleak eager look.

It was cold and I found I kept breaking into uncontrollable shivers, but I knew it was nothing to do with the night air. Marie-Ange seemed suddenly calm, however, as though she had decided to argue no longer.

As we waited for morning, we could hear the guns muttering away to the west and see the flickering lights against the horizon that indicated the front line. After a while I noticed that the sky behind us was growing paler.

'Fun'll start soon,' Sykes said. 'The early morning boys'll be off and we'll be able to see what happens.'

More lights were appearing now by the hangars, one of them

bobbing among the line of aeroplanes. A square of yellow appeared, as though someone had opened a door.

'Gone for their hard-boiled eggs,' Sykes said.

He seemed altogether too flippant about the whole thing but I knew it didn't mean anything. He was probably as nervous as I was and was trying to hide the fact. Then suddenly, the silence was split by the roar of an aeroplane engine starting up.

'We're off,' Sykes said. 'Warming up for the early patrol.'

Marie-Ange was crouching silently beside me and, glancing at her in the growing light, I saw there were tears on her cheeks.

'Why, Marie-Ange?' I asked. 'Why?'

She shrugged, in a peculiarly Gallic gesture. 'Because you are much brave and silly,' she said.

Another engine started up. 'Expect it's the same at Bayeffles,' Sykes said.

'I wish I were back there,' I commented without thinking, and saw Marie-Ange look quickly at me.

Another engine started and I could see the field taking shape now and the dark blocks of the huts and a thin streamer of smoke rising into the sky.

'Any minute now it'll be daylight,' Sykes said.

I had been silent and listening and I gave him a jab. 'Dry up,' I said. 'Listen!'

He cocked his head and caught the sound I'd heard – the faint hum of aeroplane engines.

'Somebody up early,' he said.

'Yes. And what's more, they're coming this way.'

Automatically, I put my arm round Marie-Ange's shoulders and pushed her closer to the ground. There was a long pause. The low hum was still audible and across the field where the hangars were it had clearly not yet been heard above the clatter of the morning duties, the clink of spanners and the noise of metal panels being removed, and the squeak of carts carrying ammunition belts.

A dog barked and I felt so tense I thought I was going to choke.

The hum of aeroplane engines was growing louder now and suddenly the men at the other end of the field woke up to it, too. There were staccato shouts and I saw them starting to run. Almost at once we heard the snarl of engines approaching from beyond the trees at tremendous speed and the sudden clack-clack of machine guns.

I grabbed Marie-Ange and thrust her down into the bushes. 'For God's sake,' Sykes was saying furiously. 'It's the Navy!'

Four black triplanes were coming over the trees at the far end of the field and I saw the earth erupt near the huts as bombs fell, then a second later the triplanes were howling past our heads.

'The swine!' Sykes roared furiously, pounding at the top of the bank with his fist. 'They've done it across us! They'll double the guards now and we'll never pinch anything.'

The triplanes were turning in a steep bank now a quarter of a mile away for a second run across the field. One of the huts at the far end was blazing and in the growing daylight I could see men running. Then I saw that one of the Albatroses had got away and was moving towards us down the field to get into position for a take-off into wind. It was a grey-and-green machine with a large letter K on the fuselage just behind the Maltese Crosses.

'Damn them!' Sykes said furiously, staring at the sky. 'They've got the sea! What more do they want?'

The grey-and-green Albatros was still moving towards us, its wings rocking as its wheels rolled over the uneven surface of the field. Several more were following it but the triplanes were coming down again now. I saw a hut go up in a shower of planks and debris, then three of the moving machines were hit, one after the other. A bomb dropped alongside one of them and it flipped neatly over on its back and burst into flames. The pilot scrambled clear and began to run from the path of the other two, but another triplane screamed down, its guns rattling, and I saw him go head over heels like a shot rabbit and one of the following Albatroses bumped over his body and then that one was hit, too, and burst into flames. The pilot of the third machine also seemed to have been hit because he was careering about the field in an indeterminate way, and he finally crashed into the machine which had flipped over on to its back. I heard the crunch as he ploughed into the starboard wings, even above the crack of the bombs and the clatter of machine guns and the shouts across the field.

The triplanes had gone now, as suddenly as they'd come, and the grey-and-green Albatros was near the end of the field immediately in front of us, swinging round to take off after them, its propeller idling, as though the pilot were trying to make up his mind which way to go to avoid the debris scattered across the centre of the landing area. Suddenly I realized Sykes was struggling out of the haversack and thrusting it at Marie-Ange. Then he wrenched off the old coat she'd acquired for him and threw it down.

'Now,' he screamed. 'Now!'

I knew at once what he intended and I swung round and kissed the startled Marie-Ange full on the lips. 'Run!' I yelled. 'Get away from here as fast as you can!'

We didn't even have a chance to say goodbye because she was already thrusting through the bushes away from the airfield while I was wrenching off the coat I was wearing and scrambling with Sykes over the lip of the rise to where the Albatros waited.

It stuck out a mile that there was a chance for one of us to escape right there in front of us, because there seemed to be complete confusion at the far end of the field. One of the hangars and two of the huts were blazing and, as I scrambled over the rise, I could see the gap where a bomb had removed another hut. The aeroplanes there were all mixed up together, facing in every possible direction, as though in their haste to get clear they had simply got in each other's way, and mechanics were frantically dragging at them to swing them round so they could head for the take-off area.

The grey-and-green Albatros was turning now to head diagonally across the field. I heard the engine roar and thought we were too late, but then I saw Sykes jump on the wing, and, throwing an arm round the German pilot's neck, reach past him into the cockpit. The engine blared but even as the machine moved forward it died again and the aeroplane slowed to a stop, its tail swinging wildly.

'For God's sake,' Sykes yelled. 'Hurry, Brat!'

I had grabbed a piece of stone from the bank as I had jumped over its lip and the next moment I was plunging through the slipstream as the engine died and on to the other wing. The German was fighting furiously under Sykes' grip, and was still threshing away with his free arm when I hit him over the head with the stone.

He immediately slumped in the cockpit. 'I've killed him,' I said.

'Shouldn't think so,' Sykes panted. 'But he's going to have a headache. Get him out, for God's sake!'

The German was a big man and neither Sykes nor I were, and it was harder than I'd ever imagined. I'd helped lift injured men from cockpits before but there'd always been plenty of assistance and plenty of time, and this time there was neither and he seemed to have his legs jammed somewhere inside. Sykes was panting and cursing in a way I'd never heard before as we fought to drag him free.

'How are we going to do it?' I shouted in a panic of excitement and fright. 'One of us riding on the wing? We'll never get away with it.'

'No – oh, for God's sake, this damn' man! – two in the cockpit! You on my knees! I've got longer legs!'

'Two in the cockpit!' I tried to reach past the German to free him. 'Can't be done.'

'It's a big cockpit.' Sykes' voice came in a panting rush. 'Albatroses are. It's not a Pup and neither of us is a giant. Do it like we learned to fly. In the old Longhorns.'

I knew at once what he had in mind. In the Farman Longhorn, the instructor had sat in front, while the pupil sat behind, his legs on either side feeling the extra rudder bar, his arms holding on to extensions to the controls. I knew at once it would work if we could only get the German free.

'For God's sake,' Sykes yelled. 'Hurry Brat'

Inevitably the struggle had been noticed by this time and I could see men running across the field, and then a car burst out of the confusion round the hangars, its engine howling. A shot was fired and I heard the bullet 'whack' past and whine away into the distance.

We nearly had the German free by this time, but he seemed to be bent backwards like a bow and his feet were now under the dashboard somehow and he was beginning to come round and struggle feebly.

Sykes yelled as he came free at last, and I fell in a heap on the grass with him. For a second I thought we'd lose the aeroplane because the propeller was still turning but Sykes was still on the wing and was scrambling now into the cockpit.

'For God's sake,' he screamed, and I ran after him as he swung the machine into wind. Hardly looking where I put my feet I scrambled up the round belly and flopped into the cockpit on to his knees. It was a tremendous jam and there didn't seem any room to move the joystick.

'Let her rip,' he yelled and I opened the throttle immediately without really thinking of the consequences.

Sykes couldn't see a thing except round my body, but his long legs were on either side of me on the rudder bar, while I held the joystick and the throttle. As we bumped across the grass, I stared at the dials and indicators, and the *Johannisthal* plate on the dashboard that indicated the plane's origin.

'What's "Zu" stand for?' I yelled. 'And "Hauptank"?'

Fortunately, I was able to assume that the engine was warm and primed, and all I needed to do was push the stick forward as the speed built up. The German pilot was on his feet now and was dragging at a revolver. As we swung round I heard it go off and my right leg leapt.

'Oh, God,' I yelped, in a panic of fright. 'He's hit me!'

'Bad?' Sykes yelled back.

I felt sure it was but I didn't seem to be dying and I was far more concerned with the fact that at the moment we were facing directly towards the burning aeroplane. 'Rudder!' I screamed.

'Right rudder! She's swinging!'

Sykes' legs moved.

'Not too much! That'll do!'

As the speed built up the aeroplane swung wildly then hurtled forward. I couldn't read the airspeed indicator because it was set out in kilometres but I had been at the game long enough to fly by the seat of my trousers and could tell by the feel when she was ready to lift off.

The Germans were still running towards us and the car was moving in front of us now. I saw a mechanic grab for the wing but we were moving too fast by this time and I saw him go head over heels as it sent him flying. Then I pushed the stick forward and the tail came up. The car swung across our path and it looked as though there was going to be the most almighty crash. I yanked frantically on the stick although I sensed we hadn't yet built up flying speed, and the nose lifted and the wheels came off the ground. But we weren't moving fast enough and they touched again and we bounced, but I was still heaving at the stick and at last the nose lifted. I saw men jumping out of the car and a German officer standing in the back seat firing at us with a pistol. Where the bullets went I had no idea, but I heard a 'whangg' as one of them hit the cowling, then he took a dive over the side as the Albatros lifted over him.

I caught a whiff of burning oil as we flashed through the drifting smoke from the blazing aeroplanes, then we were roaring over the huts towards the trees. I saw men with rifles firing and a machine gun on a cartwheel swinging round. A little flag of fabric began to flap on the lower wing and the trees seemed to be rushing towards us, growing enormously in size until they seemed to fill the whole of my view. I headed for the smallest.

'The trees!' Sykes screamed, his mouth by my ear. 'The trees! Lift her!'

'She won't come up,' I screamed back. 'She's too heavy!'

With two aboard, the Albatros was taking a long time to climb and I saw the trees flash past on either side. For a moment I thought we'd gone through them.

'Think we clipped 'em,' Sykes yelled. 'Saw a lot of flying leaves.'

We were clear of the airfield at last and I found the rising sun and swung in a wide circle to put it behind me on course for the west. Sykes was staring backwards and downwards, looking for Germans, but my eye was searching the roads. After a while I caught sight of a small figure that I knew instinctively was Marie-Ange's. She'd not wasted time and had already put a good distance between herself and the aerodrome and I felt thankful for that. Then I saw her lift her arm and the frantic flutter of a white handkerchief as she slipped backwards, a small forlorn figure, out of sight below the wing. I realized then that I hadn't said a single one of the things I'd wanted to say to her. Nothing else but 'Run! Get away from here as fast as you can!' It hardly seemed to express what I'd wanted to say. And that chaste kiss I'd decided on had turned out to be nothing more than a hurried peck as I'd scrambled for the bank.

It was a good job Sykes was with me because he didn't give me the chance to think about it long.

'A couple of 'em are off,' he yelled in my ear. 'They're coming after us.'

Sitting on his knee I was half out of the cockpit and, with the wind flattening my hair, half-frozen in the slipstream. The Albatros felt as though she'd been crash-landed at some point in her career and they'd never been able to true the rigging up and she seemed to fly left-wing-low, while the Mercedes engine was throwing out oil which I could feel spattering my face in a fine mist mixed with odd larger globules.

'How's the leg?' Sykes yelled.

I'd almost forgotten it but now I realized it was painful and felt sure I could feel the blood running in bucketfuls into my boot. 'Numb,' I shouted.

'Better turn the wick up a bit,' Sykes suggested. 'Those two behind are catching up.'

I juggled with the throttle but it didn't seem to make much

difference.

'Won't go any faster,' I said. 'Carrying too much weight.'

'Coming up fast,' Sykes yelled and, turning my head, I saw the two Germans right behind us, climbing for height. I decided there was no point in trying to get up very high. We had only a matter of ten miles to go but I knew they were going to be the longest ten miles I'd ever flown.

'Better cock the guns,' Sykes advised. 'Might need 'em.'

It seemed a good idea.

With its extra load, the Albatros was sluggish and there was nothing I could do about it. We were only about a hundred feet up, just skimming the tops of the tall poplars, and I saw a ruined church spire flash past, all the slates missing and the laths showing. Faces were staring up at us, white against the brown earth, and I saw horses and guns moving forward to the lines, their drivers also gazing up, obviously wondering why two German aeroplanes were advancing with such menace on a third.

'Here they come,' Sykes shouted. 'For what we are about to receive may the Lord make us truly thankful!'

I heard the clatter behind and there was a whack of bullets passing through the wings and I saw the tracer trails and smelt the smoke of the bullets.

'Port,' Sykes yelled and, as he kicked at the rudder bar, I shoved the stick over and we skidded away from them.

There was another sharp ack-ack-ack behind us and I knew by the sound that the German was dangerously close by now.

'Port again!' Sykes roared and we skidded away again.

'We can't keep going to port,' I screamed. 'We'll end up back at Phalempon.'

'Have it your own way, but the Huns are to starboard!'

The rattle of guns sounded again and splinters leapt from the edge of the wing. We skidded away again, to starboard this time as the German flashed past, and for a moment I thought we were going to hit the second German who came up unexpectedly on that side. By the grace of God, he pulled away in time, and as the first one banked steeply to come behind us again, I saw we'd been given a minute or two of grace before he got into position again, and pushed the nose down to gain speed.

I could see the lines now just in front and a whole string of shell-bursts. The thought that we were going to be flying through the barrage just as the shells reached the last few yards of their downward arc made my stomach turn over but there was no chance to do anything about it. The Germans were coming up behind us again and they must have been so furious or so excited at seeing us escaping they, too, didn't bother to turn aside. I heard the machine guns go again and saw more flags of fabric flap. A bullet whanged against the engine cover some-where and I heard it scream way. A large hole appeared above my head and more splinters flew.

Between us we managed to fling the machine away from the streams of bullets but, sitting high out of the cockpit without a safety belt, I seemed to flop about like a jelly on a hot plate. My leg seemed to be stiffening, too, and I was certain now that my boot was full of blood.

'Gettin' warm,' Sykes roared. 'Can't you do anythin' about it?'

'No!'

'Thought you were a dab hand with an aeroplane?'

'If you think you can do any better,' I yelled back, 'we'll change places.'

The Germans seemed to be sitting just behind us now, potting at us every few seconds, and why neither of us was hit I couldn't imagine because the Albatros seemed to be falling to pieces about our ears. But I could see barbed wire now. It was new wire and hadn't gone rusty, and it lay over the ground like a pale blue mist. Then Sykes started hammering at my back and, turning my head, I saw him pointing. Though I couldn't get round properly, I saw the flat top wings and the dihedral of the lower wings that stamped a group of Camels coming down.

The Albatroses had seen them, too, because one of them was swinging away to bolt for home. The second seemed to decide on one last try and came in again for us. I felt sure this time that the Albatros was going to fall apart but it kept on flying even when I threw it in as tight a bank as I dared. As we came round we were face to face with the German who was going round in the opposite direction and I pressed the trigger of the guns. I smelled cordite and saw the guns jumping and he began to wobble and I saw a puff of smoke, then he had flashed past and I was too busy simply keeping the machine flying to worry about what had happened to him.

'He's gone,' Sykes roared. 'And the Camels have got the other! We're all right now . . . Oh, my God!' – his voice rose to a scream – '*no, no!*'

I didn't have to look to guess what had happened. The Camels hadn't noticed what was going on and had seen only three German Albatroses apparently larking about close to the ground. They had disposed of one and probably we had disposed of the other and now they were coming down on us.

The Mercedes engine was making weird noises now, as though something were loose inside, and I had an awful sensation that the wings were about to fall off. But we were over the German front line now and crossing the blue belt of barbed wire.

The first Camel came in so close I could see the oil on the engine cowling catching the early morning sun. The guns rattled and the Albatros took more punishment, but by the grace of God once again we weren't hit ourselves. The engine was labouring badly now, though, and I could see smoke coming in puffs from it and could even smell it.

'We're on fire!'

'Keep it up,' Sykes roared. 'Only a bit further!'

But the Albatros was barely flying now. I could see wires trailing and hear them twanging all round us and I knew that if I tried to dodge the next Camel that came down the wings would simply fall off. But the Camels seemed to consider that they had done all that was necessary and, probably hoping we'd land intact, they were waiting just above for us to crash. I didn't think they'd have to wait long.

I saw the shell-holes come up in front then another belt of wire and the British trenches.

'We've made it,' I yelled, then to my horror a positive fusillade came up at us. Both sides were shooting at us now. The Germans had long since spotted two heads and caught on that something was wrong and had opened up with rifles and machine guns, while the British, seeing only black crosses on the wings, were doing the same. The wings looked like sieves by this time and the engine gave one last despairing clang and stopped. The propeller jerked twice and halted in a horizontal position, and in the silence all I could hear was the hum of the wind through what wires still remained and the roar of battle about me.

I had never realized just what a lot of noise went on in the front line. I could hear machine guns rattling away steadily in short bursts and the separate pop of rifles, the whole lot backgrounded by the thump and crash of shells.

We floated over the British front line, barely flying, and I saw a shell explode just in front, then we were drifting through the smoke and the clods of earth and the spray of water it had thrown up. The ground was only just beneath us now, and there was a ruined cottage just ahead right in our path. I tried to bank to starboard but I knew I couldn't and the wingtip caught the gable end. I felt the aeroplane lurch and pieces of wood and metal fell off, then the wheels touched and the machine, still miraculously upright, rolled along what must have been the only piece of flat dry land for miles around and dropped neatly into a shell-hole. The tail came up, and I was surrounded by a violent crunching, crashing sound, then everything went black.

I came round with a pain in my face and firmly convinced I was dead. Foul-tasting water was in my mouth and eyes and nose. I tried to raise my head but a tremendous weight came down on it, shoving my face into the water again. With the desperation of the drowning, I fought free and found I was sprawling at the bottom of the shell-hole with Sykes alongside me. He had fallen out of the cockpit straight on top of me and seemed to have fared better than I had. My nose was bleeding where I'd banged it in the crash and I felt sure I was dying. Sykes didn't waste time sympathizing, however. He grabbed me by the collar and as he dragged me free from the aeroplane I realized that, just to make things complete, I was saturated with petrol.

A shell exploded just over the lip of the crater, showering us with earth and stones and water and we scrabbled in the torn surface trying to bury ourselves in the soil. I was frightened to death and almost weeping with fury that this should happen to us after all we'd been through. The water in the bottom of the shell-hole was foul and green and stank abominably, then it suddenly dawned on us that we'd made it, and, sprawling in the slime in the bottom of the shell-hole, we leapt at each other delightedly.

My leg gave way as I jumped up and I fell helplessly against Sykes, clawing at him for support. But it didn't matter that my breeches were soaked with blood. I knew no bones were broken and we were delirious with joy, pounding each other's shoulders, our faces streaked with dirt, our hair flattened by the wind and drenched by the water, rolling and yelling and laughing, until we must have looked like a couple of drunken puppies wallowing about, both of us covered with mud and the blood from my nose.

'Beat the whole bloomin' German air force,' Sykes shouted.

'And the whole bloomin' British air force!'

'*And* the German army!'

'And the British army!'

'Navy, too, come to that!'

We leapt at each other again, but this time, the antics were brought up short by a dry rasping voice that sounded like Munro's.

'Hands up, ye Prussian bastards, or Ah'll gi'e ye four inches o' cold steel richt doon the throat.'

It brought us up sharp and we released each other to turn round and stare open-mouthed at a soldier in a mud-caked helmet peering at us over the lip of the shell-hole. He was a sergeant and alongside him two other men appeared. They were all three heavily moustached, their faces black with dirt, their uniforms and kilts covered with mud.

Sykes grinned. 'We're English,' he said. 'English pilots. We've just escaped.'

'Aye, tell me anither yin.'

Sykes looked up indignantly. 'We're wearing British uniforms, aren't we, man?' he said.

'Could ye no' be spies?'

'We *are* British!'

I scrambled to my knees and screeched at him in fury, terrified he'd shoot me after the effort we'd made to escape. 'We pinched the damn' thing and flew it back!'

'Hoo do *Ah* ken ye're British?'

Sykes looked up, gave him a brilliant beaming smile and began to swear. He used all the good old Anglo-Saxon words he had ever heard uttered by sullen privates in a cavalry stables, together with all those he'd gathered from raw-knuckled fitters crouched over recalcitrant engines on frozen mornings, and rounded them off with a few he'd doubtless picked up in the hunting field and from poachers round Hathersett village. I stared admiringly. So did the sergeant.

His moustache lifted and they all three of them began to grin. The rifles they were pointing at us dropped.

'Och, aye,' the sergeant said. 'Ah ken fine ye're British.'

The Deep Silence

DOUGLAS REEMAN

H.M.S. *Temeraire* is the latest and most advanced of Britain's nuclear submarines. Her trials are cut short and she is ordered to the Far East under the control of the Vice-Admiral Sir John Colquhoun. On their arrival, their Commander, David Jermain, is ordered to take part in an exercise to track a conventional submarine which will be attacking a Polaris boat. But then the exercise goes wrong.

Jermain listened to the brisk passing of orders as the helm went over and like a circling aircraft the *Temeraire* swam round in a tight turn on to the new bearing. Half aloud he said, 'Just as I thought. The enemy must have known about the fishing boats and has been sculling about behind them all day. Just waiting his chance!'

'Course one one zero, sir.'

'Very good. Increase to twenty knots!' He looked at Wolfe. 'As soon as we cross into deep water I'll dive to three hundred feet!'

Wolfe nodded and tapped the planesman's shoulder.

The admiral was on his feet. 'Can you head him off?'

'Should be easy, sir. He's taken too long to make his attack.

Nemesis will be making her next turn in five minutes, so he'll have to crack on speed. I shall close the range as for two homing torpedoes and then loose a grenade.' He smiled in spite of his earlier uncertainty. 'All parties will hear the grenade and know that the hunter has been hunted!'

He watched the gyro repeater as the admiral said, 'That'll make 'em sit up! You see now why I wanted your boat on this exercise? To me it's more than a show of force, Jermain, it's the only way to prove our worth out here!' He rubbed his hands. 'I might get a couple more nuclear boats under my command in the near future. That'll stop any possible chance of our authority being undermined!'

Mayo called, 'Crossing the Shelf now, sir! Eight hundred fathoms in five minutes!'

Jermain heard Drew's harsh voice on the intercom as he goaded his torpedo party into the final part of the attack drill. He did not really care what the admiral saw in the exercise. The important thing was that the crew had behaved extremely well, and at no time had a single defect been reported. Now perhaps they could get on with the business of training undisturbed.

The sounding recorder began to swing slowly and then more steeply as the sea bed fell away. Maybe at their present depth of one hundred feet they would make a slight shadow across the treacherous cliff edge as they swam into safer waters.

Without warning there was an insane screech of metal, like a bandsaw across solid steel, and as the deck gave a warning tilt to port the nerve-searing sound was followed by a violent, shuddering lurch which threw some of the men from their feet.

Jermain reeled against the periscopes, his ribs aching from a blow against the greased metal, his mind momentarily stunned as the hull received a full jolt as if from a solid object. For an instant he imagined that they had collided with another submarine. Already the depth gauge was rotating wildly, and he heard Wolfe yelling hoarsely at the coxswain.

Jermain forced his mind to hold steady. 'Slow ahead! Watch your gauges!'

Jeffers, the second coxswain, sounded breathless. 'Can't hold her, sir! The planes is jammed!'

'Diving, sir!'

Wolfe was gripping the planesman's seat, his eyes glued to the dials.

Jermain felt the deck corkscrewing beneath him and heard Wolfe say tightly, 'One hundred and fifty feet, sir! One hundred and seventy-five feet!'

As if to emphasize the danger, the hull shuddered again and more violently. It was like hearing an oil drum being beaten with a giant hammer. And in between each boom there was the screech of metal, grating at the hull like steel tentacles.

'Emergency surfacing drill, Number One!' Jermain listened to his own voice and found time to wonder. It sounded calm and unemotional, yet he could feel his nerves screaming in time to the *Temeraire's* struggles with the thing which was trying to destroy her. 'Close all watertight doors!' The control room seemed to become smaller as the oval doors were clipped shut.

Wolfe added, 'Still diving, sir. Two hundred and seventy-five feet!'

Jeffers gasped as his control wheel slackened for a few seconds and then locked again. Every eye was fixed on the dials, and each ear was numbed by the regular booming impacts against the tough steel.

Jermain said, 'Must be one of those fish-buoys! We've got it wrapped round the fin and the after hydroplane!'

He could feel the sweat pouring between his shoulders like ice water, could sense the horror around him which already fringed on the edge of panic. The young messenger was gripping a petty officer's sleeve, his eyes filling his face like mirrors of terror, and in the chart-room entrance Mayo stood with his arms wide against the tilting hull as if he had been crucified.

Ross's voice came on the intercom. 'I'm blowing everything, sir! Can you try and free the aft-planes?'

Jermain said, 'Try opposite helm, Coxswain! See if you can shake it off!'

Twine swung the wheel, his eyes steady as he watched the gyro repeater. Twisting and turning like a snared fish the submarine thrashed wildly from one side to the other.

Only the admiral appeared unmoved, Jermain noticed. He stood against the plot table, his pale eyes empty of expression, like a man already dead.

'Four hundred feet, sir!' The man's voice sounded fractured.

Jermain dashed the sweat from his eyes and listened to the banshee screech against the hull. Down and down. Nearly five thousand feet to the bottom. No one had ever lived from a last dive. Friends of those lost in early disasters spoke glibly of a 'quick death', but who could tell? Jermain saw a seaman staring at the curved side as if expecting to see it cave in at any second.

'Four hundred and fifty feet, sir!'

There was a long-drawn-out rattle and then a violent jerk which nearly threw Jermain to the deck.

Jeffers yelled, 'It's free, sir! She's answerin'!'

The sounds were changing again. Now it seemed as if a giant piece of metal was being bounced along the casing, its trailing cable rattling jubilantly behind it.

Jermain said flatly, 'Hold her, Number One. I don't want to pop up like a cork!' He saw the needle begin to turn in their favour, and heard a seaman sobbing quietly behind him. He added, 'Keep her at periscope depth.' Over his shoulder he snapped, 'All sections report damage and injuries!'

Voices crackled and hummed through the intercom system, voices unrecognizable in strain and relief.

'Open up the boat. Stand by emergency deck party!'

Jeffers did not turn. 'Shall I be relieved, sir?'

Jermain shook his head. 'No, I want you there at the planes. We're not out of the wood yet!'

Wolfe said, 'No apparent damage, sir. Two torpedomen slightly injured in the fore-ends.'

'Very well. Pass the word for the doctor.'

Oxley's voice sounded loud over the speaker. 'Lost contact, sir. The submarine must have turned away.'

Twine said between his teeth, 'Not bleedin' well surprised, with all this row goin' on!'

Jermain met Wolfe's eye and wondered if he too had been struck by Oxley's behaviour. With the boat diving headlong for the bottom Oxley could still retain an interest in his hard-won target.

The deck party were already mustering below the bridge ladder, their expressions mixed between shock and surprise at being alive.

Sub-Lieutenant Colquhoun slung his leg over the coaming of the control-room door, his fingers fumbling with his life-jacket. He did not seem to see either Jermain or his father, but stared blindly at his waiting men.

The admiral broke his silence and said tightly, 'Well, Jermain, I hope you're satisfied!'

Jermain tore his eyes from the depth gauge. 'About what, sir?' He saw the anger flickering in the admiral's eyes, like reflections in the side of an ice floe.

'By your pig-headed stupidity you've not only lost the submarine contact, you also damn nearly sunk this boat!' He waved his hands around him. 'You should have stuck to the instructions!'

'We would have made no contact, sir.' Jermain eyed him angrily. 'At least, it would have been too late to intercept.'

Sir John Colquhoun turned away. 'We don't know for sure that Oxley did make a true contact. It might be just one more piece of damned incompetence!' he seemed to be talking to himself now. 'The humiliation! Your excuses'll cut no ice with me, I can assure you!'

'Sixty feet, sir!' Wolfe was watching the admiral, his features grim.

'Up periscope.' Jermain staggered, and for a moment he thought the steering had jammed. But as the periscope hissed from its well he saw that the weather had worsened, and in spite of the watery sunlight the lenses seemed to be shrouded in heavy mist. But it was rain, steady, torrential rain, which was beating the sea's surface into froth and fine spray.

He straightened his shoulders. 'Can't see a thing. Surface!'

He brushed past the admiral and stopped beside the deck party. 'You will have to get out on the hull. It'll not be easy, and speed will be essential.' He looked at Colquhoun's pale face. 'But no risks, understand?' He saw him nod, but there was little understanding in his eyes.

Mayo yelled, 'I'm sending up an additional rating to replace Jeffers, sir!'

The hull staggered, and Jermain swarmed up the ladder, knocking off the first set of clips and opening the hatch in automatic movements. Up the ladder with the deck party panting at his feet and then through the second hatch and on to the surface navigation bridge. The water was still draining away, and the fin's fibreglass covering was thick with crusted salt and trailers of weed.

With the rain beating savagely at his head and shoulders Jermain pulled himself the last few feet into the open cockpit at the top of the fin. The rain was as deafening as it was heavy, and the masked sunlight shimmered around the wallowing hull and made the sea seem like steam. As if the sea was angry to lose its victim and its rage had been transformed into heat.

Jermain clambered over the edge of the screen, his eyes straining astern. He saw the raw welts on the black whaleback where the trapped cable had scored through the paintwork to the metal itself. And then bobbing astern like a sea-anchor he saw the dull-coloured buoy and the last coil of wire which appeared to be holding it to the boat's vertical rudder.

He shouted above the hissing rain, 'Pass the word to the control room! We must retain this speed the whole time. If we stop the buoy may sink and wrap itself around the screw, then we are done for! Not that the Communists would mind towing us into port!' The joke had no effect, and he heard his instructions being relayed tonelessly through the intercom.

Lieutenant Victor squeezed into the cockpit. 'Number One sent me up to lend a hand, sir.' He blinked at the sea and added,

The Deep Silence

'God, what a mess!'

Jermain turned to Colquhoun. 'Are you ready?'

Colquhoun nodded dumbly.

'Right then. Take your men down to the rear of the fin, just like you did when the dinghy came aboard. I suggest you rig a tackle to the handrail and pay out two men towards the vertical rudder. Once there they should be able to hack that wire free without too much difficulty.' He gripped the boy's arm. 'I'll trim the boat as high as I can, but the men who do the job will be swimming for part of the time, so hold on to their lifelines like hell!'

'Yes, sir. I'll go myself.'

Jermain watched the little group climb down to the partly submerged deck and waited as they rigged the lifeline and huddled together for a last conference.

During all the confusion no one had reported hearing the end of the exercise, which was hardly surprising. The attacking submarine was to detonate two grenades to signify a successful strike, and no doubt at this very moment her captain was congratulating himself at this unexpected result.

Jermain gritted his teeth and plucked his sodden shirt away from his chest. All it needed now was for the unseen fishing boats to arrive and demand damages!

The Wooden Horse

ERIC WILLIAMS

Stalag-Luft III in 1943 seems to be virtually escape-proof; but John and Peter are determined to get out. They hit on the idea of using the Trojan wooden horse principle: causing a lively diversion to cover up their escape activity. They build a vaulting horse inside which they can be carried out to the same spot each day and dig a tunnel while the vaulting team do their work-out. The third man finally chosen for their break-out is Philip, a stalwart administrator on the camp escape committee.

That evening Peter made the top section of the shoring for the vertical shaft. He made it with four sides of a plywood packing case reinforced and slotted so that they could be assembled into a rigid four-sided box without top or bottom. The box would stand a considerable inwards pressure.

John stitched twelve bags for the sand. Several prisoners had made themselves shorts by cutting their trousers off above the knee. When John had sewn the bottoms together, roughly hemmed the tops and threaded string through the hem, the trouser-legs had become bags about twelve inches long. As a result of the experiment with Klim tins earlier in the evening, they reckoned that twelve trouser-leg bags full of sand would weigh about the same as one of themselves. With twelve full bags added to the weight of the horse and the tunneller, the vaulters who carried the horse back to the canteen would have to be keen types, and fit.

During the week when they were testing the Germans' reaction to the vaulting they had made two sand pits, one at the side and one at the head of where they positioned the horse near the football pitch. These pits were ostensibly to soften the shock of landing on their bare feet; actually they served as a datum mark, to ensure that the horse was always replaced on the exact spot.

The next afternoon they took the horse out with John inside it.

John crouched bent almost double, sitting on one of the removable bearers, a foot braced on each side of the bottom framework. In his arms he cradled a cardboard Red Cross box holding trouser-leg bags, some hooks fashioned from wire, one side of the vertical shoring, and the bricklayer's trowel he had stolen from the bathhouse.

The horse creaked and groaned as the four men carried it down the steps from the canteen. A smoother ride over the flat ground, more creaking as it was positioned by the sand pits. The vaulting began, with Peter as team captain standing close to the horse.

Inside, John worked quickly. Scraping up the dark grey surface sand he put it into the cardboard box and started to dig a deep trench for one side of the shoring. He put the bright yellow excavated sand into the bags and suspended them from the wire hooks which he had poked up between the boards and canvas padding of the top of the horse.

As the trench got deeper he had difficulty in reaching the bottom. He made it wider and had to bank the extra sand against one end of the horse. It was hot and stuffy in the confined working space, and he began to sweat.

He finished the trench and dropped the plywood sheet in position, with its upper edge six inches below the surface. He replaced most of the sand, ramming it down with the handle of the trowel, packing the shoring as tight as he could, to prevent any telltale subsidence.

Standing on the framework of the horse he carefully spread some of the remaining sand over the plywood sheet, packing it down hard. He was left with enough surplus sand to fill one trouser-leg bag.

Finally he sprinkled the grey surface sand from the cardboard box over the whole area, obliterating his foot and finger marks.

Calling softly to Peter, he gave the word that he had finished.

The vaulters inserted the bearers and carried the horse back into the canteen.

Working alternately, it took them four afternoons to sink the four walls of the shoring. Then they began to dig out the sand from inside it, covering the hole each time they left it with a trap made from bed-boards and the hoarded surface sand.

Now the vaulters staggered back to the canteen carrying twelve bags of yellow sand inside the horse as well as the digger. Once there, they transferred the sand from the trouser-leg bags into long sausage-like sacks made from the arms and legs of woollen underwear. These they carried away slung round their necks and down inside their trouser-legs.

The sand was dispersed around the compound, some finding its way by devious routes to the *aborts*, some buried under the huts, some sprinkled through special trouser pockets over the tomato patches and dug in by the kriegie gardeners.

When they reached the bottom of the plywood shaft Peter realized they had to dig deeper still; and they made another night sortie to the unfinished bathhouse to get bricks, which they later wedged under the four corners of the shoring to support it. He was not satisfied until they had a shaft five feet deep and two feet six inches square. They had dropped the plywood walls twelve inches as they worked. The tops of the walls were now eighteen inches below the surface of the ground. The eighteen inches of sand above the wooden trap gave them security from the probing-rods of the ferrets and deadened any hollow sound when the trap was walked on. But it was too much sand to remove each time before reaching the trap. To make this easier they filled bags, made from woollen undervests, and placed them on top of the trap before covering them with merely six to eight inches of surface sand. The bags were thin enough not to impede the progress of the ferret's probe, and enabled them to uncover and recover the trap more quickly.

The plywood box stood on four brick piles two feet high. On three sides the shaft below the box was shored with pieces of bed-board. The fourth side was left open for the tunnel.

They found that it was possible to stand in the shaft – with head and shoulders up inside the horse – but it was not possible to kneel; so they removed the bed-boards between the bricks on the side opposite the tunnel entrance and dug a short burrow into which they could thrust their feet.

For the first seven feet the tunnel was lined with bed-boards, to take the force of the impact of the vaulters landing heavily on the surface. Peter made this shoring piecemeal, in the evening, in the security of their room; using as tools a table knife and a red-hot poker. To assemble it he lay on his back in the darkness of the narrow tunnel, scraping away sufficient sand to slide the main bearers into position before inserting the boards. He had to work slowly and carefully and was fearful all the time that a sudden fall of sand might bury him. Even a small fall would be enough to pin him, helpless, on his back in the tunnel.

Once the shoring was in position they had to fill the space between the roof of the tunnel and the wooden ceiling with sand. If this were not done, sand would trickle down and the roof become higher and higher until the subsidence of the ground above would reveal the path of the tunnel.

After the first seven feet the tunnel ran on without any shoring whatever.

The tunnel was very small. They had quickly seen that the

progress of the work would be determined by the speed with which they could get the excavated sand away. The smaller the tunnel the less sand they would have to dispose of and the faster the work would go.

While one of them supervised the vaulting the other dug in the tunnel. He worked alone. Once he got into the tunnel with his arms stretched ahead of him he had to stay like that; he could not get his arms behind him again. Nor could he crawl with them doubled up. It was fingers and toes all the way until he got to the end. There he scraped some sand from the face with the trowel and crawled backwards along the tunnel, dragging the sand with him. When he got back to the vertical shaft he had brought enough sand to fill half a bag. And there were twelve bags to fill.

There was no light in the tunnel and very little air. He spent his spell of digging in a bath of sweat. He worked naked because it was cooler; and if he wore even the lightest clothes he would scrape a certain amount of sand from the sides as he crawled along. Each bag of sand that was scraped from the sides meant one bag fewer taken from the face. As he sweated the sand caked on him. He got sand in his eyes, in his ears, in his nose and under his foreskin.

And so they worked until they had dug a tunnel forty feet long. They grew skegs on their elbows and knees and broke their fingernails. As the tunnel grew longer the work became more difficult and the air more foul. They did not put up air holes for fear of the dogs.

After forty feet they could do no more. They were taking two hours to fill the twelve bags, and they had reached the limit of their endurance.

Not only were the tunnellers exhausted by the twenty-four times repeated crawl in both directions along the tunnel, but the vaulters – who had been vaulting every afternoon of the two months that it had taken to dig the forty feet – were exhausted too. The tunnellers were issued with extra rations by the Escape

Committee, but the vaulters were not, and they had little energy to spare.

Peter and John had devised games and variations on the theme of vaulting. The whole time one of them was below ground the other would be trying to make the two hours that the horse stood there appear as natural as possible. It was not easy, especially when a ferret was standing within earshot, watching the show.

They organized a medicine-ball and a deck-tennis quoit and the twelve-man team stood in a circle round the horse throwing these to one another. They even organized a run round the circuit – leaving the horse unguarded and vulnerable, with the trap open below it.

It was a considerable physical strain working in the tunnel; yet both of them preferred it to organizing the P.T.

The end came one afternoon when John was in the tunnel. It was ten minutes before they were due to take the horse in. Peter had left the vaulters and walked over to the main gate to ask the duty pilot how many Germans were in the compound. There were two ferrets, nowhere near the horse or the canteen. As he walked back he was met by David, pale-faced and running.

'Pete—'

'What's wrong?'

'There's been a fall.'

'Where?'

'Not far from the horse.'

'Is John all right?'

'We called to him but we couldn't get a reply.'

Peter started running. A fall could mean that John was trapped. There were no air-holes. He would be caught in the end of the tunnel; suffocating, trapped by sand.

The vaulting team were grouped round a figure lying on the ground. Peter glanced quickly at the nearest watch-tower. The guard was looking down at them through field-glasses.

'Where *is* the fall?'

'Nig's lying on it,' David said. 'A hole suddenly appeared so Nig fell down on it to stop the guards seeing it. He's pretending he's hurt his leg.'

'How's John?' He bent over Nigel, speaking urgently.

'Can't get a reply.'

Oh God, Peter thought, John's had it. He wanted to overturn the horse and go down, but the thought of the discovery of the tunnel held him back. John would be furious if he panicked for nothing. 'Send someone for a stretcher,' he told David.

Two vaulters went off to the canteen at the double. Peter crouched by Nigel's feet, as near to the horse as possible.

'John,' he called. '*John!*'

No answer.

'Roll over, Nig.'

Nigel rolled over. There was a hole, about as thick as his arm, going down into the darkness of the tunnel.

'John,' he called, projecting his voice down the hole. 'John!'

'That you, Pete?' The answer was weak.

'What happened?'

'There's been a fall but I can clear it. I've taken some of the boards from the shaft. I'll have it fixed in a jiffy. Can you fill-in from the top?'

'OK. Let me know when you've got it fixed.' He pretended to attend to Nigel's leg.

'The goon in the box seems interested,' Nigel said. 'He's still watching.'

'The chaps with the stretcher will be here in a minute,' Peter told him. 'They'll carry you back to the hut. That'll satisfy him.'

Before the stretcher arrived he heard John's voice again; thinly, from inside the tunnel. 'Just putting the shoring in. You can fill-in in about five minutes.'

What a man, Peter thought. Good old John. He poked solicitiously at Nigel's leg, and Nigel simulated pain. The two vaulters returned with the stretcher and a first-aid kit. Peter made a business of bandaging Nigel's leg while the others, shuffling round, idly kicked sand towards the hole.

334

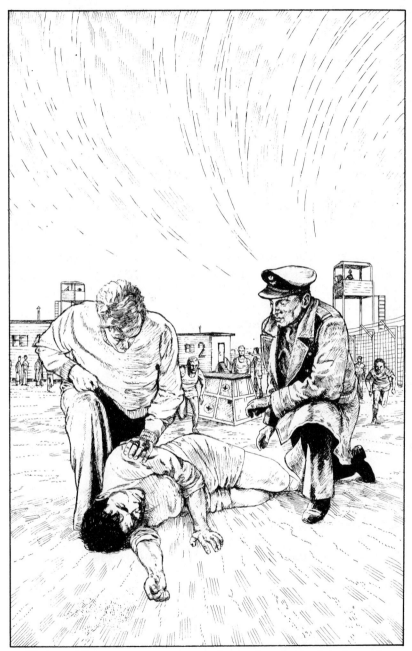

The vaulting team were grouped round a figure lying on the ground

'It'll sink a bit,' Peter said. 'We'll kick some more over it later on . . . What's the time?'

'Three-thirty,' David said.

'Christ – *appell* at four! We must get him up before then.' He got to his feet, and leaned against the horse, kicking it with his heel. 'John!' There was no reply.

The two vaulters bore Nigel away on the stretcher, the rest surged in an untidy group round the hole. The minutes passed. There was no sign from John.

Oh God, we've had it, Peter thought. If we can't get him up before *appell* we've had it. 'Come on, chaps, let's get vaulting again,' he said. 'We can't just stand around.'

They began to vault, with David standing by the hole as though waiting to catch the weaker ones and help them to their feet. Suddenly Peter heard John's voice, tired but triumphant, from inside the horse itself. 'Hey, Pete, what's the time?'

'You've got five minutes.'

'It's a hell of a mess.'

'Don't worry. Get ready.'

At the end of five minutes they carried the horse into the canteen. John could hardly stand. 'It's the hell of a mess,' he repeated. 'There's a bit of tree root there and the vaulting must have shaken it loose. I've jammed it up temporarily but it needs proper shoring.'

'I'll take some down with me tomorrow,' Peter said.

The tunnel was choked with sand, soft shifting sand that continued to fall as he worked. He worked on his back, entirely by feel, and the air was so bad that he panted, gasping for breath. Sand fell into his eyes, his nostrils, his mouth. He worked furiously, clearing the loose sand and fitting the new shoring into position.

When it was securely fitted he managed to pack some of the sand between the shoring and the sides of the tunnel. The rest he spread about the floor, lying flat on his belly and pressing it down with his hands.

When he got back to the horse he could hardly find the strength to climb out of the shaft and replace the trap. Wearily he put it back, placed the woollen sacks filled with sand on top of it, and spread the surface sand. He gave John the signal that he was ready to be taken in. The journey back across the compound was a nightmare and he never knew how he was able to balance on the framework. When they reached the canteen he crawled out from under the horse and fainted.

That evening, after *appell*, he reported to the camp hospital. He knew he had taken too much out of himself with the digging, the vaulting and the worry. The British doctor examined him and ordered a week's complete rest in bed.

For the next twelve days there was an Indian summer, and they were able to take the horse out every morning and afternoon. Working up to a crescendo of effort they dug faster and increased the number of bags to be carried back at a time from twelve to fourteen and finally fifteen. With the extra weight the bearers were beginning to stagger as they carried the horse up the steps into the canteen; and Peter wondered how they would cope when they had three men inside. The smallest and lightest of the regular vaulters was a New Zealander called McKay. When they asked if he would come out and close the trap after them he agreed immediately.

They decided to break on Friday the twenty-ninth of October. The work went so well that they had time to make a final bulge where John would stow the baggage. They dug the bulge on the twenty-eighth; it was as far as they could go. They reckoned that between them they could dig a further ten feet after they had been sealed down the next evening.

On the morning of the twenty-ninth they brought in the second batch of fifteen bags, and recovered their civilian clothing from scattered hiding places round the camp. Ralph, the Committee Clothing Officer, handed over the phoney Marine dress uniform; to his evident satisfaction and Peter's relief, it proved a good fit. When he had removed the tacked-on stripes

337

from the trouser-legs, the patch pockets, and the epaulettes and insignia from the shoulders, it became an almost-too-good civilian suit for a foreign worker to wear in wartime Germany.

With all their gear mustered and checked, they packed it into kitbags and took them to the canteen hidden in bundles of other kriegies' dirty laundry.

At twelve-thirty John had a substantial meal of bully beef and potatoes, Canadian biscuits and cheese. At one o'clock, wearing his civilian shirt and trousers under a long khaki greatcoat, he left for the canteen with the male voice choir. Peter hurried off to see the duty pilot, who told him there were two ferrets in the compound.

'Where are they?'

'One's in the kitchen, and Charlie's hanging around outside the canteen.'

'Hell!' Peter thought for a moment. 'OK – if any more come into the compound send a stooge off to tell Phil. He'll be in the canteen.'

He ran across to the hut where the S.B.O. lived; and knocked on his door.

'Come in.'

He stood in the doorway, panting slightly. 'Sir – we're just putting Clinton down and Charlie's hanging round the canteen. I wonder if you could get him out of the way for a few minutes?'

'Let met see.' The group captain put down his book. 'The cooking stove in Hut 64 isn't working very well. I'll just stroll over and ask him to report it to the Kommandantur. He might like to smoke an English cigarette with me.'

Back at the canteen Peter found the choir lustily singing *Greensleeves*. John, Philip, Nigel and the vaulting team were standing near the door.

'Can't get started,' John said. 'Charlie's outside and he keeps walking past and looking in at the window. I think he likes the singing.'

'Let's change it to *Run, rabbit, run!*' Nigel suggested.

'There's another ferret next-door in the kitchen,' Peter said. 'The S.B.O.'s going to take Charlie away—'

'I'll deal with the one in the kitchen.' It was Winyard, whose Vorlager *dienst* had not yet broken, come to see John off.

'Fine,' Peter said. 'Then we'll get cracking.' He looked out of the window. The S.B.O. was walking across the compound, a golf club in his hand. Suddenly he appeared to see Charlie, and altered course. 'Here comes Groupy.'

The group captain and Charlie exchanged a few words and they both walked away towards Hut 64. They could hear Tony Winyard chatting with the ferret in the kitchen. Hurriedly John doffed his coat and pulled the long black combinations on over his shirt and trousers. He pulled black socks over his shoes and a hood which he had made from an old undervest dyed black over his head. 'It's bloody hot in this clobber,' he whispered.

'You look like the Ku Klux Klan,' Peter said. 'Ready?'

With the choir singing more loudly than ever, they both crawled under the vaulting-horse; Peter holding a blanket, a cardboard box and fifteen empty bags, John sinister in his black outfit. The three kitbags hung between them, suspended on hooks wedged under the top of the horse. They crouched with their backs to the ends of the horse, their feet one each side on the bottom framework. Then the bearing poles were inserted and the horse was lifted. As they lurched down the steps and went creaking across the compound towards the vaulting pits, they held on to the kitbags to prevent them from swaying and falling off the hooks.

With a sigh of relief the bearers placed the horse in position and withdrew the poles. The vaulting began.

John crouched in one end of the horse while Peter piled the kitbags on top of him. Peter then spread the blankets on the ground at the other end and began to uncover the trap. He collected the top layer of grey sand in the cardboard box, and threw the damp subsoil on to the blanket. Feeling round with his fingers he uncovered the bags of sand on top of the trap and removed them. He scraped the remaining sand away from the damp wood. As he lifted the trap he smelled the familiar damp mustiness of the tunnel. He lifted the kitbags off John's crouching figure and balanced them on top of the trap on the pile of sand.

'Down you go.' He crouched astride the hole while John dropped feet first into the shaft. 'My God, those clothes stink!'

'It'll be worse by the time you come down,' John said. 'It's the dye. Must have gone bad or something.'

As John crawled up the tunnel Peter detached the metal basin from the end of the rope and tied one of the kitbags in its place. One by one John pulled the kitbags up to the face and stowed them in the bulge. Peter then re-tied the basin, and John sent back enough sand for him to fill the empty bags.

While Peter was stacking the bags in the body of the horse, John crawled back for his last breath of fresh air. It was the first time he had been in the tunnel wearing clothes and Peter could hear him cursing softly as he struggled to get back. His feet came into view and then his body, clothed and clumsy in the black combinations. Peter crouched inside the horse looking down on him as he emerged. The shouting of the vaulters outside and the reverberating concussion as they landed on the canvas padding above his head seemed louder than usual.

John straightened up, head and shoulders out of the trap. He had left the hood at the end of the tunnel and his face was flushed. He looked strange with short hair; smaller, older. 'It's hot down there with clothes on.'

'Take it easy,' Peter said. 'For Christ's sake don't overdo it. I don't want to have to carry you once we get outside.'

'I'll be all right. You seal me down now and I'll see you after *appell*.'

'OK – don't make the air hole bigger than you have to.'

He watched John's feet disappear down the narrow tunnel and then he closed the trap. He replaced the heavy bags of sand over it and stamped the loose sand firmly on top of them. He didn't like doing it. It's burying a man alive, he thought. He heard an urgent voice from outside.

The Wooden Horse

'How's it going, Pete?'

'Five minutes, Phil.'

He started to hang the fifteen bags full of sand from the top of the horse. He gathered the blanket in his arms and spread the rest of the sand evenly over the ground under the horse. He sprinkled the dry grey sand from the cardboard box over this, and smoothed it carefully. Finally he gave Philip a low hail that he was ready. The bearing poles were inserted and he was carried back towards the canteen. He could hear the voices of the choir: '*He shall give His angels charge over thee . . . lest thou dash thy foot against a stone . . .*' In the dark belly of the horse he laughed softly, releasing tension.

With a last creaking lurch they were up the steps and inside. The old horse is falling to pieces, he thought; hope it lasts out this evening.

One end was lifted. Before crawling out he passed the bags of sand to Philip. They began to carry the bags into the band practice room where the choir was going at full blast.

'. . . *the young lion and the dragon . . . there's a ferret passing the window,*' sang David.

'There bloody well would be,' Peter said. 'Keep an eye on him. Is Nig in the roof?'

David nodded and went on singing, '. . . *because He hath known my name . . .*'

'Right – we'll just pass these bags up to him and then we're in the clear.'

Nigel's anxious face was peering down from the trapdoor in the ceiling. Peter held out his fist, thumb extended upwards, and grinned. Nigel grinned back, and lowered his hand for the first of the bags.

'. . . *with long life will I satisfy Him . . .*'

Back in the mess Peter first trimmed, then shaved off his beard. In the mirror he had made from a smoothed-out Klim tin and nailed to his bunk, he watched his features emerge, round and unlined. John had looked years older with cropped hair. Without his thick wiry black beard he himself looked younger

than his thirty-two years, innocent and inexperienced. Somehow, discarding the beard was his final commitment to the
escape; and he was impatient to get on with it. This two hours'
wait with John sealed down the tunnel was going to be the worst
time of all. It was touch and go now. At any moment until they
reached the shelter of the trees the scheme might be blown. At
any moment the four-and-a-half months of back-breaking effort
might go for a Burton.

Stretched out on his bunk he stopped worrying while he
wondered about the origins of 'gone for a Burton'. Airmen used
the phrase, or said 'bought it', as euphemisms when fellow
airmen were killed. Both must have stemmed from that brewers'
advertisement *Where's George? Gone for a Burton.* What would
the first beer taste like? He turned his thoughts back to the
escape. Once they were outside it wouldn't matter so much; it
was the next few hours that mattered. Outside anything might
happen, and they would have to rely almost entirely on luck. It
was no use making detailed plans like they'd done for the tunnel.
They had a rough idea of what they wanted to do – get to Stettin
and board a Swedish ship – but that was all. From the moment
they broke out of the tunnel they would have to adapt their
actions, maybe their policy, to the conditions and even the
people they met.

Always reluctant to ponder imponderables, he let his mind
run over the list of things he was taking with him. There was the
'dog food', a hard cake made from dried milk, sugar, Bemax and
cocoa; it had been packed in small square tins saved from the
Red Cross parcels, and he intended to wear a girdle of them
under his shirt. Next there were the linen bags containing a dry
mixture of oatmeal, raisins, sugar and milk powder; mixed with
water it would swell and fill the stomach, preventing that hollow
aching sickness that comes from eating ill-balanced, concentrated food. He had sewn one of these bags into each armpit
of his trench coat as an emergency ration in case they became
separated from the attaché-case which held the bulk of their
food.

The Wooden Horse

The attaché-case was already down in the tunnel, at the bottom of his kitbag. Mentally he re-checked its contents: the food, clean socks, shaving gear, rollneck sweater, soap, a few sheets of paper, and pen and ink for minor alterations to their documents. German cigarettes and matches.

He got to his feet and went through his jacket pockets: the wallet which held the papers and the Reichsmarks, the pocket compass and torch supplied by the Committee, two handkerchiefs, cigarettes bought in the town by one of the tame guards, a length of string, a pencil, a pen-knife, his beret and a comb.

It was no use, he couldn't be still. He went out on the circuit and walked round, over the tunnel; thinking of John moling away down there, sweating, not knowing the time, not knowing whether the tunnel had been discovered, out of touch with everyone. John digging away, trying to get as much done as possible before he and Philip joined him.

He went unnecessarily to the abort, checked with Philip on the timing of the diversion for the break, and then walked with Nigel round and round the circuit while they waited for *appell*.

Nigel broke a long silence. 'David and I . . .' he hesitated, diffident. 'We thought we'd have a bash at the tunnel tomorrow – that's if you don't mind. The chaps could take us out after lunch and we'd stay down there until dark.'

'But – what about your leg? We wanted to ask you to come in with us – before we asked Phil. But we thought—'

'I know,' Nigel said. 'John told me. I'm glad you didn't. I'd only have held you up. And Phil deserves it.'

'Are you and David going together?'

'Oh no – I'd hold him up too. I'm going as a discharged soldier – dumb from shellshock as well as wounded. Hitching lifts on my way home to Bavaria from the *Ostfront*. I'll try to get into Switzerland if I get that far. They've got the papers ready. David's jumping goods trains – heading for France.'

'Well, jolly good luck to you both,' Peter said.

'I just wanted to know . . .' he hesitated again, 'to ask whether you could camouflage the hole a bit before you leave.'

Peter could see the complication, the necessity to stay there in the light of the arc-lamps; but Nigel deserved the chance. David too. 'I'm second man out,' he said. 'Phil's the last. It rather depends on how far we can mole. If we come out in the ditch we might manage it.'

'We don't want to jeopardize your effort,' Nigel said. 'We just thought—'

'I'll talk to Phil. You have everything ready in any case. Even if we can't cover the hole there's always the outside chance. The ghosts'll take our places at morning *appell* so if the hole hasn't been seen by then you've got a chance.' If it's not been discovered by then, he thought, we shall be well on our way.

'I don't expect I shall get far,' Nigel said. 'Nowhere near any of the Death Zones. but I'd like to have a bash . . . I shall miss you after you've gone. It's been good fun, the vaulting.'

'I expect they'll take the horse away when they discover the tunnel.' Peter said. He wanted to thank Nigel for all the help and encouragement he'd given them, but he knew that he could not do it. To thank him in words would put the thing on a formal basis and it was beyond that.

'You will see my wife, Pete?'

'First thing when I get home. Don't take any risks, will you, Nig?'

'You know me,' Nigel replied. 'I'm dumb enough to forget I'm dumb and yell "Goon in the block!" when I see my first policeman.'

With *appell* safely over, the vaulters assembled in the canteen for the third time that day. Peter's knees felt loose and for a moment he did not want to get into the horse. He felt that three was an unlucky number, that the guards in the watchtowers were bound to be suspicious when they saw the horse being brought out again, after the evening *appell*.

The moment passed and he wanted to get on with it, quickly. As he pulled on the evil-smelling black combinations, he heard

Nigel instructing the four men who were to carry the horse. He looked at Philip, unrecognizable in his black hood; and then at the third man, McKay, stripped for lightness and holding the cardboard box ready for the dry surface sand which he would sprinkle over the bags on the trap after he had sealed them down.

Nigel came over and handed him a bottle of cold tea for John. 'Give the child my love,' he said, 'and tell him to write.' He turned abruptly and limped over to the window.

Peter and Philip crawled under the horse, stood crouching one at each end, and held McKay suspended between them. The bearer poles were pushed into position and they braced themselves on these. The four men lifted the horse. It creaked protestingly and seemed to Peter to sag in the middle. One of the bearers slipped as they came down the steps; recovered his balance; and the horse went swaying and jerking across the football pitch.

Once the horse was in position over the shaft Philip sat on McKay's back at one end while Peter removed the trap. As he lifted the wooden boards he listened for sounds of movement at the end of the tunnel. It was silent. He turned to Philip.

'I'll carry on up the tunnel and see how John's doing. You fill some bags from the bottom of the shaft for Kiwi to take back, and then stay down this end. I'll send the stuff John's dug back in the basin and you leave as much as you can this end, then spread the rest along the floor of the tunnel as you come.'

'Right. It's sixteen-oh-five now.' Philip was looking at the Rolex wristwatch he had borrowed from a member of his mess. 'We'd better get cracking.'

Peter dropped feet first into the vertical shaft. McKay, stoically silent in the discomfort of the journey from the canteen, eased out from under Philip and spoke at last.

'My bloody oath!' He was staring in wonder down at the tunnel entrance. 'Is it as small as that all the way?'

'Smaller.' Peter slid to his knees, edging his legs and feet into the back burrow. 'Thanks a lot, Kiwi. Don't forget to smooth the surface sand—'

'My bloody oath! good luck, mate.'

Stooping awkwardly in his tight clothing Peter managed to get his head under the lintel of the opening and slipped head first into the tunnel. He waved his legs in farewell, and squirmed inch by inch along the hundred feet that had taken them so long to dig. Now that it was finished and he was crawling down it for the last time, he was almost sorry.

He switched on the torch. Stafford had been right about the battery. Even so, it was a help. As he inched forward he could see heaps of loose sand dislodged by John's clothing. He noticed all the patches of shoring, built with difficulty in darkness, strangely unfamiliar in the light. Near the end of the tunnel he flashed the torch ahead and called softly to John. He was afraid to call loudly for he was now under the wire and not far from one of the watch-towers.

He came to the bend where they had altered course, and saw the end of the tunnel. Where he had expected to find John there was nothing but a solid wall of sand.

John must have been digging on steadily and, banking up the sand behind him, had completely blocked the tunnel.

Peter began to bore through the wall of loose sand. After about three feet he broke through. A gust of hot fetid air gushed out; and there was John, sweaty and sand-covered, hands and face streaked with black dye. A fringe of hair, wet and caked with sand, plastered his forehead. He looked pale and exhausted in the yellow light of Peter's torch.

'Where the bloody hell have you been?' he asked.

'It's not four-thirty yet.'

'I thought it must have gone six. I seem to have been down here for ever. I thought the roll-call had gone wrong and I'd have to go out alone.'

'Everything's under control,' Peter said. 'Nig sent you some tea, with his love.' He pushed the bottle through. 'I'll just get this sand back to Phil and then I'll join you.'

He pulled the empty basin up the tunnel and sent the first load back to Phil, who filled the empty bags they had brought out and stacked them in the shaft. When all twelve were ready he hung them in the horse, and gave McKay the word to replace the trap and seal them in.

As Peter and John worked on they had a certain amount of fresh air from the air hole under the wire. Philip, back in the vertical shaft with the trap closed above him, had none. When he found himself gasping for breath he crawled up the tunnel and joined in the moling.

They worked feverishly, trying to get as much as possible done before the breaking time. John, in front, stabbed at the face with the trowel and pushed the damp sand under his belly towards Peter, who lay with his head on John's heels collecting the sand and squirmed backwards with it to Philip, who banked it up as a wall behind them. They were now in a narrow stretch of the tunnel about twenty-five feet long and two feet square, ventilated by one small hole three inches in diameter.

They were working for the first time in clothes and for the first time without the fresh air pushed up the tunnel from the open shaft by the movement of the basin. They were working three in the tunnel and they were anxious about the air; Peter and Philip especially, because they knew from flying how lack of oxygen could create a sense of euphoria so that a man got careless and made stupid mistakes. They were working for the first time by the light of a torch, and in the light the tunnel seemed smaller and the earth above more solid. By now the prisoners had been locked in their huts for the night. If the tunnel collapsed the three of them would be helpless.

They worked fast, and steadily. None of them wanted to be the one to break the rhythm of the work. And they worked silently, conscious that without the vaulting as cover the slightest sound might be registered on the seismographs.

At five-thirty Peter called a halt. 'Half an hour to go,' he whispered. 'We'd better push up to the top.'

John nodded his agreement, and began to push the tunnel uphill, towards the surface. It proved farther than they had expected and they thought they would never get there. Then

John broke through – a hole as large as his fist. Through it he caught his first glimpse of the stars. The stars in the free heavens beyond the wire.

'I'll dig out the whole width of the tunnel,' he whispered, 'just leaving a thin crust over the top. Then we can break that quickly at six o'clock exactly. There'll be less risk of being seen while we wait.'

Peter gripped his ankle in reply and squirmed back to Philip to warn him to get ready. He retrieved John's kitbag from the third bulge, pushed it ahead of him up the tunnel, and tied it to John's ankle. He returned to the bulge, extracted his own bag, and got Philip to do the same for him. He dragged it behind him towards the mouth of the tunnel where John was resting. Philip followed, pushing his own gear ahead of him, in front of his nose. It was five-fifty, and they were ready.

At six o'clock John broke through to the open air, pulling the dry sandy surface down, choking and blinding himself and making him want to cough. As the sand settled they heard the sound of the diversion coming from the huts nearest the wire. There were men blowing trumpets, men singing *My Brother Sylveste*, men banging the sides of the hut and yelling at the top of their voices.

'They're overdoing it,' John whispered. 'The silly bastards'll get a bullet in there if they're not careful.'

'Go on! Go now!' Peter said. He was scared. It was too light. The hole was some feet short of the ditch, on the edge of the outside sentry's path.

John hoisted his kitbag out of the tunnel and rolled it towards the ditch. He squeezed himself up out of the hole and disappeared from view.

Peter stuck his head out of the tunnel. He looked towards the camp. It was brilliantly floodlit, he had not realized how brilliantly. The high watch-towers were in darkness and he could not see whether the guards were looking into the camp, at the noisy huts, or in his direction. He pulled out his kitbag and pushed it into the ditch, wriggled out of the hole and dragged himself full-length across the open ground and into the ditch. He expected every second to hear the crack of a rifle and feel the tearing impact of its bullet in his flesh. He lay, out of breath, in the shallow ditch and looked back.

The hole was in the full light of the arc-lamps. It would be impossible for Phil to stay and cover it.

The diversion in the huts reached a new crescendo of noise. He picked up his kitbag and ran blindly across the road, into the pine forest where John was waiting.

Acknowledgements

The publishers would like to extend their grateful thanks to the following authors, publishers and others for kindly granting permission to reproduce the extracts and stories included in this anthology.

THEY HAVE THEIR EXITS by Airey Neave. Copyright 1953 by Airey Neave. Reprinted by permission of Hodder & Stoughton Limited and Curtis Brown Ltd.

THE SCARLET PIMPERNEL by Baroness Orczy. Reprinted by permission of the estate of Baroness Orczy and Hodder & Stoughton Limited.

THE BALD ARCHAEOLOGIST from *The Thirty Nine Steps* by John Buchan. Reprinted by permission of Lord Tweedsmuir and William Blackwood and Sons.

FLIGHT TO FREEDOM by Michael Donnet. Reprinted by permission of Ian Allan Ltd.

AN ACT OF GOD from *Joe Burkinshaw's Progress* by Geoffrey Kilner. Reprinted by permission of Methuen Children's Books Ltd.

WHERE EAGLES DARE by Alistair MacLean. Reprinted by permission of the author and William Collins Sons & Co Ltd.

ROGUE MALE by Geoffrey Household. Reprinted by permission of the author and Michael Joseph Ltd.

DEAD CERT by Dick Francis. Reprinted by permission of the author and Michael Joseph Ltd.

ESCAPE TO NOWHERE by Francis S. Jones. Reprinted by permission of The Bodley Head.

THE OPEN WINDOW by Georgette Elgey. Reprinted by permission of The Woburn Press.

FLYING COLOURS by C. S. Forester. © 1938, 1939 by Cecil Scott Forester. Reprinted by permission of A. D. Peters & Co Ltd and Little, Brown and Co.

FREE AS A RUNNING FOX by T. D. Calnan. Reprinted by permission of Macdonald and Jane's Publishing Group Ltd and The Dial Press.

Acknowledgements

THE BOILING WATER from *The Strode Venturer* by Hammond Innes. Reprinted by permission of William Collins Sons & Co Ltd and Alfred A. Knopf Inc.

WHITE COOLIES by Betty Jeffrey. Reprinted by permission of the author and Angus & Robertson (UK) Ltd.

THE SILVER SWORD by Ian Serraillier. Reprinted by permission of the author and Jonathan Cape Limited.

CAPTAIN OF FOOT by Ronald Welch. Reprinted by permission of the author and Oxford University Press.

THE CRUEL SEA by Nicholas Monsarrat. Reprinted by permission of the Estate of the late Nicholas Monsarrat and Alfred A. Knopf Inc.

THE WOODEN HORSE by Eric Williams (revised and expanded edition)© Eric Williams 1949 and 1979, published by William Collins Sons & Co Ltd and Bantam Books, Inc, reprinted by permission of the author.

Every effort has been made to clear all copyrights and the publishers trust that their apologies will be accepted for any errors or omissions.